ETHICS FOR THE JUNIOR OFFICER

The U.S. Naval Institute Blue & Gold Professional Library

For more than 100 years, U.S. Navy professionals have counted on specialized books published by the Naval Institute Press to prepare them for their responsibilities as they advance in their careers and to serve as ready references and refreshers when needed. From the days of coal-fired battleships to the era of unmanned aerial vehicles and laser weaponry, such perennials as *The Bluejacket's Manual* and the *Watch Officer's Guide* have guided generations of sailors through the complex challenges of naval service. As these books are updated and new ones are added to the list, they will carry the distinctive mark of the Blue & Gold Professional Library series to remind and reassure their users that they have been prepared by naval professionals and they meet the exacting standards that sailors have long expected from the U.S. Naval Institute.

ETHICS FOR THE JUNIOR OFFICER

Selected Cases from Current Military Experience

Second Edition

A Gift from the USNA Class of 1964 to the USNA Class of 2005

Founding Editor
Dr. Karel Montor, Professor of Leadership, U.S. Naval Academy
1925–1998
USNA Class of 1964 Project Manager
CAPT Gordon H. Clow, USNR (Ret.)

Editors
Col Michael F. Campbell, USMC
LCDR Aaron L. Johnson, USN
Dr. Albert C. Pierce

Naval Institute Press
Annapolis, Maryland

Naval Institute Press
291 Wood Road
Annapolis, MD 21402

Library of Congress Cataloging-in-Publication Data
Ethics for the junior officer : selected cases from current military experience / founding
editor and case-compiling author, Karel Montor ; editors Justin R. Mostert . . . [et al.].—
2nd ed.
p.   cm.
"A gift from the USNA class of 1964 to the USNA class of 2005."
Includes bibliographical references and index.
ISBN 1-55750-241-2
1. Military ethics—Case studies. I. Montor, Karel.
U22.E83427 2000
172′.42—dc21   00–51121

Printed in the United States of America on acid-free paper ∞
12 11 10 09 08 07 06 05   12 11 10 9 8 7 6 5

Contents

SUPERINTENDENT
UNITED STATES NAVAL ACADEMY

Dear Members of the Class of 2005,

The book *Ethics for the Junior Officer* is being presented to you by the members of the Class of 1964. It is an important resource that you should read and reflect upon as you become officers in the Fleet and the Corps. It will reinforce the ethical foundation you laid during your time in the Brigade. Its lessons are both timely and timeless. Discussing the cases with your subordinates and peers will help provide indications and warnings when ethical plots need to be refined or when major course corrections are required. In this demanding and complex time of the Terror War, many recent graduates are experiencing new and complex challenges to their moral courage. It is more important than ever to ensure that we have leaders of character in the naval service.

You have seen the country at war in Afghanistan and Iraq, fighting to defeat the forces of evil and terror. Our nation's armed forces have displayed incredible military power while simultaneously taking great risks to ensure the safety of noncombatants. Your profession is about leading men and women in the operating forces in combat. You are tasked to protect those under your charge, as well as noncombatants. We expect you to do the right thing under adverse and trying circumstances. This book will help you refine your ethical decision-making skills.

The Naval Academy, and all who work here, are committed to preparing you not only for commissioned service in the Fleet but also more broadly for leadership to the nation—in uniform, in government and public service, and in the private sector. From its earliest years, the Naval Academy has insisted that the leadership we aspire to is *ethical* leadership and that we aim to produce officers who are technically competent leaders of character.

Thanks to the generosity of the Class of 1964, you will now have an additional tool in your kit as you move on to the Fleet and beyond. Use it often. Use it wisely and well, not only for your own enrichment but also for the training and education of your peers and subordinates.

I want to thank and commend the Class of 1964 for taking the initiative many years ago to launch this valuable project. They have since been joined by the Class of 1984 to sponsor this book and the dinner at which it is presented. I also thank and commend the Center for the Study of Professional Military Ethics, who edit this book and make it available to you, the future leaders of our Navy and Marine Corps.

With best wishes for your success as officers and in your many endeavors in life.

Sincerely,

RODNEY P. REMPT, VADM, U.S. Navy
Superintendent

Letter from the Class of 1964

The U.S. Naval Academy Class of 1964 presents this ethics book to each graduating midshipman as a result of a class project started in 1991. This project was chosen by the Class of 1964 Executive Committee in consultation with the superintendent, RADM Tom Lynch, also a member of the Class of 1964, who concurred in the conceptual plan. The Class of 1964 wanted to sponsor a project that would professionally benefit our future U.S. Navy and Marine Corps leaders.

You are that future leadership, and as you embark upon your initial tour of duty, you will be presented with choices as a commissioned officer that, on occasion, will pose an ethical challenge. Your selected course of action, be it in a professional, social, or even an academic setting, will be observed and contribute to that intangible known as your "service reputation." The choice you confront will not always be easy to discern. On occasion a situation will even require an immediate response on your part. The case studies in this book will not cover every situation with which you might be confronted, and certainly will not guarantee that you will make the right choice. However, each of the cases conveys a lesson, and in each you will see the course of action chosen and the results thereof.

The Class of 1964 owes a special debt of gratitude to the late Prof. Karel Montor, who conceived and assembled the original *Ethics for the Junior Officer.* Professor Montor epitomized the traits we expect from our officer corps—the highest standards of ethical behavior, a tireless work ethic, and the willingness to voice his opinion (tactfully and diplomatically) when he thought it helpful in the decision-making process. Professor Montor died unexpectedly on 13 March 1998. The members of the Class of 1964 will always remember our friend and honorary classmate. We have been privileged to help bring to fruition a project that was his lifelong dream, and we are committed to ensuring that Professor Montor's unswerving devotion to the development of the nation's officer corps will live on through this publication.

You have a wonderful career ahead of you. Your country has invested much in you and has high expectations of an effective return on that investment. As commissioned officers, we truly are held to a higher standard of conduct and accountability than our civilian counterparts. The Class of 1964 sincerely hopes that this book helps each of you live up to the higher standard established by generations of leaders who preceded you in Annapolis.

The Class of 1964 will always be deeply indebted to Prof. Karel Montor for his dedication in creating this book, and to CAPT Gordon H. Clow, USN (Ret.), our classmate and the project manager for this book.

Good luck and Godspeed,

CAPT. DAVID F. TUMA, USN (Ret.)
President, Class of 1964
U.S. Naval Academy

To the USNA Graduating Class

As you join the active forces, the Naval Academy Class of 1964 provides this volume prepared especially for you. It is intended to guide you in the years ahead, that you may uphold the ethical traditions of our military profession. Reading the foreword by VADM James Stockdale will explain the importance of military ethics and how best you may use this book.

We, the Class of 1964, dedicate this volume to our own beloved superintendent, RADM Charles Cochran Kirkpatrick, USN, who inspired us as midshipmen and throughout our careers by his devotion to duty and the way he met ethical challenges during his long and distinguished career.

Admiral Kirkpatrick, a submariner, USNA 1931, served as commander in chief of the U.S. Pacific Fleet. As commander of the submarine *Triton,* he conducted three successful war patrols during 1942–43 and was credited with sinking 22,949 tons of enemy shipping. For extraordinary heroism and outstanding courage during enemy action, he was awarded three Navy Crosses, the Distinguished Service Cross (Army), the Silver Star Medal, the Legion of Merit with Combat V, and the Purple Heart.

As you start your career, we share with you the knowledge that during our careers we have been privileged to serve with honorable officers from all our armed forces. These officers have contributed to the esteem, respect, and confidence the American public has in our military profession.

This places great responsibility on you to maintain this fine tradition so that our nation may continue to have the greatest confidence in our word and be assured that we shall always act responsibly, with integrity, and be accountable for our actions.

The more you read this book, the greater will be your understanding of the part ethics plays in the daily life of an officer and the greater your ability to have an ethical impact on your unit. The volume will provide a rationale for thinking through ethical dilemmas. You are encouraged to make use of the index at the back of the book to identify particular issues with which you may be wrestling.

We know you are prepared to give your life for your country. We also ask you to be prepared to give your career, if need be, to ensure that ethical actions are taken. The good deeds and heroics of a million service personnel will be overshadowed if one individual puts his or her self-interest before that of their ship and shipmates. Our job is to be prepared to defend our nation. We need to be ready. It is we who set the moral and ethical standard for our service; there can be no weak link in the integrity chain.

RADM T. C. LYNCH, USN
Superintendent, U.S. Naval Academy
15 September 1993

Preface

This book is a basic ethics reference designed to provide newly commissioned officers with true ethical dilemmas faced by junior officers of the armed forces of the United States. Hundreds of officers have provided detailed accounts of real ethical dilemmas in which they were involved to be used for personal reading and reflection or to serve as training material for you and your subordinates on issues of personal and professional conduct. To use the book for training, pick a case that presents an issue or controversy you want to address with your subordinates. Have your students read it and identify its points of tension or conflicts. Then, in a controlled but open forum, discuss the moral dilemma, making sure that you cover your main points in the discussion. Displaying the points on a board can help you keep the discussion on track. Once your students have identified all the issues and tensions, have them develop a course of action or make a decision and discuss their reasons.

Close your discussion by evaluating the course of action or decision. At this point, you have the opportunity to explain to your subordinates where you as well as the Navy or Marine Corps stand on the issue. What are the acceptable behaviors or actions? What are the organizational standards, and what is their moral basis? These case sessions can also help you to learn more about your subordinates and help them to learn about you, their leader. By working through a good case study together, your subordinates reveal how they would solve an ethical problem, and you can communicate your standards and expectations. Use this book to its fullest to develop yourself and your unit into an efficient combat team.

Leadership requires expertise in many areas. This volume provides officers with strategies that they can use to arrive at ethical decisions. Other aspects of leadership are covered in two companion volumes: *Naval Leadership: Voices of Experience,* and *Fundamentals of Naval Leadership,* both published by the Naval Institute Press.

Foreword
VADM James Bond Stockdale

This book contains actual leadership dilemmas faced in modern times by junior officers of the armed services of the United States. It was commissioned by the U.S. Naval Academy, Class of 1964, to be bequeathed annually to upcoming graduates of their alma mater. It is designed for reflection and reference throughout a person's first few years as a commissioned officer. Periodically, the case studies of the volume will be reviewed for timeliness and applicability, with an eye toward keeping the book up-to-date and on the mark.

Underlying all these cases are ethical considerations that go a long way in the final determination of whether the young officer's real-life solution to the dilemma served our country ill or well. In fact, the focus of the whole book is to dramatize for Navy ensigns and Marine second lieutenants and their junior officer counterparts in other services just exactly what constitutes ethical behavior and what does not. Each case appears in two areas of the book. The facts of a situation are laid out first, in sufficient detail to allow the reader to take on the problem as a personal challenge and form a tentative solution. Then a section bearing on the ethical considerations of the case follows. This part at least makes sure the reader is aware of the ethical issues involved so that he or she may reconsider a tentative way of handling it. Lastly—and sometimes with surprise—the real-life results are delineated. Cases were picked based on their potential to stimulate discussions in the junior officer quarters and, on occasion, the advice of willing seniors, JAG Corps officers, and chaplains—when appropriate—independently queried in the interest of our readers' self-education and their speedy assimilation of the "feel" for what is expected of them in their new profession.

These real-life case studies were solicited from the Navy inspector general, the Naval Safety Center, and senior officer sources of the Army, Air Force, Marine Corps, Coast Guard, and Navy. Their presentation and organization in the original edition underwent an extensive editorial review process under the direction of the late Karel Montor, Ph.D., Professor of Leadership at the Academy.

I hope this book serves to create in each of your hearts a happy understanding of the down-to-earth "rules of the game" of this life of American military officership on which you are embarking. It is fitting that the focus of the whole book is on the military ethic because that is the core value of every operational specialty of every service. Whether you go forth from the Naval Academy to fly or submerge or fight on the surface, or go ashore with the Marines or the SEALs, you have to be worthy of the trust of both your seniors and juniors, or all is lost for you.

I've sat on many selection boards for officer promotion, read the candidates' jackets, heard the briefs and board discussions on many people of high operational qualification, advanced engineering degrees, and other intellectual badges of distinction. You should know that once the board agrees that a history of indirectness or deviousness is in the record of an aspirant, the probability of that person's promotion all but vanishes. All considerations fall before that of personal integrity. It is the core value expected of an American military officer. If it does not come naturally to you, be honest with yourself and choose some other line of work.

You might question my use of the word *happy* as a descriptive adjective in understanding all of this. I use it because if you develop the right "hang" of things, you will be happy as you realize that the military ethic in most units—certainly in all good ones—is not the nagging, nitpicking, hairsplitting bother that we hear complaints about in other professions. The military ethic comes naturally to people of many personality "cuts," many "cuts of their jib." The idea is not to hammer everybody into one mold; the services are rich in the diversity of leadership styles of their better officers. It's just that the people under them are our most precious asset, and they must be treated in a manner above reproach. We insist that they deserve leaders with integrity.

There's that word again. It's not just a good-sounding term. The original meaning of *integrity* was "whole," a unity, as opposed to a broken thing, or something in parts only. The readers of Plato and Aristotle will relate it to those ancients' distinction between "living" and "living well." It refers to the possibility of living according to a strong and coherent sense of oneself as a person whose life, considered as a whole, reflects a definite and thoughtful set of preferences and aspiration. If well composed, the person who possesses it knows he or she is whole, not riding the crest of continual anxiety, but riding the crest of delight.

This ethic is natural to, not artificially grafted to, the profession of arms, the profession of warfighting, in which friendships are consumed by the more powerful and generous force of comradeship. This was an idea propounded by philosopher Jess Glenn Gray, who spent all of World War II as a ground soldier in Europe. He noted how men in battle would lay down their lives for unit companions they were known even to dislike. People of integrity facing a common danger coalesce into a unity that surpasses friendship. It is not a willful change of heart; it happens as a function of human nature. And I've seen it happen. J. Glenn Gray, in his book *The Warriors: Reflections on Men in Battle* (New York: Harcourt, Brace, 1959), writes, "Loyalty to the group is the essence of fighting morale. Friendship is not just a more intense form of comradeship but its very opposite: While comradeship wants to break down the walls of self, friendship seeks to expand these walls and keep them intact." So whereas an "ethics program" may seem unnecessary or foreign to some professionals (we read of businessmen who think it is foreign to those engaged in free enterprise), the profession of arms is at home with it. Our major product, you might say, is comradeship in the heart of battle. And in our business, how we lavish our skills of leadership on comrades is "bottom-line stuff."

Am I old-fashioned, in this post–Cold War period, to use the heart of battle as the control point for a personal strategy of how to live? The United States has never been far from wars, and now as the world's only superpower, we're the natural choice to resolve knotty problems in the world. Geoffrey Perret wrote a book about America and wars past titled *A Country Made by War* (New York: Random House, 1989). In the 217 years between 1775 and 1992, we were involved in ten major wars. In more than 20 percent of the years of our existence, we have engaged in major wars (the Indian Wars, Philippine Insurrection, Mexican War of 1916, etc., excluded). Between 1945 and 1993, the proportion of years we've engaged in major wars has been considerably higher than 20 percent. So keep your powder dry.

In tight spots in this service life of ours, the higher the pressure gets, the greater is our need for mutual trust and confidence. And the more trust and confidence among us, the more power we draw from one another. Oliver Wendell Holmes Jr., for nearly thirty years one of America's favorite Supreme Court justices, was famous for his tales of life as a young officer in our Civil War. In *The Mind and Faith of Justice Holmes* (Boston: Little, Brown, 1943), he says, "Perhaps it is not vain for us to tell the new generation what we learned in our day, and what we still believe."

The essence of what I learned and what I still believe came about not in some grand office, but more than twenty-five years ago, face down in a prison cell, leg irons attached, signaling under the door to my comrades across the courtyard during those few early morning minutes when the guards were too busy to watch us. It was the third anniversary of my shoot down, and I had just got the message, swept out with strokes as my ten comrades, one at a time, scrubbed their toilet buckets: "Here's to Cag for three great years. We love you; we are with you to the end." And I said to myself, "You are right where you should be; thank God for this wonderful life."

Holmes was more eloquent about what he learned and what he still believed:

> That the joy of living is to put out all one's powers as far as they will go; to pray, not for comfort but for combat; to keep the soldier's faith against the doubts of civil life; to love glory more than the temptation of wallowing ease, but to know that one's final judge and only rival is oneself with all our failures in act and thought, these things we learned from noble enemies in Virginia or Georgia or on the Mississippi, thirty years ago; these things we believe to be true.

Jim Stockdale
20 August 1999

[*Biographical note:* VADM James Bond Stockdale was born in Abingdon, Illinois, in 1923. After graduating from the U.S. Naval Academy in 1946, Vice Admiral Stockdale served on active duty in the regular Navy for thirty-seven years, mostly as a fighter pilot aboard aircraft carriers. Shot down on his third combat tour over North Vietnam, he was the senior naval prisoner of war in Hanoi for seven and a half years—tortured fifteen times, in solitary confinement for more than four years, and in leg irons for two. Stockdale was serving as president of the Naval War College in 1979 when physical disability from combat wounds forced him to retire from military service. He was the only three-star officer in the U.S. naval history to wear both aviator's wings and the Medal of Honor. His twenty-six other combat decorations include two Distinguished Flying Crosses, three Distinguished Service Medals, four Silver Stars, and two Purple

Hearts. When the admiral retired, the secretary of the Navy established the Vice Admiral James Stockdale Award for Inspirational Leadership, which is presented annually to two commanding officers, one in the Atlantic Fleet and one in the Pacific Fleet.

As a civilian, Stockdale served as president of the Citadel for a year, as lecturer in philosophy at Stanford University, and as senior research fellow at the Hoover Institution at Stanford for fifteen years, where he is now emeritus. His writings focus on how men and women can rise in dignity to prevail in the face of adversity. Aside from numerous articles, with his wife, Sybil, he cowrote the book *In Love and War,* now in its second revised and updated edition (Naval Institute Press, 1990). In 1987 NBC produced a drama based on this book starring James Wood and Jane Alexander. Admiral Stockdale has also written two books of essays: *A Vietnam Experience: Ten Years of Reflection* (Hoover Press, 1984), and *Thoughts of a Philosophical Fighter Pilot* (Hoover Press, 1995). Both of his essay collections won the George Washington Award from Freedoms Foundation at Valley Forge.

In 1989 Monmouth College in his native state of Illinois named its student union Stockdale Center. The following year, during a ceremony at the University of Chicago, Stockdale became a laureate of the Abraham Lincoln Academy. He is also an honorary fellow in the Society of Experimental Test Pilots. In 1993 he was inducted into the Carrier Aviation Hall of Fame, and in 1995 he was enshrined in the U.S. Naval Aviation Hall of Honor at the National Museum of Aviation in Pensacola, Florida. In 2001 the U.S. Naval Academy honored him with its Distinguished Graduate Award. Admiral Stockdale also holds eleven honorary degrees.]

Acknowledgments

Many individuals eagerly contributed to this and previous editions. We are truly indebted to those who gave their time, creativity, experience, and efforts to this endeavor. Special thanks is owed to CAPT Gordon H. Clow, USNR (Ret.), who, as project manager for the Class of 1964, coordinated all activities between the Naval Academy and the Class of 1964 and oversaw every phase of the project from review and revision of issues to final proofreading.

After founding editor Dr. Karel Montor passed away in 1998, the leadership of the Class of 1964 asked Dr. Albert C. Pierce, director of the Center for the Study of Professional Military Ethics, if the center would take responsibility for editing and updating *Ethics for the Junior Officer.* Dr. Pierce readily accepted. With this updated printing of the second edition, a gift to the USNA Class of 2005, the center enters its sixth year overseeing production of the book.

The current editors are listed on the title page in descending order based on the amount of time and effort spent working on the volume. We also wish to acknowledge the valuable contributions made by those who worked on previous editions and whose work continued to enrich this newest printing. Listed alphabetically, they are Maj. Christopher Breslin, USMC; CDR Richard A. Cataldi, USN; Ms. Rose Ciccarelli; LCDR Michael C. Cosenza, USCG; Dr. Aine Donovan; Dr. Shannon E. French; CDR Justin R. Mostert, USN (Ret.); LCDR Eric Rice, USN (Ret.); LtCol Gary E. Slyman, USMC (Ret.); LtCol William T. Stooksbury, USMC (Ret.); and LT Glenn Sulmasy, USCG.

For their contributions of articles to this volume, we thank ADM Hank Chiles, VADM James Bond Stockdale, RADM Marsha J. Evans, RADM Gary Roughead, and CAPT James Campbell. We especially recognize ADM Arleigh Burke for his article "Integrity," which is the classic essay on this subject in the naval service.

This book was developed for junior officers, and all who read it are invited to send constructive suggestions and additional situations to: Director, Center for the Study of Professional Military Ethics, U.S. Naval Academy, Annapolis, Maryland 21402.

Military Ethics

The exploration of ethical issues is an ancient pursuit. Throughout history brilliant philosophers, theologians, and sages of every nationality have wrestled with questions such as, How ought we to behave toward each other? How can we live good and meaningful lives? What virtues define an excellent character? What are our duties and obligations to one another? How we answer these critical questions says a lot about who we are as a society and as individuals.

In the new millennium, the study of ethics has become even more practical and focused. Broad theoretical foundations are still important, but much ethical inquiry now also pays attention to specific ethical dilemmas that arise for the practitioners of various professions. Traditional codes of behavior are receiving renewed scrutiny (either praise or criticism) just as modern advancements and emerging technologies are raising previously unimaginable ethical concerns. Ethicists worldwide currently address their talents to a wide range of specialized fields in applied or professional ethics, including biomedical ethics, media ethics, ethics in education, ethics in government, sports ethics, business ethics, and military ethics.

The study of military ethics begins with the assumption that those who volunteer for the profession of arms will face a unique set of ethical challenges. All branches of the U.S. military make an effort to encourage continuing character development and reinforce positive values among those in uniform so that they will be prepared to face these challenges. Everyone who serves is expected to keep his or her moral compass well aligned, accept strict personal accountability, and display moral courage. The actions of military personnel are constantly reviewed and evaluated. And, due to the oaths they take and the enormous responsibility they assume, members of the military are generally held to a higher ethical standard than the rest of their community. As ranks and duties increase, the bar is raised even further, because society expects more from those who are trusted to lead others.

To suggest that every military officer stands to benefit from the frank discussion of complex issues in military ethics is not in the least to imply that military officers suffer from any ethical deficiencies. On the contrary, as the famous Greek philosopher Aristotle once explained, the ideal student of ethics is not an unethical person but someone who already has a strong commitment to doing the right thing at all times yet acknowledges, as we all must, that it is not always a simple matter to figure out what the right thing is. In order for ethical inquiry to have any value at all, Aristotle argues "the soul of the student must first have been cultivated . . . with a kinship to excellence, loving what is noble and hating what is base" (J. L. Ackrill, trans., *Nichomachean Ethics,* bk. 10, chap. 9, ll. 25–30).

We should all consider ourselves to be lifelong students of ethics. It is not the kind of subject that a person can just master and move on from, like simple arithmetic. No human being has all the answers when it comes to ethics. Life is much too complicated for that. But we can all benefit by considering the arguments, opinions, and experiences of others in light of our own values and experience.

With that idea in mind, this book has been put together as a means to present those currently in uniform with a valuable collection of arguments, opinions, and experiences related to the challenges of modern military life. We hope that this work will give junior officers in particular an interesting opportunity to reflect on issues in military ethics that have arisen in the recent past and are likely to remain relevant throughout their years in uniform, and beyond. The cases assembled here are all drawn from real events, with details garnered from the actual officers who lived through each crisis. A certain amount of commentary is included with each case in order to stimulate analysis and debate, but the ultimate conclusions are left up to you.

As you make your way through the text we encourage you to keep in the forefront of your mind some general points regarding the ethical obligations of military officers:

    1. Many of the situations recorded in this text clearly show that there are seldom, if ever, any "victimless unethical acts" when it comes to serving in the armed forces as a commissioned officer.

    2. Officers who follow an unethical course of action are frequently aware that they are doing something wrong, but they allow themselves to rationalize or make excuses, often persuading themselves that they are acting as their superiors would

wish, or that no one will be hurt by their actions, or that their actions will produce some benefit which outweighs other considerations.

3. Rules are not written lightly and should never be broken lightly. On rare occasions, it may be ethically correct to make an exception to a rule, if no other alternative will satisfy the ethical requirements of the situation. It should be remembered, however, that an exception to a rule does not necessarily disprove the rule; rather, it establishes that further evaluation of the rule may be needed.

4. When an officer fails to act ethically, negative consequences spread both up and down the chain of command. When an officer acts unethically, it will reflect badly on his or her superiors. It will be assumed that too much authority was delegated, not enough responsibility was exercised, and supervision was lax. An officer's unethical behavior will also create trust and morale problems among subordinates. On the other hand, when officers do the right thing, they establish a command climate that encourages all members of the command to be ethical.

5. Ultimately, all members of the military answer to the society they have sworn to protect. When an officer acts unethically, it may cast doubt on the integrity of the officer corps in particular and the military in general, raising doubts, perhaps serious doubts, about the quality of the U.S. military in the eyes of the citizens, voters, and taxpayers who support it.

6. Military professionals are dedicated to serving their country, even losing their lives in its defense, but, curiously, some may consider it more difficult to risk losing their careers. Having true moral courage, however, means always being prepared to do the ethical thing, even if it means damaging or losing one's military career.

7. An officer's accountability can never be delegated or diminished. The fact that those who serve under you are also individually responsible for their actions does not lessen your responsibility to or for them.

8. Not every difference of opinion should be viewed as a moral crisis. Command decisions may have subjective elements, so if your commanding officer chooses a course of action different from what you judge to be correct, you should not *automatically* conclude that his or her decision was *necessarily* morally wrong.

9. An officer's professional reputation begins the day he or she is commissioned and may be affected by every ethical decision he or she makes, in or out of uniform, from that point on.

10. Since an officer who is not a member of the Judge Advocate General's Corps cannot be expected to know all of the laws governing the actions of federal employees and military personnel, the advice of a JAG officer should be sought in all instances in which an individual is not positive that what he or she intends to do is legally correct. But that individual should also bear in mind that what the law requires may be less than what ethics demands. Ethical obligations are not always legislated, and the law may only represent absolute minimum behavioral requirements. Military personnel are encouraged in the Standards of Conduct to avoid any action that might create even the appearance of impropriety, whether or not it is specifically prohibited.

11. The importance of operating within the chain of command cannot be overemphasized. At the same time, however, officers must never hide behind their strict observance of the chain of command, using it as an excuse for moral negligence or as a way to rationalize their failure to do everything in their power to prevent unethical behavior.

12. Finally, religious, racial, gender, and ethnic biases have no place in the American military. Upholding and defending the Constitution requires respect for the dignity of all persons.

The following saying was prized by the late Karel Montor, original editor of *Ethics for the Junior Officer:*

Sow a thought, reap an act,
Sow an act, reap a habit,
Sow a habit, reap a lifestyle,
Sow a lifestyle, reap a destiny.

All of our ethical decisions are important. They help shape who we are and what we can become. We often cannot predict the consequences of our actions, but when we look back on the choices we have made, it is not the moments of moral courage we regret. We never have to make excuses to ourselves for doing the *right* thing. In that sense, at least, ethical behavior is its own reward.

TRUTH TELLING

CAPT James Campbell, USN
Director, Character Development Division
U.S. Naval Academy

*[A military officer] has veracity if, having studied a question
to the limit of his ability, he says and believes what he thinks to
be true, even though it would be the path of least resistance to
deceive others and himself.*

—S. L. A. Marshall

The foreword to *Ethics for the Junior Officer* states that it is "designed for reflection and reference throughout a person's first few years as a commissioned officer." Your Second Class leadership course spoke of reflection as a framework for understanding the contributions of both experience and education in your development. Hopefully, this short article will provide you insight and knowledge to aid you in analyzing past and future situations and help guide you in your first few years of commissioned service.

The Moral Reasoning, or "Ethics," course at the Naval Academy is intended to prepare you to think and reason through the complex issues and situations that will confront you in the profession of arms; in short, to learn to reason well. As you no doubt concluded, the study of military ethics is not easy, and reasoning to find the "right" answer can be very troublesome and challenging. This article would be much easier to write if we could categorically state that an officer must never lie and always tell the truth. Is this statement categorically true, or are there times when truthfulness does not serve the best interest of the common good or is, in fact, not the right thing to do? In his book *Morals under the Gun*, James Toner devotes many pages to addressing this question. "But if ethics is more than figuring out who wins and loses in particular circumstances— if ethics is a matter of knowing and applying the right *rules,* regardless of circumstances—are there any rules that *always* apply?" Most of us would agree with Toner that the answer to that question is "yes." But what are those rules, to which "there are and can be *no exceptions*? . . ." Are there rules that have exceptions, exemptions, and overrides? More importantly, under which category does truth telling fit? Many learned philosophers and theologians, such as St. Augustine and Kant, would rule out all lies at any time, consequences and probable outcomes aside. At the other end of the spectrum, some reason that only circumstances and probable outcomes can determine whether lying is justified. Described here are the absolutist and the relativist concepts you are familiar with from your education at the Naval Academy.

In the context of our profession, the profession of arms, we frequently encounter conflicting obligations, or what Toner calls, "dueling duties." Let us review again the classic encounter discussed in your ethics class, and explored by Toner. "You are Polish and a Warsaw resident in 1939, and you are harboring two Jews in your basement. An SS officer knocks on the door and asks you whether you have seen any Jews. May you lie to protect the Jews you are hiding?" You are now faced with a conflict of duties—to protect innocent human life or to protect the virtue of truth telling. Most of us would feel it appropriate to lie to the SS officer and protect the innocent lives. The question then is, *why* would you not tell the truth in this particular situation?

The absolutist would speak the truth and place the lives of those innocent people at risk. The relativist would lie, being driven by the problematic circumstance and probable outcome. As a military professional, it seems that there should be some point between these extremes that can help resolve this conflict of "dueling duties." Toner would offer the "universalist" position. The universalist is the individual who "chooses according to circumstance, intuition and insight, rules, and reasoned judgment." As Toner points out, the decision of a universalist "flows from wisdom or prudence," and may give us some insight as to why prudence is the first of the classic cardinal virtues.

One reason not to tell the truth in this case is that the SS officer, by his actions and intentions, has forfeited his right to the truth. So, we have considered lying to save lives. Is the sanctity of life, then, always central to whether or not to tell the truth? Let's consider another case study with which you should be familiar. Air Force Major Hal Knight, directing

B-52 raids over Vietnam in 1969, is asked to redirect the bomb runs to Cambodia, destroy the targeting information, then report false information back to the Strategic Air Command. It was known that North Vietnam was using Cambodia as a staging ground to launch attacks into Vietnam, putting U.S. soldiers at risk, unfairly, since Cambodia was still "neutral." I am sure that you have all been asked during the course, "You are Maj Hal Knight, it is 2130, what do you do?" Do you follow the orders and lie to help save U.S. lives? Major Knight did follow orders that night and many subsequent nights. Was he right? Most of us would agree that he was not right. Sadly, this was not the only case of falsification of records during the Vietnam War, prompting Air Force Chief of Staff, Gen John Ryan, to issue this statement in 1972: "Integrity . . . is the keystone of military service. . . .Therefore, we may not compromise our integrity—our truthfulness. To do so is not only unlawful but also degrading. . . . Any order to compromise integrity is not a lawful order. . . ."

With lives at stake in both instances, what are the criteria to use to determine whether or not to be truthful? You have, I hope, learned those criteria through your education, but now you must be able to apply them. In one case, it is right to lie; in the other, it is wrong. As educated and thinking officers, we should recognize that truth telling, like other moral obligations is neither culturally relative nor absolute, yet our first instinct *must* be toward the truth. We are not searching for the middle ground in the spectrum of lying and truth telling. The ground we seek is very close to the absolutist. When our decisions and actions are no longer determined by intuition, insight, rules, and reasoned judgment, but guided by poor judgment and self-serving motives, then we no longer are true servants of the public.

> Other than the officer corps, there is no group within our society toward which the obligation of the nation is more fully expressed. Even so, other Americans regard this fact with pride, rather than with envy. They accept the principle that some unusual advantage should attend exceptional and unremitting responsibility. Whatever path an American officer may walk, the officer enjoys prestige. Though little is known of the officer's intrinsic merit, the officer will be given the re-

spect of fellow citizens, unless that officer proves to be utterly undeserving.

—S. L. A. Marshall, *Armed Forces Officer*

Trust is at the heart of our profession. That trust resides at several levels: between military members, both up and down the chain of command, and between the military and the public we serve. The 2002 Gallup poll shows the military at the top of the list of organizations garnering the American public's trust and confidence. Our profession sits atop the list with 79 percent, and near the bottom is big business with 20 percent. While this fact should give each of us a sense of satisfaction, we should also recognize that this trust and confidence could be eroded over time or even lost in an instant. We will lose that trust and confidence if our decisions and actions, either individually or collectively, reflect selfishness, or our public senses that we no longer understand our "exceptional and unremitting responsibility." When we, as officers, no longer struggle to resolve conflicts of duty in favor of honesty, and we lie or hide the truth to protect programs, to follow our own agendas, to prevent embarrassment to a command or to ourselves, or to support a misguided loyalty, we will quickly find ourselves compared to big business. We owe our public more, much more.

Case 1: The Canteen Tops

This case focuses on three related issues. First, what constitutes a lie? Is only an intentionally false statement a lie, or is misrepresenting facts also a lie? What about omitting facts? Second, how important is "looking good" compared to "being good"? Third, how critical is it for higher echelons in the chain of command to be aware of the problems their forces are facing?

A stateside installation was picked to be the first Marine Corps site to implement a new Table of Organization, with an emphasis on logistical responsiveness to generated needs. The installation's new commanding general (CG) held the Medal of Honor.

The new CG conducted personal inspections of every unit, down to companies within battalions in his division. One item he focused on was the lowly canteen top. Even though it costs only a few cents, it's vital to the Marine in the field, who survives on water. A canteen without a top will lose water as the Marine conducts field operations.

During an inspection of one company, the CG asked the company commander about canteen tops. The company commander was able to answer truthfully that he had all the canteen tops he was supposed to have. But that wasn't the whole story.

During his regular inspections, the CG had been asking company commanders, platoon leaders, and individual Marines about the status of canteen tops. The CG had learned that tops were scarce because the contracts for ordering them weren't a high priority among professional supply officers, who were more concerned with getting the big-ticket necessities. However, to a Marine in the field, a canteen top *was* a necessity. The system wasn't as responsive as it should have been.

Because he knew his company was due for inspection by the CG, the company commander in this case went to his peers in other units and persuaded them to lend him some canteens and tops for the inspection. He promised to return them later.

On the day of the inspection, the company commander was ready. Each Marine in his company had a canteen with a top.

Turn to page 147 to find out what happened.

Case 2: Travel Orders

This case points out what can happen when someone decides that the end justifies the means, and that not getting caught is more important that doing the right thing.

Lieutenant Commander James was an officer with eleven years of service who was much admired by the junior officers. He had gotten married recently and was now stationed overseas, well into an unaccompanied tour. His wife, who was living alone back in the United States, was unhappy about their separation.

Lieutenant Commander James considered resigning from the military for the good of his marriage, but Personnel Headquarters required him to complete the full overseas tour before leaving the service. James felt he needed to talk with his wife about the situation face-to-face, and he received leave to do that. He tried to get a seat on a space-available flight to the United States, but it was full. Next, he tried to get priority as a courier, although he didn't have courier status. He still couldn't get a flight.

Meanwhile, his wife made it clear in overseas phone conversations that their marriage was in jeopardy, and he felt he needed to get home immediately. Perhaps he could make her understand the benefits of his finishing his twenty years of service in order to attain retirement benefits.

Lieutenant Commander James was under a lot of emotional pressure, and he felt that the Navy owed him air transportation. He decided to do something he considered a very minor offense—and better yet, undetectable. He forged a set of flight authorization TDY orders, figuring that his actions really didn't hurt anyone and that saving his marriage was the most important thing. Besides, if by some remote chance he got caught, he thought his senior officers would understand the necessity of his going home and consider his past contribution to the service. Those two factors ought to mitigate any punishment.

Turn to page 148 to find out what happened.

This is our special duty, that if anyone specially needs our help, we should give such help to the utmost of our power.

—Marcus Tullius Cicero

Case 3: The Fitness Report

This case is about a commanding officer (CO) who misses the forest for the trees. He concentrates so much on the good of his squadron that he doesn't see the larger picture.

O-4 rankings during the annual October fitness report cycle are one of the most competitive and influential set of marks received in the course of a career. This set of marks can determine who is selected for O-5 and command. For an officer who is a senior O-4 and about to go before a selection board, this fitness report cycle is critical.

In a particular squadron, there were nine O-4s who were assigned as department heads. Based upon the size of the year groups, five department heads fell into year group A and four were in year group B.

For group A, the October fitness report ranking was the last one before the O-5 selection board met in the spring. The squadron CO, Commander Whitley, realized that the ranking and report of fitness on the five department heads would make or break the majority of people's chances for selection, but the instruction was very clear: the department heads must be ranked, and reported, from one to nine.

Whitley had worked with all of these officers every day and felt that each one was more than qualified to be an O-5. Based on their performances, they deserved selection. However, Whitley also knew that the promotion rates would be approximately 60 to 65 percent for year group A and probably less the next year for year group B.

Whitley considered his options. He could:

(1) Do the ranking and reporting as instructed. This would reinforce and improve the current system that requires all the fitness reports to be submitted at the same time and returns any piecemeal submissions.

(2) Come up with a plan to take care of everybody. If he ranked the department heads competitively only within their year group and then double-ranked both within the year group and between year groups, he could ensure that each person in year group A was ranked one or two. After all, the squadron CO has the best opportunity to observe the department heads and

ought to be the most qualified to determine who gets promoted. Historically, if someone isn't ranked 1 or 2 as a department head, the chances for promotion are reduced. Whitley also knew that by sending in his fitness reports piecemeal, instead of as a group, his chances of being caught were reduced.

(3) Submit a proposal to overhaul the rating system so that cheating won't work. It might improve the behavior of some raters. This approach assumes, however, that cheaters won't be able to figure out how to beat the system.

If you were the CO, what would you do?

Turn to page 149 to find out what Commander Whitley did.

Oh, what a tangled web we weave,
When first we practice to deceive!

—Sir Walter Scott

ETHICS FOR THE JUNIOR OFFICER

Case 4: Certification

This case is about taking responsibility for a mistake, even when there is little chance that it will be noticed. In fact, the senior officer in this case urges the junior to ignore the incident, assuring him that the error will go undetected.

Lieutenant Thomas is assigned to a Pacific-based aviation squadron. He is the tactical coordinator, as well as the mission commander for his crew, so he's responsible for the accomplishment of the mission.

His plane was involved in an annual mining certification readiness inspection. The mining run up to this point had gone perfectly. As Lieutenant Thomas reached the next to last target, he released a mine. The computer made a mistake and dropped the last two mines together into the target. There were no mines to drop on the last target.

Lieutenant Thomas's department head is a senior lieutenant commander, qualifying as a mission commander. He told Lieutenant Thomas that radar wouldn't detect the error and his score would remain 100 percent.

Lieutenant Thomas wasn't sure what to do. On one hand, his aircrew had received outstanding marks in other inspections and chances were that the error wouldn't be noticed. After all, Lieutenant Thomas thought, the department head had been around long enough to judge the situation better than him.

On the other hand, Lieutenant Thomas was the mission commander. He had the overall responsibility for the aircraft. Regardless of rank, he was in charge in the air. He was accountable to his seniors, his crew, and himself for accomplishing the mission.

Turn to page 150 to find out what the lieutenant did.

Responsibility is the test of a man's courage.
　　　　　　　　　　—Lord ADM John Jervis, Earl of St. Vincent

Case 5: Takeoff Time

This case focuses on the pressure a senior officer places on a junior officer to obey an illegal order.

Captain Storace is in the Air Force, working as the flight examiner who administers flight evaluations at one of the major Air Force commands in Europe. For a flight of two or more aircraft to be considered on time, it can take off at zero minutes early or up to two minutes late.

One day there was a mechanical failure, and one crew had to transfer to a spare airplane. The flight took off six minutes late.

Captain Storace radioed the command post and reported that the takeoff time was 0606 hours.

"Sir, please change that to 0602," a voice replied.

"Look, there was a mechanical failure," Storace said. "The crew did a highly professional job of changing planes, but the takeoff time was 0606."

"It has to be 0602, sir," the voice repeated.

Correct reporting was a requirement of the captain's job. He took a deep breath and said, "The right takeoff time has to be entered in the log."

"I can't, sir."

"What's your name and rank?" Storace asked.

"Corporal Morgan, sir. I've been given instructions that all times have to be listed within the prescribed limits."

"Well, corporal, I'm an Air Force captain, and I refuse to report something that isn't true."

There was a pause in transmission, then Storace heard another voice.

"This is Colonel Stanley, Captain. Report the takeoff time as instructed. It's within my authority, so let's get this done so we can move on to something important."

Storace realized that while he probably had more time in service than the corporal, the colonel not only outranked him but had more experience. The captain asked the colonel for an explanation for the wrong reporting.

"I don't have time to explain," Colonel Stanley snapped. "Just get on with it if you know what's good for you."

Turn to page 151 to find out what happened.

ETHICS FOR THE JUNIOR OFFICER

Case 6: Reporting Ready Status

This case focuses on a junior officer trying to decide what to do about a minor reporting discrepancy. The command knows about it and approves it, and the misreporting doesn't seem to be affecting operations. Is it worth raising a fuss about?

Lieutenant Commander Lee was the new assistant maintenance officer in a fighter wing in Europe. After being in the position for a few weeks, he discovered that his midnight shift in maintenance control had been submitting a daily report at 0300 to higher headquarters. This daily report listed more aircraft in operationally ready status than there actually were at 0300.

Lieutenant Commander Lee questioned this practice and was told that it had been going on for a long time. More ready aircraft helped the wing commander look good to headquarters. In fact, the attitude seemed to be that since the minimum number of operationally ready aircraft needed to maintain the wing were normally ready between 0600 and 0700, what was the big deal?

Lee realized that even though operational procedures are relatively constant throughout Air Force operations, local commands may vary their procedures. He decided to check all of the lower echelons to see whether they were doing this kind of reporting too. Lee found out that this was the standard operating procedure. He confirmed that the maintenance officer himself knew what was happening, as did the wing commander.

Lieutenant Commander Lee wondered what to do. It wasn't a policy he would have implemented. He knew, however, that fighting the system at this point might jeopardize his career. He might be making a lot of fuss over what was a pretty innocent stretching of the rules. Finally, he decided to discuss the misreporting with his boss. His boss told him not to worry about it. Operations have never been affected by these inaccurate reports.

Turn to page 152 to find out what happened.

I would lay down my life for America, but I cannot trifle with my honor.

—ADM John Paul Jones to A. Livingson, 4 September 1777

Case 7: Missile Test Firing

This case illustrates a situation in which there are a lot of good reasons for lying and not a single reason for telling the truth.

An important test firing of an air-to-air missile had been delayed a number of times. The missile was now scheduled for launch on 30 September, with a 1 October backup date. The launch was funded by O&M,N (Operation and Maintenance, Navy) with one-year money that was to expire on 30 September.

On 27 September a meeting was held to decide what to do if the shot didn't happen on the thirtieth. All the players, including the range director and test director, discussed shooting on 1 October and backdating the range and telemetry costs.

The test was important, and new money wasn't available in the next fiscal year. They were all willing to go ahead with the backdating plan.

Everyone wanted the test to take place. The Navy testers, the missile's builder, and even the Range Directorate stood to gain something from the test. The consensus was that the O&M,N money was meant for this test, so why turn it back in over a one-day delay?

The participants in the meeting—two O-4s, one O-5, and two GS-13s—made the decision to proceed on 1 October if necessary and "adjust" the accounting later.

Turn to page 153 to find out what happened.

God grant that men of principle shall be our principal men.

—Thomas Jefferson

ETHICS FOR THE JUNIOR OFFICER

Case 8: The Exam

In this case, a student lets his personal needs dictate his actions, rather than his sense of what's right and wrong. He considers falsifying records so that he can get away for the weekend.

Ensign Peterson was an officer student at a service school. His sister's wedding was coming up on Saturday, and Peterson wanted to take leave for four days so that he could go home and attend. Unfortunately, his grades weren't high enough to meet the normal standards for leave.

Also, a big exam was scheduled two days after the wedding. Part of the preparation for this exam involved reviewing classified materials that couldn't be taken from the base. The ensign hadn't finished studying for this exam.

Peterson thought it might be worth trying to obtain leave, although he knew his request would probably be refused. Perhaps, he considered, his request would be approved if he promised to improve his studying and performance. On the other hand, if he was turned down, then he would have drawn attention to himself, making it impossible to leave.

Of course, if Peterson just took off, chances were that no one would miss him over the weekend. He could fill out study logs, stating that he studied all weekend long. The ensign wouldn't get caught because the logs didn't have to be countersigned. Plus, Peterson thought, the logs just certify that he studied—it just wouldn't be *at school,* as the logs implied. Anyway, Ensign Peterson decided he needed some time off. The exam was important, but so was his sister's wedding.

If you were Ensign Peterson, what would you do?

Turn to page 153 to find out what happened.

Faults done by night will blush by day.

—Robert Herrick

Case 9: The Lone Ranger

This case examines whether certain modifications to a procedure are in the best interests of efficiency, the command, and the Navy—or are these modifications, like other examples of misreporting, unethical behavior?

Lieutenant Salamon was newly assigned to a squadron, and he was a junior mission commander. He was asked to "pencil whip" crew qualifications, so that the squadron's readiness would look good to the wing.

Lieutenant Salamon believed this practice was wrong, and he discovered that other officers were falsifying records about crew qualifications. Salamon found it ironic that some of these officers, once they had completed their assignments, were receiving "prime" orders for their next ones.

As a junior officer, the lieutenant also realized that reduced defense budgets were sure to mean fewer command slots in the future. He also knew that he needed good orders—for example, to make department head—in order to keep advancing in his career. Lieutenant Salamon wondered what, if anything, he should do about the falsification of records.

Some issues that Lieutenant Salamon might consider are: (1) Long-standing practices are established by senior officers, and perhaps time and experience dictated modifications that are in the best interest of a given command. (2) When an individual thinks everyone else is out of step, some introspection is needed to be sure the concern, whatever it is, is realistic. (3) The armed forces are based on trust, and if one junior officer perceives that the command is failing in a particular area, perhaps more specific knowledge and experience is needed. (4) In making a decision, a junior officer must consider the effect of his or her actions on the good of the command. Is it better to wait until you've achieved higher rank and then make policy changes to prevent this problem? If you were Lieutenant Salamon, what would you do?

Turn to page 154 to find out what happened.

ETHICS FOR THE JUNIOR OFFICER

Case 10: The Parking Pass

In this case, an officer is faced with the temptation to commit fraud. His fellow officers, knowing the situation, weigh in with their opinions.

Lieutenant (jg) O'Neill wanted a better parking spot, one that would cost fifty-five dollars a year. He decided that it would be a wonderful joke if he could produce his own pass and get the space for free. To him, this wasn't fraud as much as it was just being savvy.

O'Neill borrowed a legitimate pass from a friend and made several copies. With painstaking work, he was able to create one that looked exactly like the real thing. When he showed the fake pass to his friends among the other junior officers, they complimented him on the skillful job he had done. The officers warned him, though, that if he got caught, he would be punished, and probably severely.

Lieutenant (jg) O'Neill considered what to do. He figured if he used the pass only a few times a week and at random times, no one would notice. The other junior officers still advised him against it. O'Neill was certain, however, that none of them would turn him in.

He realized that it wasn't right to use a fake pass for illegal parking. However, he was much less concerned with getting caught than with what his friends and fellow officers would think of him if he went ahead and used the pass. He also hadn't considered how much trouble could come out of what he considered to be just a prank.

Turn to page 156 to find out what happened.

The easiest person to deceive is oneself.

—Edward Bulwer-Lytton

Case 11: Lost Documents

In this case, classified material is missing, and there's no record of its destruction. The officer involved debates whether to recreate the material's destruction record. The issues include the falsification of records and the ethics of dragging a friend into the situation.

Lieutenant (jg) Walker couldn't account for some classified documents that had been signed for. Walker actually believed the material had been destroyed but the record of destruction had been lost.

Rather than admit he had lost control of this material, Walker tried to reproduce the destruction record. By reproducing this record, he would get the receipt he needed for the material that he believed was destroyed.

Two signatures were needed to verify destruction, so he asked a fellow officer and friend to sign—knowing that the other person hadn't participated in the assumed destruction.

The friend, Lieutenant (jg) Shane, was positive that Walker must have destroyed the material, because it couldn't be located. She thought that the only possible explanation was that the receipt had been lost.

If the material ever turned up, both Shane and Walker would be in serious trouble. On the other hand, if Walker came forward and admitted that he had lost control of the documents, there would be an investigation. That would hurt his career, and legal action could be taken against him.

There wasn't much time to make a decision, and Walker wanted an answer fast. If you were the friend involved, what would you do?

Turn to page 157 to find out what happened.

Case 12: To Fail Oneself

This case examines the conflict an officer has with coming clean about his past, especially when he knows the truth will derail his career aspirations.

Ensign Parker was an officer candidate who worked hard to develop both academic knowledge and professional skills. He was accepted into the Nuclear Power Program. After being commissioned, he was asked to answer a few administrative questions before he went to his first submarine.

One question asked whether he had ever used marijuana. In his earlier academic schooling, he had smoked pot twice. Parker was certain that if he said no, he would be able to continue with his career. If he admitted to smoking pot, however, it might result in punishment or the end of his career.

What issues should be considered? The reader might want to consult the article written by ADM Arleigh Burke that appears in appendix A for some insights into approaching the subject of integrity. The opening section is particularly applicable.

One of the many lessons to be learned in life is that you can never go back and retrace your steps. The past, even if we're the only ones who know our secrets, is with us forever. Even though it's hard to imagine now what it will be like to be forty, and age sixty seems unimaginably long off, the reality is that you may live to be at least ninety! That's a long time to live with something you've done.

If Ensign Parker says nothing, he may be able to continue with his career. Even if he reaches four-star status, Ensign Parker will have thirty to forty years to live with himself after retirement. Being an officer is something to be proud of, but his secret will be something he can't forget, and it may tarnish all his other accomplishments.

If Ensign Parker owns up to the mistake, his military career may be over, but his chance for a successful life is not. Many industry and government executives have admitted smoking pot in their youth, but that hasn't stopped them from holding some of the highest positions in our society. Being honest about what they did removes any burden of guilt they might carry for the rest of their lives.

If you were Parker, what would you do?

Turn to page 158 to find out what happened.

Case 13: Training

In this case, several units are falsifying their training data, not so much to please the CO, but because "everyone is doing it." The officer in this case has to decide whether to do the same in order to level the playing ground.

This officer's predecessor and fellow officer had worked in the Training Department. He would routinely add a certain percentage of hours to the command's required report, to improve his unit's standing among other units. His unit stood out as better than they actually were.

The fellow officer decided that the better the numbers were in the report, the better the chances were that his unit would get an award in that particular area. He wanted his unit to achieve a standard of performance higher than the other units.

Now the officer in this case was assigned to take this officer's place. He had to decide whether to continue the practice.

The officer thought about possible consequences. If he didn't continue the practice of inflating the numbers, his unit might still win the award.

He also knew that a reporting office in the second-place unit was reporting its numbers correctly. If he kept inflating his numbers, his unit would beat that unit again. All the members of his command were certainly working very hard to stay on top and win the award.

Of course, when this officer took over, no one said anything about fudging the figures. Still, the command climate was very competitive. The CO tried to excel in every area, and awards of any type served as outside recognition of the unit's hard work. The command pursued awards to cement its image as the best unit around.

This officer realized the unit was operating very well, but if he stopped reporting inflated numbers, their self-confidence might be affected. If there was an investigation, it would hurt not only his predecessor but also the CO.

He investigated further and found out that several other units were also falsifying data. Maybe, he thought, my unit deserves to be first anyway. He also found out that his fellow officer wasn't especially trying to please anyone. He had thought that since everyone else was doing it, he should inflate his numbers as well, to give his unit a fair shot.

Turn to page 159 to find out what happened.

ETHICS FOR THE JUNIOR OFFICER

Case 14: Travel Claim

In this case, an officer wants to take his spouse along on a trip, and he's tempted to figure out a way to have the government reimburse both his travel costs and those of his spouse.

Major Trevor was assigned to travel to a distant city on official business. The city was a vacation spot, so he thought it would be nice to have his wife come along.

He knew that the government would reimburse only his costs, but he didn't have enough money to pay for his wife's transportation.

If you were this officer, what would you do?

Turn to page 160 to find out what happened.

The measure of a man's real character is what he would do if he knew he would never be found out.

—Lord Thomas Babington Macaulay

Case 15: Specifications

In this case, an officer debates about whether to report an out-of-specification reading on a piece of equipment. The issues involved include the officer's concern about how he and his work center will be perceived versus the career consequences and eventual cost of the repair if he doesn't report the situation and it's discovered later.

Lieutenant Commander Hyatt noticed an out-of-specification reading on a piece of equipment for which his work center was responsible. The normal procedure was to report incidents like this to the CO. The records kept might indicate a trend in either equipment failure or the quality of the work center's output.

By reporting the problem, however, Hyatt realized that the work center might be perceived as unable to maintain equipment properly. His reputation for competently running the center might also be affected.

Hyatt felt that the work center had been doing good work, and so he was concerned that reporting the out-of-spec equipment would displease the CO. Beyond that, he thought that the equipment reading would eventually correct itself. Consequently, it wasn't worth spending time trying to fix a piece of equipment that was probably operating properly.

He did consider that the equipment might not be operating properly and that the out-of-spec reading would be noticed eventually. If he failed to report the condition, and it was later discovered, his CO might view him as untrustworthy. Hyatt also thought about the possibility that the longer the problem went undetected, the higher the cost of the repair would be in time and money, compared to correcting the problem now.

Turn to page 162 to find out what happened.

The one permanent emotion of the inferior man is fear—fear of the unknown, the complex, the inexplicable. What he wants beyond everything else is safety.

—H. L. Mencken

ETHICS FOR THE JUNIOR OFFICER

Case 16: The Fall

This case examines whether an ensign should report a potentially disqualifying injury when all indications are that he's recovered and in perfect health.

An ensign had just graduated from the Naval Academy and was scheduled for flight training. He was scheduled to arrive in Pensacola after thirty days of leave. In a stopover at his home, he joined some of his high school buddies for beer at a local night spot. He had too much beer and fell after leaving the club. His head hit the back of a concrete step, and he lost consciousness.

When he came to, he was in a local hospital, and a neurologist was giving him tests. The results of one test revealed the reason he had been unconscious for a little over an hour. He had a small contusion on a frontal lobe of his brain and symptoms that included loss of his sense of taste and smell, all caused by the jolting the brain received from the fall.

When he reported to Pensacola, he had recovered totally and felt ready to start flight training. All that was left was to complete a questionnaire about head injuries. When he read through the Navy Air physical qualifications, he learned that (1) a head injury that results in a loss of consciousness for less than fifteen minutes is not disqualifying, (2) a head injury that results in a loss of consciousness for greater than fifteen minutes but less than two hours is disqualifying for at least two years, and (3) a head injury that results in loss of consciousness for more than two hours is permanently disqualifying.

He wondered how he should answer the questionnaire. He had always wanted to fly, and now his dream was within reach. By the time he reported to Pensacola, he had recovered his sense of smell and taste. The advice of everyone he spoke to was the same: as long as he was okay, he should not disclose the injury. After all, if there was anything really wrong, the EEG physical taken at Pensacola would reveal it anyway. Navy Air was getting more and more competitive, and slots were disappearing as the Navy was downsized. His chances of continuing his Navy Air career would be slim to none if he reported the fall.

Even the neurologist who had treated him agreed that the two-year rule seemed unduly bureaucratic and unbending. EEGs weren't advanced significantly enough that they could even detect that a fall had taken place. In addition, an exam given by a private physician showed that his eyes and overall physical condition were perfect.

The ensign knew that if the Navy heard about his injury, he could be disqualified for at least two years. Yet he felt great. There were no marks or other indications of injury. There was no apparent way the Navy would find out unless he offered the information.

He agonized over the decision. On the one hand, telling the Navy was the honest thing to do. On the other hand, it seemed so unfair, since he was fully recovered and felt as well as he ever had. Should he really let his life-long dream go, even though he believed he was in excellent health?

Turn to page 163 to find out what happened.

Honest men fear neither the light nor the dark.

—Thomas Fuller

Case 17: Zeroing the Truth

Two pilots willfully perform a flying maneuver prohibited by the aircraft operating manual. Their actions result in overstressing the aircraft. The senior officer covers up the evidence of the incident and doesn't report it. What does the junior officer decide to do?

The CT-39E Sabreliner aircraft is used by the Navy to provide rapid transport of both personnel and small cargo. It's flown by two pilots—a transport aircraft commander (TAC) and a transport second pilot (T2P)—and an aircrew member. The TAC is responsible for the aircraft, its crew, and the overall mission. The T2P handles navigation, communications, and other operational or emergency functions for the aircraft.

One day, for a local training flight, the TAC was Lieutenant Gage, while the T2P was Lieutenant (jg) Tallarico. This kind of flight usually involved flying the aircraft through various maneuvers so that the pilots could maintain their proficiency in all regimes of flight. NATOPS (Naval Aviation Training and Procedures Standardization) states that the Sabreliner airframe can withstand only a predetermined number of Gs. It also prohibits certain maneuvers so that the aircraft isn't inadvertently overstressed. Among these are any acrobatics, such as rolls, loops, and spins, as well as any maneuver that causes the aircraft to fly inverted.

Sometime during the flight, Gage, who was also serving as the instructor pilot, thought it would be fun to test their skills in this aircraft by flying a modified loop. Both pilots rationalized that this was right to do because they had heard that factory pilots had done a modified loop in a civilian Sabreliner.

As the aircraft was coming on the downside of the loop, the airspeed increased dramatically, to nearly the maximum limit. To keep from overspeeding, Lieutenant Gage pulled harder than he normally would on the yoke. He just managed to recover the aircraft as it rapidly shot out from the bottom of its loop. When the two pilots checked the cockpit accelerator, they realized their speed had significantly overstressed the aircraft. Since it was possible to reset the meter to zero, they did that and then returned to base.

Both pilots knew the dangers associated with prohibited maneuvers, including the possible loss of life and equipment. They also knew that they had acted against orders. If they reported this, their careers might end. They would probably never fly again. Lieutenant Gage, the senior officer, decided not to tell Maintenance Control.

Several days went by. Lieutenant (jg) Tallarico felt guilty about not reporting the incident. He tried to decide what to do. He realized that Lieutenant Gage was also his fitness report evaluation senior.

After their training flight, the overstressed aircraft flew several passenger flights without incident. If you were Tallarico, what would you do?

Turn to page 164 to find out what happened.

He who permits himself to tell a lie often finds it much easier to do it a second time and third time, till at length it becomes habitual; he tells lies without attending to it, and truths without the world's believing him. This falsehood of the tongue leads to that of the heart, and in time depraves all its good dispositions.

—Thomas Jefferson

ETHICS FOR THE JUNIOR OFFICER

Responsibility and Accountability

RADM Gary Roughead, USN
77th Commandant of Midshipmen, U.S. Naval Academy

Navy Regulations, Article 0701, states, "The responsibility of the commanding officer for his command is absolute."

That one phrase sets us apart as a profession. This recognition of a commanding officer's responsibility is codified in Navy Regulations, and has been recognized by seafarers since the beginning of history. With absolute responsibility comes authority commensurate with that degree of responsibility, and, ultimately, accountability for the exercise of authority in furtherance of responsibility. Some are drawn to command because of the responsibility and accountability it requires. Others avoid command for the same reason, concluding the rewards of command do not outweigh the burdens. Some may not think they will command during their time in service, or reason there will be ample time and a series of assignments that will groom them for the day when, with a crew assembled before them, they will be privileged to say, "I relieve you." The nature of the profession of arms, however, especially as applied to naval officers, demands that we be comfortable with responsibility and be prepared to assume command at any time in our careers. Command can be ours in a heartbeat, and circumstances may require us to lead as ensigns or admirals, second lieutenants or generals. When those above us have fallen or communication is impossible and action is required, duty will call you to command.

Your preparation for command has been underway for some time. You have studied leadership and practiced it to a degree. You possess a level of tactical and technical competence. These factors are all important in command, but the real key to your preparation for command is your readiness to assume responsibility *and* your acceptance of the fact you will be held accountable for your exercise of authority. Of the two, responsibility is easier to address because you already know what it means to be responsible for others and for mission or task accomplishment. As officers in command, you will be charged with various duties, ranging from ensuring the well-being of your subordinates to killing in combat.

Our exposure to responsibility as naval officers begins early on in our careers with tasks commensurate with our experience. We learn more, demonstrate greater proficiency and competence, and as a result are given more responsibility. How quickly that happens depends on a number of factors such as circumstance, our capacity for taking on more responsibility, our desire for more responsibility, and how possessive we are of the responsibility that we are given. This possessiveness should become a passion—an abiding commitment to your people, job, unit, and service. That passion allows you to thrive on increased responsibility; indeed, it causes you to seek more challenge and responsibility leading to the exercise of absolute responsibility or command. The underpinning of command is accountability. Accountability carries with it sanctions, both self-imposed and administered by others, but moreover, immeasurable rewards.

I once had a discussion with a very senior Army officer during which he opined that naval officers take accountability to the extreme. This was not the first time in my career I had heard this opinion expressed by an officer serving in a different armed force or by a civilian with no experience working with the Navy. Although our standards often appear cruel and unreasonable to others, for those who go to sea and in harm's way, there is no alternative to strict accountability. Some individuals may argue that in today's technologically connected world, the need for such a degree of accountability is unnecessary and is an anachronism. On a small ship in a large ocean, however, when things are not going well and lives are on the line, trust and confidence are not sought outside the lifelines. This is truly what accountability, to naval officers and to the sailors and Marines serving under them, is about—trust and confidence. Trust and confidence in your unit, in your service, and in you as a leader.

Regrettably, accountability is most often discussed in the context of affixing blame when things have gone wrong. This is one aspect of accountability, to be sure. Critically more important, however, is recognition that the substance of the naval profession, the essence of leadership and the ability to command, lies in a sense of accountability—a personal commitment to allow decisions to be made, positions to be taken, and actions to be carried out, knowing you have the strength of character to stand by those actions and claim them as your own. This sense of accountability and its inseparable component, integrity, are the touchstones of our professional ethos as naval officers. Accountability and integrity can be talked about, lauded in speeches, and sworn to as oaths of affirmation, but the only thing that matters, in the end, is what you do: It is your personal statement of action that tells the world who you really are. You cannot be accountable for only that which is "important." You must possess and epitomize a sense of accountability throughout your professional and personal life because, in the end, your sense of accountability, like your integrity, must be a comfortable habit. Additionally, you must think through and comprehend, ahead of time, the magnitude and the potential consequences of decisions you will be called upon to make as a naval officer. This awareness of the decision-making process and the development of your sense of accountability will give you the confidence needed to recognize what must be done when the situation arises and to act instinctively with respect to the issue of accountability. Those you lead will be confident in their ability to carry out their assigned duties because they will know you have recognized and appropriately weighed all factors affecting the issue at hand and will stand by your decisions. For the sake of those you lead, if you are not willing to accept the consequences of your decisions, do not enter the arena.

What about the seemingly harsh standard of accountability in the naval service? The consequences of decisions you will make as a naval officer are significant because ours is a high-risk profession. It is not a question of a failed investment or a late delivery on a contract. Decisions you will make on a daily basis at sea involve life and death and the security of our nation. No other profession thrusts this degree of responsibility upon young men and women. The sailors and Marines you will lead are well aware of the risks, and they are the ones who will suffer the consequences of poor plans and decisions. To gain the degree of trust and confidence required for sailors and Marines to place their welfare, indeed their lives, in your hands, your sense of accountability must be absolute, and they must know your standard is inviolable.

Your professional and personal reputation will rest upon your sense of accountability and your integrity. It allows others to take what you say to the bank, to know that your part of the operation will go as planned, or you will promptly and voluntarily acknowledge your shortcomings. With this sense of accountability and integrity, well-informed decisions to continue or to alter plans can be made. Further, a sense of accountability that freely acknowledges error serves as the basis for improvement. Those who identify problems, even when such identification reveals organizational or personal weaknesses, enable progress and ultimately save time by eliminating the need for anyone else to search for the basis for the error.

Assess, every day, where you stand with regard to responsibility and accountability. Do not allow concern for your personal fortunes to influence controversial decisions, but rather think carefully about your sense of responsibility and accountability, and about your willingness to step into the arena. Remember, as a leader, you are in the arena all the time.

Case 18: Letter from Home

This case raises issues of responsibility and accountability. Every responsible moral agent should be held accountable for his or her own actions and choices. In an ideal world, individuals would always monitor their own behavior in order to meet necessary standards of conduct. There would be no need for us to monitor one another. In the real world, however, we cannot always rely on others to act responsibly 100 percent of the time. Even the most well-intentioned and generally reliable people will occasionally act irresponsibly. Therefore, in high-stakes situations, particularly when lives are on the line, it becomes the responsibility of everyone concerned to closely observe, judge, and, if necessary, correct someone's behavior. As you read this case, consider how many people can be held accountable fairly for the outcome of recorded events.

Two aircraft were scheduled to fly a formation flight together. Because the aircrews had worked together before, they thought they would make a good team for this particular mission. On the day of the flight, a normal briefing session was held. Before the flight, both aircraft were in good condition, and the aircrews appeared to be in good spirits overall, with the exception of one copilot.

While most of the preflight preparations seemed unremarkable, there was something amiss. The copilot of one of the aircraft was clearly exhausted. During the briefing session, he read a personal letter from home instead of paying attention to the material being presented to him.

The pilot's behavior was a clear violation of NATOPS, aviation discipline, and professionalism. However, no one said anything to correct the pilot, or even to draw attention to his irresponsible behavior.

Turn to page 165 to find out what happened.

Case 19: Computers

Can an officer who takes on a civilian job to supplement his salary really give his all to the military? This case looks at the ethical quandaries that result when an officer starts his own business.

Lieutenant Cunat was assigned to an administrative position at a shore command. He decided to supplement his military income by running a private business on the side. He checked with a judge advocate officer, who advised him that he could run a business as long as it didn't interfere with his professional responsibilities, and he had the permission of his CO.

A few months later, Lieutenant Cunat requested leave to take care of a personal family matter. Actually, he wanted the time off so that he could make a trip to enhance his business.

Meanwhile, one of his co-workers had been noticing that Lieutenant Cunat was using a government computer to help with his personal business. The co-worker thought that it was unfair for Lieutenant Cunat to use equipment that is intended solely for government projects.

The co-worker had also noticed that Lieutenant Cunat worked on his personal business during regular working hours, weaving it in with his military responsibilities. To top it off, Cunat received personal business calls during government working hours. When the co-worker heard about the trip, she made a "hot-line" report.

Turn to page 166 to find out what happened.

Every violation of truth is not only a sort of suicide in the liar, but is a stab at the health of human society.

—Ralph Waldo Emerson

ETHICS FOR THE JUNIOR OFFICER

Case 20: The Thief

In this case, a friend and fellow officer is guilty of a crime. Similar crimes have happened over the past few years. Does the friend confront the officer and ask if she's guilty of those crimes as well?

Second Lieutenant Keller was caught shoplifting at the base exchange. Second Lieutenant Roland was a good friend of Keller's, and she wondered if Keller was also responsible for other thefts from fellow officers in their unit over the past two years. The missing items had included credit cards, money, wallets, and other personal effects.

Second Lieutenant Keller was Roland's best friend and a friend of her family as well.

Roland wondered if she should ask Keller about the other missing items. If she didn't ask, they would keep the relationship and regard they have for each other. She could assume this theft was a one-time thing.

If she did ask, she in effect would be saying that she thinks Second Lieutenant Keller is a longtime thief, not just someone who made a mistake once. If she confronted her, Keller would never ask Roland for help later on if she needs it.

However, Roland realized that if she didn't confront Keller, everyone in the unit would remain under suspicion for theft.

Turn to page 168 to find out what happened.

Every rascal is not a thief, but every thief is a rascal.

—Aristotle

Case 21: Private Information

This case examines what a junior officer's options are when he overhears private personnel information being shared inappropriately at a party. Does he let the situation go? Does he talk to his senior officer privately? Or does he report the incident to the chain of command?

Lieutenant McCullough was entrusted with private information about personnel in the command because he had a need to know that information. By chance one day, Lieutenant (jg) Schultz overheard Lieutenant McCullough repeating private information to other officers at a party in the Officer's Club.

The nature of the information was such that it shouldn't have been disclosed. Schultz was junior to McCullough. In fact, his next position could really be affected by his relationship with McCullough.

Lieutenant McCullough was the personnel officer for the unit. The question for Schultz was, should he (1) ignore the situation since more senior officers were there and had heard what had been said, (2) challenge McCullough about how he was doing his job and thus affect his relationship with him, or (3) report the matter through the chain of command and take the risk of hurting the lieutenant's career, especially if Schultz had misunderstood what was said. Schultz would then look foolish, and that would affect his future assignments.

If you were Lieutenant (jg) Schultz in this situation, what would you do?

Turn to page 168 to find out what happened.

Case 22: The Notepapers

This case focuses on the importance of SWO (surface warfare officer) qualification during the first tour of duty in order to be selected for SWO Department Head School. These qualifications signify the upward mobility of the young officer and may lead to an eventual sea command. What is one junior officer willing to do to get those qualifications?

During Surface Warfare Officers School, students review many classified publications involving various threat parameters, procedures, and equipment capabilities. That information, along with other class requirements, makes it easier for the student to have the SWO Personal Standards Booklets filled out and signed at the first command after school graduation. The booklets have to be completed, signed off through validation at school or by a qualified SWO, before the board is convened on the ship to conduct an oral examination.

In all the courses at SWO basic school, students take classified notes, which stay within the confines of the school, thus protecting the security of the information while allowing students to study for tests. After students complete school and graduate, their notes are sent, using standard security procedures, to the officers' ships or station for more study. They can review the notes as they complete their PQS (Personnel Qualification Standards) Booklets.

Ensign Rivers was a newly commissioned officer in the U.S. Navy. As an ensign, he recognized that it was imperative for him to attain warfare qualifications in order to remain competitive for promotion.

Ensign Rivers decided that the classified notes were so important to him that he bypassed the security arrangements and carried these notes to his first command. He wanted to make sure they weren't lost during the standard transmission of classified documents. Knowing that people would ask questions about his security arrangements, he decided to keep his notes at home, with his other professional papers. That way, Rivers felt his notes would be secure, and he wouldn't have to answer questions about their location.

In the years that followed, Ensign Rivers moved six or seven times. Each time a moving company moved those notes, along with his books and other papers. Some years later, and now as an O-4, Rivers came across his notes.

Rivers had basically three options from which to choose. He could (1) turn the information in to be burned, risking that a security violation would be reported, (2) burn the information without anyone's knowledge, or (3) keep his notes.

He realized that most of the systems and equipment spelled out in his notes were no longer in use. Plus, if Rivers told someone about the situation, he risked ending his career for a mistake he made years ago. He also realized that the security of the United States hadn't depended on his actions, then or now. His primary concern was his ability to compete against other competitive officers.

Rivers had become very successful after the basic course, qualifying as an SWO in the shortest possible time and selected to Department Head School well before his peers.

If you were Rivers, what would you do now?

Turn to page 170 to find out what happened.

I hope I shall always possess firmness and virtue enough to maintain what I consider the most enviable of all titles, the character of an "Honest Man."

—George Washington

ETHICS FOR THE JUNIOR OFFICER

Case 23: Sleeping on Watch

This case examines what happens when an officer and senior enlisted unintentionally break a rule. The officer is the only one who knows. Does he report them both to the CO or not?

The engineering duty officer (EDO) on a nuclear submarine had worked for many years to obtain his position of responsibility and authority. The watch standers who reported to him also had worked hard for many years and were professionals in all respects.

A new CO had recently reported to the ship. The EDO was impressed with the CO's abilities and sense of fairness. He was enthusiastic about supporting the new CO's policies. The CO stated unequivocally that sleeping on watch was unacceptable. All offenders would be processed for administrative separation from the Navy.

While a shutdown nuclear submarine is in port, typically the only watch stander in maneuvering is the shutdown reactor operator (SRO). The EDO's work here is in mostly maneuvering, with coming and going allowed as necessary.

In this case, the SRO was a senior experienced enlisted electrician who had been very helpful to the EDO in the long and tedious process of qualification. The SRO was always willing to answer questions and to help the EDO research answers. As the SRO's division officer, the EDO knew that the other members of the division looked to the SRO for answers. On days off, the SRO often came to work to help others. The SRO had spent more time at sea than the EDO had in the Navy.

It was 0500, and the EDO had been on watch for twenty hours with only two hours of sleep. The SRO had had roughly the same amount. Their lack of sleep was due to the fact that they were coordinating a complex propulsion plant testing. The EDO and his watch standers successfully conducted this training. He had just gotten off the phone with the chief engineer, who congratulated him on doing a good job during the night. The EDO passed the good word on to his watch standers.

He was filling out the turnover sheet for the incoming EDO, who was scheduled to appear in a few hours. While writing, his eyes shut and his pen drew along the paper. No one else saw him, and his eyes had been shut for no more than a few seconds.

He completed the rest of his paperwork and decided to stand up and get a cup of coffee. While standing up, he knocked a book off the shelf, which hit the floor with a loud bang. The EDO noticed that the SRO, with his chin on his chest, eyes shut, and limp arms and legs, didn't move at all.

The EDO woke the SRO, and the two of them went to get coffee. The EDO thought about whether to report the two of them for sleeping. He knew he wanted to support command policy, maintain his own integrity, and possibly identify a policy that leads to sleeping on watch.

On the other hand, he considered the possible damage to or the end of his career, and the damage to or end of the SRO's career. That would influence the morale of the electrical division and disrupt the entire crew as two key watch standers were removed from the stand bill.

If the EDO reported himself and the SRO for sleeping on watch, he couldn't know ahead of time what the results would be. He expected, as a minimum, that the CO would hold Mast for each of them. It was possible that they would both be administratively separated from the Navy. But it was also possible, given his honest admission, that the CO would be lenient.

Turn to page 171 to find out what happened.

Divine Providence has granted this gift to man, that those things which are honest are also the most advantageous.

—Quintilian

Case 24: The Party

In this case, a junior office mentions something potentially troubling to her senior but doesn't go into detail. In a few days, the senior officer finally realizes how serious the situation is. Who's at fault for the lack of communication?

During a party hosted by military personnel, a lot of alcohol was consumed. Some of the guests behaved in a criminal fashion, and the other guests were annoyed and angered.

Lieutenant Takesako, who had been at the party and served as a subordinate of a senior military official, complained the next day to him that a wild party had gone on the night before. She didn't elaborate.

The senior, who had a lot on his mind, listened to her but didn't ask more or take any action. Three days later, when Takesako went into more detail, he realized that things had really gotten out of hand and that he needed to take further action.

Turn to page 172 to find out what happened.

God is with those who persevere.

—Koran

Case 25: Government Equipment and Services

A civilian friend of the command asks for a small favor. Can one of the command printers be used to print out a report?

Jack, a civilian, was a good friend of the base's CO. He also helped out the command with a wide range of activities and offered advice to different members of the command on boating repair, a hobby of his. All of Jack's activities were legal.

The command had purchased several business computer programs that were used every day. Jack had the same programs at home, but his printer was broken. He brought in a floppy disk and asked his friend the CO if it was alright to print out a particular report on one of the office printers. The CO directed one of his juniors, an O-3, to help Jack. Jack supplied his own laser printer paper for the copy.

If you were the O-3, what would you do?

Turn to page 174 to find out what happened.

Case 26: Motivation Isn't Everything

This case study examines a commanding officer's responsibility in judging the fitness of one of his subordinates. At what point does loyalty to a subordinate become a problem for the command?

Lieutenant Danton was one of the pilots in Commander Petrina's squadron. Commander Petrina, the CO, was concerned to see that the lieutenant was having a hard time concentrating on his job.

When the CO talked to Lieutenant Danton, he found out that the young man was excited because he and his girlfriend had just gotten engaged. Commander Petrina congratulated Danton.

Petrina decided that Danton's absentmindedness wasn't a problem. The lieutenant was committed to being a good pilot. He seemed to be motivated to do things the right way, and so the CO allowed him to keep flying.

Turn to page 175 to find out what happened.

Case 27: The Drug Test

In this case study, a competent sailor confesses to using cocaine once. The division officer must decide how to handle this revelation. Can you reconcile the Navy's zero-tolerance policy with compassion for a good sailor?

Petty Officer Edwards was an E-5 nuclear submarine technician and a good, solid performer. He went to his division officer after a random unit-sweep urinalysis. Edwards explained to the division officer that he was under stress because of problems at home, and he had used cocaine for the first time in his life. Edwards deeply regretted it.

The results of his urinalysis turned out to be negative.

The division officer had to decide what to do. There was insufficient evidence of drug use. He wondered if Edwards had really used drugs or if he was just trying to ask for help. If Edwards did use cocaine and wasn't caught, would he try it again? And if the division officer didn't take action, what kind of message was this sending to the other sailors?

The division officer had to consider the petty officer's job in relation to the unit's security and safety. He realized also that if sailors can't trust officers with their problems, they may not open up about them at all. If you were this division officer, what would you do?

Turn to page 176 to find out what happened.

Any man can make mistakes, but only an idiot persists in his error.

—Marcus Tullius Cicero

Case 28: Drinking Contest

In this case study, several officers decide to operate a bar. Is there anything unethical about allowing their customers to become intoxicated?

Several officers decided to supplement their income during off-hours by operating a bar in town. One evening, the patrons started a drinking contest, and several customers became legally intoxicated. Assuming that no fights break out, have the officers done anything wrong?

Turn to page 177 to find out what happened.

Case 29: Interaircraft Communications

This case study focuses on what happens to two pilots who skip some of the paperwork and preparations before going on a flight and makes the point that paying attention to detail is an ethical obligation.

Two pilots were assigned to fly a formation flight in hazardous mountain terrain. Both pilots were impatient with the required paperwork and procedural follow-ups, so they rushed through some of the preparations for the flight. They felt they knew what they were doing, and neither pilot had ever experienced a mishap.

During the flight, the two aircraft collided, and both were destroyed. Fortunately, no one was injured.

Turn to page 178 to find out what happened.

For nothing goes for sense or light
That will not with old rules jump right.

—Samuel Butler

Case 30: Transportation

In this case study, a senior officer asks his junior officers to help a civilian friend with his move. They use a government van for the move.

Commander Jay was a senior officer at a base. He was also very concerned about the welfare of his junior officers and thus quite popular with them. Commander Jay often complimented the people who worked for him on their outstanding performances.

Over the years, Commander Jay had also developed friendships with members in the civilian community. One of his friends in town, who was slightly disabled, had entertained officers without charge, as a goodwill effort. He had also opened his home for overnight guests who were visiting the base.

Commander Jay's friend came to him and asked if Jay could help him move some furniture sometime, at the convenience of the motor pool and Jay's personnel. Later that day, a few junior officers asked Jay if they could borrow a government van to use on a night out. They thought it would boost morale.

Jay thought about both of these requests. He realized that his success at the base was due largely to the devotion of and extra hours worked by his juniors, as well as the goodwill efforts of his civilian friend.

Commander Jay checked and found that a government van was available on the evening the juniors wanted to go out. Even if additional requirements came up, other vans were available that night. He called the motor pool and found out that a truck was available on the day that his civilian friend wanted it; in addition, other trucks would be available that day.

The commander considered how he could give his civilian friend the assistance for the move. Furniture was going to be too heavy for this man to handle.

Turn to page 179 to find out what happened.

Case 31: The Bus to Liberty

In this case study, a Morale, Welfare, and Recreation (MWR) officer has planned an approved trip, but only one family shows up. Is it ethical to use the bus, and an enlisted driver, to go on the trip anyway?

Lieutenant Boyle was the unit's MWR officer. She was always looking for chances to create pleasant off-duty experiences for members of the unit and their families. She surveyed the unit's members and discovered that a trip to a family theme park in the area would be a very popular outing. The theme park was several hundred miles away.

Lieutenant Boyle planned the trip and distributed notices about the departure and return times for a bus. The notices also gave information about the expected incidental costs. The bus for the trip was drawn from the motor pool and filled at the pool's gas pump early on the Saturday of the trip.

The departure time was 0700 that morning, and Boyle arrived a half-hour early to be sure that everything was ready when the service personnel and their families came. By 0730, only one family had arrived—a more senior officer with his spouse and children. Lieutenant Boyle realized that this family, Boyle's husband, and Boyle herself would be the only ones going to the park.

Lieutenant Boyle tried to decide what to do. She liked the senior officer, who worked extremely hard. He and his spouse had done a lot for the enlisted in the command. She knew they had been looking forward to this trip. In fact, they had even changed some other plans in order to be free to go. Boyle added to that the fact that the senior officer was her fitness report evaluation senior.

The use of the bus had been approved. Lieutenant Boyle didn't know why no one else was there, but was positive—as was the senior officer—that everyone had received word about the proposed trip. If you were this officer, what would you do?

Turn to page 180 to find out what happened.

ETHICS FOR THE JUNIOR OFFICER

Case 32: Crew Assignments

In this case study, an XO has to decide how to assign two new ensigns to two different billets.

Commander Berben was the executive officer on a ship. Two ensigns reported for duty, one female and the other male. As XO, Berben's job was to assign them to a working billet. Two billets needed to be filled: an administrative billet and a damage control assistant billet.

Commander Berben had to decide which ensign to assign to which billet, keeping in mind the best interest of the Navy, the ship's crews, and each individual officer.

Commander Berben considered the billets and the candidates. The Damage Control Division involved a lot of manual labor as well as comprehension of some complex technical information. The female ensign had recently transferred from an administrative billet, where she had done an extraordinary job. Berben also reviewed the male ensign's experience. The XO recognized that it was his duty to develop young officers to their maximum potential. Not only was assigning the best person to the job important, but Commander Berben also felt strongly about not perpetuating past Navy stereotypes. He didn't want to erode the morale of ambitious female officers and enlisted crew members who desire more technical positions.

Turn to page 181 to find out what happened.

He saw with his own eyes the moon was round,
Was also certain that the earth was square,
Because he had journeyed fifty miles, and found
No sign that it was circular anywhere.

—Lord Byron

Case 33: The Combination

In this case study, two junior officers circumvent security procedures by obtaining both of the combinations to a security container that was used to transport COMSEC (Communications Security) material.

During a West-Pac deployment, two junior officers, Lieutenant Falk and Lieutenant (jg) Lawson, worked with classified information. In fact, Lieutenant Falk was the new command security manager, and he had recently completed Communications Management Security School.

Part of their job was to secure and transport classified material in a container. The container had two different combination locks, requiring both to be present in order to retrieve the material inside.

For the sake of convenience, Falk and Lawson gave each other their combinations, so that each of them could still get into the security container when the other person wasn't around to open the second lock. Having both combinations gave them each access to material that was guarded by procedures meant to ensure two-person integrity.

They reasoned that having both combinations made things easier and faster if the second person couldn't be found. They didn't want to inconvenience other officers by making them wait for authorized access.

Both Falk and Lawson were hardworking officers who spent more time on the job than most. Neither had ever been in trouble before, nor did they intend to use the security information for any purpose other than what was intended.

One day, a third junior officer came into the communications center just in time to see Lieutenant Falk opening both locks on the security container to retrieve classified material.

Turn to page 182 to find out what happened.

Case 34: The Performer

A junior officer has to decide how much counseling is enough for a troubled enlisted member. How far can you let someone's performance slide before it has an effect on the rest of the crew?

A petty officer second class (PO2) had a difficult time of it when growing up. Now he was part of a twenty-one person work center on a ship deployed to the western Pacific. The PO2 was recognized as an outstanding performer, even though he had trouble getting along with his fellow workers.

Because he performed above and beyond his peers on this cruise, the command advanced him to the next higher pay grade. Right after this, the PO2's performance went downhill.

Lieutenant (jg) Naville counseled the petty officer for indebtedness, lateness, and lack of interest in assignments. Then the PO2 went UA (unauthorized absence) in Australia.

When the PO2 returned, he was placed on report, sent to the Captain's Mast, and awarded a fine, restriction, and reduction in rate (grade). The violations continued.

Naville continued to counsel the petty officer, who didn't change his behavior. Naville made sure the PO2 knew Uniform Code of Military Justice (UCMJ) regulations. The lieutenant thought the PO2 should be treated like anyone else, even though the PO2 had received superior performance awards. The rest of the work section was watching what would be done to this enlisted crew member.

Naville debated about what to do next. It could be that the PO2 was pushing the system too far. He doubted if the PO2 was ever going to change. In fact, he felt that perhaps the PO2 had received too much attention for his outstanding work.

Naville thought about the people in the work center. If the PO2 were court-martialed, it would send a message. Twenty individuals could be saved versus one lost, and the ship would be better off.

If you were this junior officer, what would you do?

Turn to page 183 to find out what happened.

Case 35: Off-Duty Employment

This case study focuses on the ethics of having another business during off-duty hours.

Lieutenant Colonel Snyder was the director, Personnel and Community Activities, at a stateside Army post. His deputy was Major Gale, a conscientious, hardworking, and loyal officer.

Gale had just leased a building in the nearby community and opened an antique shop. Gale's wife operated the shop. Snyder knew about the shop because his wife had bought and sold several items there.

The night before, the post commander had spoken to a group of local business and community leaders about contributions the post was making to the local community. Lieutenant Colonel Snyder was in the audience and was surprised to hear a local antique dealer claim that Gale was hurting his business because of unfair competition.

The matter didn't end there. The post commander received a letter signed by two antique dealers several days later. They alleged that Major Gale attracted customers from the post by using his official position and contacts. They also claimed that Gale was buying and selling antiques on TDY trips, and that he sometimes wore his uniform at the store.

Snyder decided to check with the base JAG officer, who reported that it was legal for an officer to have an outside interest in a business, as long as that business didn't interfere with his assigned military duties.

"Even though it may be legal," the JAG pointed out, "there is the question of the appearance of wrongdoing that's causing these complaints."

It would be improper, the JAG officer continued, if, in fact, the major is actually soliciting business and wearing his uniform while carrying on transactions.

Snyder wondered what to do. The major was one of his hardest workers, an inspiration to his subordinate troops. When Snyder asked Gale for his side of the story, the major said that he needed the money to send to his ailing parents. He added that he knew of others who were also involved in a business, and he wondered why he was being singled out.

If you were Lieutenant Colonel Snyder, what would your next step be?

Turn to page 184 to find out what happened.

ETHICS FOR THE JUNIOR OFFICER

Case 36: Flying a Scheduled Mission

This case study looks at the ramifications of a senior officer deciding to change a training mission without proper clearance. Is the flight leader, a junior officer, obligated to speak up?

An air-intercept flight had been scheduled on a squadron's flight schedule. The mission commander, Commander Harlan, was known for his overbearing personality. Harlan decided to change the mission and briefed the pilots for air combat maneuvers (ACM) without clearing that change through the operations department or the commanding officer.

Harlan's wingman was a young lieutenant. He was also the flight leader, but he didn't challenge the change.

The mission began. Two fighter aircraft were conducting air combat maneuvers against each other, and during a roll, Harlan lost sight of his wingman.

As Harlan continued into a rolling pull-up, he tried to regain visual contact with his wingman. When he regained contact, he tried to reengage, despite being nose high and at a very slow air speed. Harlan also noticed that his aircraft wings were rocking, and he attempted to recover from this inflight condition.

Although Commander Harlan recognized his situation, he was too low to effect a recovery, so he ejected.

Turn to page 185 to find out what happened.

Case 37: The Missing Item

In this case study, a missing part on an inspection checklist can't be located. What does the junior officer decide to do?

A junior officer was getting ready for an upcoming inspection. He couldn't find one item on the inspection checklist—an obscure spare part for an essentially discontinued piece of equipment.

First, he searched for the spare part, but it didn't turn up. He found out that the shipping time to replace it would be a year or more. He felt that if he told the CO about the missing part, it would be like admitting he couldn't accomplish even the simplest task. If you were the JO, what would you do?

Turn to page 187 to find out what happened.

I seek the truth, whereby no man was ever harmed.

—Marcus Aurelius

Case 38: Civilian Attire

A junior officer spots a minor infraction. Is it worth reporting?

Second Lieutenant Moffitt was a junior officer who saw two enlisted personnel on liberty status wearing inappropriate civilian attire. She knew that the command routinely inspected liberty parties for proper attire.

Moffitt realized that the two hadn't seen her. If she didn't report them, she would avoid provoking the enlisted personnel in her unit. There was also the question of which rules should be enforced and which shouldn't.

She also wondered if she would be accused of improper action if she spoke to the enlisted directly. After all, they were not in her direct chain of command.

If she took action, would she get the people who inspect the enlisted before they go on liberty into trouble? She also thought there might be rules about distance from the base and time factors that might affect when an officer was supposed to take action.

If you were Second Lieutenant Moffitt, what would you do next?

Turn to page 188 to find out what happened.

The keenest pangs the wretched find
Are rapture to the dreary void,
The leafless desert of the mind,
The waste of feelings unemployed.

—Lord Byron

Case 39: The Valve

In this case study, an engineering duty officer finds a valve out of place and decides to fix it himself rather than report it. Then he finds another valve out of place, indicating a more serious problem with procedures. Now what?

During a submarine shipyard overhaul testing program, Lieutenant Dunn found a valve out of position in the engine room. As the engineering duty officer, Dunn was required to stop all work and inform the shipyard, the engineer, and the commanding officer.

Next, a critique would be held and corrective action would be taken. A resolution must be issued before continuing work. This process normally takes one shift or more. In this case, Dunn decided to reposition the valve without informing the shipyard because the cause was known, and it didn't affect the engineering plant.

Then Lieutenant Dunn found a second valve out of position in the same area. He was concerned now about conditions in the plant, even though he knew this matter could be easily corrected.

He realized that if he reported the second valve out of position, he should also report the first valve. If he didn't report the first valve, people would be less concerned about the second valve.

On the other hand, reporting the first valve's condition now would mean he would be censured. He shouldn't have corrected the problem without notifying the shipyard. Also, if he reported only the second valve out of position, a lot of time would be wasted because of an insignificant problem with a known cause and an easy fix.

His options were (1) to report the second valve immediately, (2) to correct both out-of-position valves (and any subsequent ones) without reporting them, (3) to report the situation after the second valve was corrected, or (4) to report the second valve out of position immediately and report the first valve as well.

Turn to page 189 to find out what happened.

ETHICS FOR THE JUNIOR OFFICER

Case 40: First-Time Use

An enlisted member with many years of good performance tests positive for cocaine in a random urinalysis screening. The administrative discharge board has some hard choices to make.

Senior Chief Jengeleski was an E-8 with sixteen years of active service. In a random urinalyis screening, he tested positive for using cocaine. He was disciplined at nonjudicial punishment, and an administrative discharge board was convened.

The board consisted of an O-4, an O-2, and an O-1. Jengeleski didn't explain what had happened, although he adamantly denied using drugs. "It must have been in my food or drink," he maintained, "as I have never used drugs." Zero tolerance and mandatory discharge processing is military policy.

The investigation showed that the urinalysis was sound. It was indeed Jengeleski's sample, and the level of cocaine was consistent with use. The government's counsel asked for an other than honorable (OTH) separation.

First, the board had to decide if Jengeleski had committed misconduct due to drug abuse. If it found he hadn't, it had to decide if he should be retained or separated. If the board decided on separation, it then had to determine the type of discharge.

Each officer on the board had to work independently, based on the evidence. They were allowed to talk to other board members and consider mandates from the CO. Personal stereotypes had to be avoided.

The records indicated that Jengeleski was a 4.0 sailor who had been recommended for promotion to E-9. He had no prior misconduct and no history of abuse. He was married with two children, and he was the only source of income for the family.

All of the officers testifying before the board understood that drug abuse couldn't be tolerated. Still, Jengeleski's chain of command testified that his performance was outstanding. The drug abuse was described as uncharacteristic and unbelievable.

The defense counsel asked for a finding of no misconduct. If the board recommended separation, the defense counsel wanted an honorable discharge. If you were the O-2 on the board, how would you have voted?

Turn to page 190 to find out what happened.

Case 41: Software

This case study concerns a civilian contractor spending government funds on research and development to create software for a government computer. A JO joins the project and thinks it's possible that the software already exists. What's the next step?

A civilian contractor was developing software for a government project. A highly competent JO was assigned to the project as the assistant to the military project officer. The JO believed that workable software for this computer might already exist and be owned by the government.

If there were software that the government already owned that could be used, dollars could be saved from research and maintenance costs and time could be cut from the delivery time for the system. When the JO approached the contractor with this idea, the contractor rejected it. The contractor didn't want to renegotiate a lower-priced contract, and he didn't want to lose follow-on maintenance contracts.

The project officer in charge had never worked with this system before and knew very little about it. The project officer considered the JO a threat because the JO was able to give guidance to the civilian employees, work the budget, outline project parameters, and determine requirements for the project. The JO's relationship to the rest of the command was professional and productive. The personnel in the command found the JO easy to work with and resourceful.

When the JO approached both the contractor and the project officer with ideas about how to save money, they told the JO not to make waves.

The JO had to decide what to do. Factors that encouraged the JO to push ahead included (1) loyalty to the government and fellow officers who might be affected by the system, (2) knowledge that the system could be produced less expensively and more safely, (3) a sense of mission accomplishment, and (4) avoidance of a possibly inferior product.

The arguments for not making waves included (1) a senior officer's stand on the issue, (2) the necessity of providing a unified front to a civilian contractor, (3) the fruitless investigation into the ethical practices of the contractor and some senior officers that might result, and (4) the negative effect the whole business might have on the individuals who originally made the basic contract for programming services.

If the JO pursued the matter, some senior officers and the contractor might think the JO was a troublemaker. There would be a lot of extra work and long hours to make the case, along with extensive travel and research. Also, the JO realized that the senior officer might retaliate on the junior's next fitness report.

Turn to page 191 to find out what happened.

I praise you when you regard the trouble of your friend as your own.

—Plautus

Case 42: Dealing with a Vendor

This case examines a civilian who is working as a government purchasing agent for a commissary officer. The civilian accepts a gift from a sales agent who also happens to be a good friend. How should the commissary officer handle the situation?

Larry Masters was a civilian who worked for a commissary officer who delegated to him all command purchases. The commissary officer made sure that all qualified vendors were able to bid on contracts to provide goods and services.

The sales agent for the company that won the award was polite and personable; it was generally a pleasure to do business with him. On one occasion, while making a delivery, he congratulated Masters, whose wife had just had a baby.

By this time, Masters and the sales agent were good friends. The vendor had some baby food available, and it seemed only reasonable to give it to Masters after his child's birth. The food was still good, but it would have been out of date before it could have been delivered to other stores. Masters accepted the gift because he felt he would be personally insulting the sales agent if he didn't.

If you were the commissary officer, how would you handle the situation?

Turn to page 193 to find out what happened.

Reason and judgment are the qualities of a leader.

—Tacitus

Case 43: Component Parts

This case study focuses on the investigation of a hot-line complaint made by a vendor. Have the contracting personnel done anything wrong?

A vendor made a hot-line complaint because she felt she hadn't been given a proper opportunity to bid on material that the military required. An investigation indicated that instead of putting the material itself up for a bid, Navy procurement personnel chose to purchase the material's component parts individually.

It appeared that they had circumvented the requirements for a full and open competition.

Turn to page 194 to find out what happened.

Case 44: Fund Raising

In this case study, a CO has to decide how to best handle a charitable request. Is there anything wrong with donating a ride on one of the base's vehicles as an auction item?

A church burned down in a city with a military base. Members of the congregation asked merchants to donate various items for use in a charitable auction to raise money. The congregation also contacted Captain Bloom, the base commander, to ask if there was some service that the military could provide that could be auctioned off.

Bloom asked the JAG for an opinion. The JAG sent back a carefully crafted five-page statement. Bloom read the whole opinion, which ended with the comment that the decision as to whether to give away a service in the form of a ride on one of the base vehicles was up to the CO.

Bloom read the JAG's opinion paper quickly, focusing on the last sentence, which implied that the final decision was up to him. He decided to go ahead with donating the ride for the church auction.

Turn to page 195 to find out what happened.

A man of character in peace is a man of courage in war. Character is a habit. The daily choice of right and wrong. It is a moral quality which grows to maturity in peace and is not suddenly developed in war.

—Gen Sir James Glover

Case 45: Overpayment

As officers move from one station to the next, they may be paid more than they are entitled to receive through administrative errors. What's the most ethical way to handle that situation?

An officer arrived at her new duty station. She wanted to "hit the deck running" at her new station, so she immediately immersed herself in work.

A short time later she discovered that she was being overpaid. She hadn't noticed immediately because the deposits were made directly to her bank account. The press of many high-priority operations delayed her from bringing the matter immediately to the finance officer's attention.

Turn to page 197 to find out what happened.

Public office is a public trust.

—Grover Cleveland

Case 46: The Christmas Gift

This case study focuses on whether the traditions of a host country and a good professional working relationship justifies stretching the regulations a bit.

A Civil Engineer Corps officer was working in construction on a contract in Italy. When he returned home, he found on his doorstep an unsolicited Christmas gift from an Italian construction contractor. The basket of fruit and other food and drink items was worth approximately two hundred dollars.

The officer worried that refusing the gift outright would be a personal affront to the Italian contractor. The two of them had developed an excellent working relationship on the project.

He knew that gifts like this were common in the construction industry, especially overseas. However, officers are subject to the Standards of Conduct and government ethics; they aren't allowed to accept gifts.

The Standards of Conduct and ethics information was provided to all construction contractors in bidding documents and is repeated to successful bidders during preconstruction conferences.

It was a very nice gift and difficult to turn down. The officer was sure that no one would know if he kept the gift since it had been delivered directly to his home. Also, he believed that the contractor understood that the gift wouldn't influence his decision making on the project in process or on any future work. The contractor's gift was just a sincere, friendly gesture.

If he went to the headquarters legal counsel, the officer thought, they might say the gift had to be returned. That would tarnish the working relationship between the contractor and the officer.

He had to figure out a way to properly dispose of the unsolicited Christmas gift without jeopardizing the working relationship with the contractor. He also had to satisfy the Standards of Conduct requirements, which are in place to prevent undue influence by any particular contractor.

Turn to page 198 to find out what happened.

Case 47: The Gift

This case study focuses on whether an officer has a duty to immediately put an end to unethical behavior, even if it is boosting morale.

In a government program office, for as long as anyone could remember, whenever a military person was reassigned, or a civilian retired, the support contractor, as a gift, had a caricature made of the person leaving. The artwork presentation was the high point of the farewell ceremony, since the artwork also included references to the person's personal and professional life.

A newly assigned financial manager (FM) arrived in the office. She had completed a tour in an inspector general's office and questioned the propriety of such a gift. Office personnel, including the program manager (PM), assumed the gift was relatively inexpensive, since similar caricatures could be purchased for under $75. He also assumed that the gifts were part of the contractor's normal public relations effort. The PM thought that this practice was an important morale booster in the office and didn't believe there was any reason to stop doing it, even if it was marginally incorrect.

The FM investigated and found that the contractor had been providing these gifts for at least thirteen years, at a cost of nearly $400 per gift, and that the contractor charged the expense against contract work. She told the PM about all this, and they agreed to stop the practice.

Within a week of this decision, one of the division heads decided to retire on short notice. This man was considered an office icon, with over thirty-five years of government service, virtually all of it in the same program office. His division personnel began planning for the party, intending to present him with a caricature.

When they contacted the contractor, he told them that the new FM had discontinued the practice. This caused an office uproar, leading to a meeting in the PM's office. The argument was that even if they had to stop giving the caricatures as gifts, this supervisor was special and should be the last one to receive the gift.

The PM decided that office morale would suffer if this particular supervisor didn't get a caricature, but the size of the office ruled out raising $400 to pay for the present. He decided that as long as the FM didn't think it was illegal as opposed to unethical, he would allow one more caricature. The practice would end with this last party. The contractor then completed the artwork for $270 and charged the work against corporate profit instead of against the contract.

This particular program office had been scrutinized before this. The PM, in order to correct what he felt were marginal practices, had asked for an FM with a background in an inspector general's office to investigate these issues. This was one of many practices that the FM discovered and corrected during her tenure. Her efforts made the relationship between the support contractor and the office more professional and less personal.

While the civilian support personnel had been with the office for many years, the contractor and military personnel had turned over many times, producing a general uneasiness, bordering on animosity, between the military and civilian personnel. That's why the PM felt that the effect on office morale was an important consideration in allowing one more gift. The FM advised him that the gift was clearly *unethical,* but since the contractor apparently agreed on the giving of the gift, it wasn't clearly *illegal.*

After the decision was made, office morale improved. The retirement party was a success, and, as always, awarding the caricature was the high point of the evening.

Turn to page 199 to find out what happened.

The morale of the force flows from the self-discipline of the commander, and in turn, the discipline of the force is reestablished by the upsurge of its moral power.

—BGEN S. L. A. Marshall

Case 48: Working with a Contractor

In this case, a government contractor offers an officer free accommodations and food. Should he accept?

First Lieutenant Ames was involved with procuring government equipment. On one project, he found that he had to make repeated visits to the contractor's place of business. Because the meetings were conducted over a two-day period, he needed a place to stay overnight.

Turn to page 200 to find out what happened.

Every compromise was surrender and invited new demands.

—Ralph Waldo Emerson

Case 49: The Disbursing Officer

In this case study, a disbursing officer keeps coming up short. Should she make up the difference out of her own pocket or report the problem?

Ensign Colbert was assigned as an afloat disbursing officer at a forward-deployed site. Her job required a large on-hand balance of U.S. and foreign currency at all times (approximately $300,000 to $500,000). The documentation of transactions was excellent, as were the procedures for turning over money to the cashiers and balancing out accounts after the completion of check cashing and currency exchange.

When handling this amount of cash, in this many transactions, it was inevitable that sooner or later someone would come up short or over. On a couple of occasions, Ensign Colbert came up short by approximately $20 to $50—not much when the total amount of cash handled was considered. Both times, she made up the difference from her own pocket. Because she felt personally responsible for the money, and the dollar value was relatively small, she chose not to report the losses.

Ensign Colbert's senior officers were the supply officer and the assistant supply officer. They were both level-headed people who looked on disbursing as a business, the same way they viewed other accountable jobs in the department. They understood that people made mistakes. As long as a verifiable audit trail existed, and people used an organized approach to problem solving, her seniors could live with human error. Colbert's CO was also level-headed.

One day, Ensign Colbert purchased additional foreign currency and simultaneously had to revalue the exchange rate. She was in a hurry when she did the calculations. In her speed, she transposed the fourth and fifth digits in her calculations resulting in a $100 loss.

Had she reported the loss, she would not have been allowed to cover the loss out of her own pocket and close the matter. A report would result in an evaluation or, if necessary, an investigation by SECNAV. Because the error was her fault, she felt obligated to personally cover the loss.

Soon after that incident, the ensign went through her cash after a payday and came up about $1,000 short. Ensign Colbert examined both her books and her safe for three days. She couldn't find the problem. She remembered that with the exception of small shortages, she had always successfully re-solved the discrepancies before. She thought back over those discrepancies.

This tender handled a higher number of cash transactions than stateside tenders because of the few places to cash checks off the ship. Paying agents were trained to handle check cashing and foreign-currency exchanges. En-sign Colbert felt bad about the losses because she had always been ex-tremely meticulous in her handling of money. She was reluctant to report these small losses; if she came up short by a significantly greater amount in the future, she would feel compelled to report it, and she didn't want to have an established track record of losses. She decided not to report the losses.

On two other occasions, she came up over instead of short. Both times, she reported the overages, of approximately $100 to $200, according to the established procedures.

The only other times Colbert's operations experienced losses was when other agent cashiers made mistakes handling her money. She always stressed to cashiers that they had nothing to fear about reporting shortages to her. The two times it happened, they never found the money, but again they reported the small shortages as required, which involved sending a let-ter to SECNAV via everyone else in that chain.

Colbert's entire chain of command handled these incidents profession-ally. Neither she nor her people were punished. In fact, even with these doc-umented overages and shortages, her operation received the highest grade possible—"outstanding"—for the two supply management inspections.

But losing $1,000 was a significant shortage. Three days had already passed, and Colbert realized she couldn't continue to sit on the problem. She went to see the assistant supply officer and told him she suspected she was short about $1,000. He was very calm and sent her back to recount after they had talked. Since she had already been over the cash and books a few times, she wasn't optimistic about finding the money.

Turn to page 201 to find out what happened.

Case 50: The Flight

A flag officer wants to attend a reunion, and one of his subordinates makes it happen by arranging for the flag to go along on a check flight. Has the subordinate gone too far to please his senior officer?

A flag officer and his wife decided to attend his high school reunion. The school was located many hundreds of miles away. The flag had a very busy schedule and was expecting important visitors the day after the reunion, so there wasn't enough time to drive to the distant city and get back.

Hearing about the situation, one of the flag's subordinates arranged for one of the airfield's officers to take a check flight that would go from the base to an airport close to the reunion. The subordinate, after making these arrangements, told the flag officer that another officer would be flying back late that night.

The flag officer thanked the subordinate for taking the trouble to find out about the flights that he could use. The flag officer attended the reunion and came back on the check flight.

Turn to page 202 to find out what happened.

The wise man is informed in what is right. The inferior man is informed in what will pay.

—Confucius

Case 51: The Hotel

In this case, an officer is entitled to special PCS rates at a motel chain. His brother works for the same chain and can get the officer an additional discount as well. Is it ethical to take both discounts?

Second Lieutenant Meister was a hardworking officer whose brother worked for a motel chain. When Meister received his transfer orders, he heard that his brother's chain had special rates for military who are on PCS orders.

The next time he talked to his brother, he mentioned that he would be traveling from the East Coast to the West Coast and staying at his brother's motels because of the military discount.

Several days before Second Lieutenant Meister and his family left to travel across country, his brother called. He told Meister that if he mentioned a special code number each time he checked into a motel, he would get an additional 25 percent discount. The code number was the brother's discount number, and he gave Meister permission to use it. Meister's brother was not an official of the motel chain.

If you were Second Lieutenant Meister, would you use the extra discount?

Turn to page 203 to find out what happened.

Case 52: Submarine Pictures

This case study looks at how far it's appropriate to go in order to accomplish the mission for your CO.

Ensign Michaels was a Supply Corps food service officer on his first retrofit before a cruise on an SSBN submarine patrol. His CO needed one hundred pictures of the submarine, which its submarine tender was to provide. This was a very hot issue for the CO, and Michaels was eager to please him.

Michaels approached the tender's ship superintendent, who was responsible for all maintenance, repair, and photo requirements. The superintendent was cordial but said that he didn't think he could provide all of those pictures according to the schedule. He added, however, that "two bags of shrimp would certainly speed up the process."

Michaels knew that it wouldn't be any trouble for him to get the shrimp. Chances were that the crew probably wouldn't even miss it, and two bags of shrimp were a small price to keep his CO happy. Ensign Michaels realized that, since he was a very junior officer, it was in his best interests to keep his visibility low and avoid making waves.

The ensign also considered what taking an ethical stand with the ship's superintendent would mean. The superintendent could refuse altogether to supply the pictures, jeopardizing the maintenance and repair schedule.

Would his CO really appreciate him standing on principles over two bags of shrimp? Also, if he made a stand and failed to get the pictures, would that in turn embarrass his CO with the CO's seniors? Would the CO decide that Michaels was immature because he made an issue out of something that was probably standard practice for the ship's superintendent?

Turn to page 204 to find out what happened.

Case 53: The Junior Officer

A junior officer in charge of BOQ/BEQ reservations experiences a lot of resistance from the senior and junior crew members, who don't want to make advance reservations. Does he continue to follow the rules or compromise his ethics?

Lieutenant Ward was a junior officer and new member of a fifteen-person aircrew. He was in charge of the BOQ/BEQ reservations at the unit's TAD site and made the necessary advance reservations. Senior and junior crew members fought with him about making them because, they insisted, "We don't stay on base, just hotels in town." Lieutenant Ward also heard them say things such as "We don't reserve ahead of time, so the quarters are filled when we arrive" and "The former JO did it the right way, and other crews do it. It's an unwritten rule."

The advance reservation practice directly affects the amount of money each crew member receives. Lieutenant Ward doesn't think the CO really wants to know what's going on, and the prevailing attitude seems to be that what the CO doesn't know won't hurt the command.

According to the written guidelines, Ward should make early BOQ/BEQ reservations to keep TAD and per diem costs down, since government quarters and messing would be available and rental cars wouldn't be needed.

Lieutenant Ward thought about what to do. If he followed the regulations, he would (1) avoid compromising his personal pride, (2) ensure his reputation as a honest officer with integrity, (3) avoid undermining his ability to lead and discipline later, (4) help to change the command and crew climate to a more ethical one, and (5) gain personal satisfaction.

On the other hand, if he kept on making advance reservations, he could almost count on (1) getting a reputation as someone who rocks the boat, (2) fielding reprisals from peers, juniors, and seniors, (3) winning this particular battle but losing the war, (4) costing everyone money, (5) making sure no one would have a rental car, and (6) making sure everyone had to stay in government quarters rather than a nice hotel.

He realized that following an ethical course of action would make him stronger in the long run. It could change the command climate by bringing out ethical behavior in other people. It may even enhance his reputation for years to come. Perhaps the CO would appreciate the command's attempts to clean up its act. He might view Lieutenant Ward as a leader.

Still, Ward felt he was taking the risk of being shunned by peers, juniors, and many seniors. If you were Lieutenant Ward, what would you do?

Turn to page 205 to find out what happened.

Case 54: Extra Labor and Equipment

In this case study, a junior officer realizes that he's not being supervised by his seniors. Does a lax ethical command climate give one permission to be unethical? Does ethical behavior matter only if there's a chance of getting caught for behaving unethically?

Lieutenant Commander Purbaugh was working as a department head at an overseas installation. He had supervisory responsibility for a labor and equipment division. This division had, among other groups, an automotive group that worked on government vehicles. This division also had a group of laborers who performed maintenance services, such as taking care of the grounds.

Purbaugh soon realized that the command climate was loose—almost anything went. He wasn't even being supervised. Maybe, he thought, being in an overseas location means paying less attention to details.

Lieutenant Commander Purbaugh decided that it was alright to use his subordinates, almost all of whom were foreign nationals, to cut the lawn and trim the shrubs at his military quarters and work on his car, all at the government's expense.

Turn to page 205 to find out what happened.

Case 55: Cheat

This case study involves the common decision about whether to use the office copier for personal use. The officer's choice has some unusual ramifications.

Ensign Montarelli, a young O-1, reported to her first duty station. She was a solid performer, full of esprit de corps. Montarelli was single at her commissioning, but she became engaged to a civilian within her first year of active duty. Both she and her fiancé pursued graduate degrees at a nearby university.

When Montarelli was promoted to O-2, she received an on-base transfer and was married. She continued with her graduate courses, as did her husband. When it came time to submit her thesis, she agonized over the expense of copying all the proposals and drafts to all the members on her thesis board. (She had grown up in a frugal household and still worried quite a bit about money.)

There was a government copier at her office. Although she had recently heard the command legal officer speak on Department of Defense standards of conduct and conflicts of interest, she decided that there wasn't a problem with copying materials for her thesis on the office copier during working hours. After all, she reasoned, the service encourages us to continue our schooling.

Since her husband was enrolled in a similar graduate program, she wondered if she shouldn't copy her husband's thesis documents at the office as well. She remembered that the military's policy of taking care of its service families and decided that this instance applied. Besides, she thought, wouldn't she be a good example to the enlisted in the office? They should be impressed by the disciplined effort she and her husband were making to continue their educations.

Turn to page 206 to find out what happened.

ETHICS FOR THE JUNIOR OFFICER

Case 56: The Computer

Is it wise for an officer to sell a used home computer to an enlisted member? Is it ethical?

An officer allowed a junior enlisted to buy and finance the purchase of the officer's home computer. The financial terms covered an extended period of time, during which the enlisted was to make monthly payments on the computer to the officer.

Turn to page 208 to find out what happened.

The officer should wear his uniform as the judge his ermine, without a stain.

—RADM John A. Dahlgren, USN, on the night of his death,
12 July 1870

Case 57: The Dinner

A government contractor invites an officer, who's the government's representative on a construction project for the military, to a dinner to celebrate the end of the project. Is it ethical for the officer to attend?

First Lieutenant Jaso was a government representative on a rather large private industry construction project being done for the military. He had maintained an outstanding rapport with the firm's senior management.

As a result of the contractor having completed the project, on time and within budget, they were having dinner at a local restaurant to reward the company's employees for their hard work.

A week before this dinner, Jaso had received an invitation from one of the company's senior executives. The executive wrote that the company would be honored if Jaso would attend.

First Lieutenant Jaso wondered if he should go. Because the project had been so successful, the government might assign this contractor additional work. If he refused to attend, would he be damaging any future relationship between the government and this contractor?

Jaso was aware of the government's standards of conduct rules but recognized that this was just a dinner, not a trip to Bermuda. Also, he had just received orders for a distant assignment, so he knew he wouldn't have further contact with this company. Because of that, there was no possible way that attending this dinner would mean that he would be throwing more business to this company.

Turn to page 209 to find out what happened.

There may be justification, or even a definite need, to restate in strong and clear terms those principles of conduct which retain an unchallengeable relevance to the necessity of the military profession and to which the officer corps will be expected to conform regardless of behavioral practices elsewhere.

—Gen Maxwell D. Taylor, USA

ETHICS FOR THE JUNIOR OFFICER

Case 58: Repair Parts

In this case study, an officer finds something wrong with the way supply and maintenance is being handled. Trouble is, no one seems interested in fixing the problem. What does the officer do?

On a new assignment, an officer was in charge of an activity that was responsible for the supply and maintenance of parts for military equipment. He worked with a contractor, who provided the parts that weren't available from government supply. The officer soon realized that something was drastically wrong.

When he reviewed the invoices, he thought that most of the parts seemed to be overpriced, while a few looked as if they were priced extremely low. Also, repairs were being requested and made on parts that weren't broken. The officer checked on the pricing in the contract and found out that the contractor was in fact being reimbursed at the bid price, which seemed exorbitant.

At the same time, rumors surfaced that the contractor was having his maintenance people change as many parts as possible, even when it wasn't necessary. It appeared that the contractor wanted to increase his profits by increasing the business.

Because he was new in the command and since senior personnel had been involved in awarding the original contract, the officer decided to investigate the situation further before going to the CO.

His investigation revealed that the government was indeed being overcharged for some parts. Also, the contractor was purchasing nonfunctional repair parts at reduced prices and then charging the government new part prices (which were severely inflated), as well as charging the government to have the parts repaired. Finally, the contractor had sent parts off to a subcontractor to repair, but the parts weren't broken. The subcontractor would then send them back at no cost to the contractor, who would charge the government the full bid price for their repair.

The officer went to his CO and briefed him. The CO fully supported his junior's request for a fuller investigation. The contracting shop, however, wasn't interested in getting involved, nor was the investigative agency, because a past similar investigation had caused a lot of bad press and gotten the military into hot water.

The officer believed that something had to be done to correct this illegal and unethical activity. He convinced his CO that the matter should be pursued. He called the investigative agency and was able to push them into conducting an investigation. Once the agency began investigating, they pursued the matter doggedly.

In addition to what the officer had found out, the investigative agency learned that there had been improprieties in the way the contracts were let. The contractors, in fact, were not the low bidders, as required by this particular procurement. The agency also solved the mystery of the low bid prices: instead of using all of the bid prices for award, only a randomly selected number of them were chosen. Oddly enough, these were the same prices that were the lower-than-usual bids by the contractor.

The investigating agency had predicted that the next few months would be rough, and indeed they were. The officer who reported the matter earned a reputation as a troublemaker. The contractor was hostile. The officer sometimes feared for his career, which was indirectly threatened by those with whom he had to conduct business during the investigation.

Turn to page 210 to find out what happened.

We know that there are chiselers. At the bottom of every case of criticism and obstruction, we have found some selfish interest, some private axe to grind.

—Franklin D. Roosevelt

ETHICS FOR THE JUNIOR OFFICER

Loyalty, Dissent, and Commitment

RADM Marsha J. Evans, USN (Ret.)
President and CEO, American Red Cross

No one can "make" you make an unethical choice: *You* are always in control of and responsible for your actions. You cannot blame someone else for your decisions because only you can make them.

Making the right, easier ethical choices routinely prepares you for the rarer, graver decisions. Just as exercising your physical muscles will prepare you for the physical rigors of deployment and even combat, so too exercising your "ethical muscles" will prepare you for the sometimes demanding ethical challenges you will face in the Fleet or the Fleet Marine Force.

I want to address in this brief essay three distinct but related concepts: loyalty, dissent, and commitment.

Loyalty. Loyalty is steadfast allegiance to a cause or person. Loyalty accounts for the patriotism that motivates individuals to sacrifice their lives for the nation and for the heroism that causes one sailor to give his life for his shipmates.

We often think and speak of loyalty to an individual (the boss or the captain, for example), but the real and abiding loyalties of an officer must be to the institution (the nation, the Navy, the command). The president, the secretary of the Navy or the chief of naval operations, and the commanding officer are the personification of those institutions respectively, but they are not superior to the institutions themselves.

We must have clear in our minds the *hierarchy of loyalties.* A naval officer's loyalty means he or she has the best interests of the nation, the naval service, and the command at heart. We must ask ourselves, "What is best for the nation, the naval service, the command, our shipmates, and then ourselves?" Only by understanding where our loyalties properly lie, and in what order, can we deal with the truth-versus-loyalty dilemmas that we may face.

Loyalty should be up the chain of command as well as to peers and to subordinates. Loyalty is reciprocal: If you want your sailors and Marines to be loyal to you (and you do), you must be loyal to them. The sailors and Marines you will be leading are savvy and sophisticated: they can smell a phony right away, and they will recognize the "real thing" as readily. The chances are that they will see you *as you really are.* Perceptions count, and you have considerable control over how people perceive you.

To be an excellent officer, it is not enough to be only loyal. Loyalty and trust go hand-in-hand. You inspire loyalty by your trustworthiness. Whether or not you are trusted depends on your trustworthiness. You build trust one day at a time, one action and decision at a time. Do you carry out your word? Do your actions reflect strong principles? Do you live an exemplary life? Do you put others before self? Can people depend on you to do what you say you will?

Dissent. Dissent takes many forms. From a positive perspective, it is the different point of view: "I disagree, Captain. I think the division can get all the necessary preparations accomplished and free up one watch team to go on liberty." (Naturally you've thought through very carefully your excellent, logical plan that could accomplish that *before* you spoke up.) It may be manifested in the raising of an alternative explanation for events: "XO, I believe the reason why . . ." (Again, you have the supporting facts to explain your contrary view.)

One of the worst things an officer can do is discourage the surfacing of different points of view, especially discouraging "bad news" or an unpopular view that contains critical new insight about a situation. As you make recommendations to your leadership or you make decisions, you want to be—and need to be—informed from many perspectives. That is the value of having diversity on your team, of people feeding information to you through many different perceptual lenses formed by their different experiences or perhaps racial and ethnic heritages, to help you see all aspects of an issue.

A good leader works to create a climate of open communications in which new, fresh ideas can be offered, opposing viewpoints can be discussed and fully debated, and the decision you make can be embraced. A

ETHICS FOR THE JUNIOR OFFICER

leader who "shoots the messenger" or ridicules differing ideas will soon find that critically important but negative information or fresh new perspectives are not offered. Why would someone risk wrath or ridicule? Your sailors and Marines will take cues and clues from you: Do you listen respectfully and with an open mind, or do you "shoot the messenger"? It's your choice to make, but you will have to live with the consequences of your choice.

Suppose you have offered a dissenting point of view, and you have argued your position with unassailable logic and passion, yet the captain's direction is exactly the opposite of your recommendation. You are now expected to provide the command your best support. Indeed, it is your duty to carry out your direction as if the direction were your own. George Marshall had it right: "The less you agree with the policies and direction of the senior, the greater the energy you should direct to carrying out the direction."

The opportunity to dissent does not include the right to defame, nor does it imply that a dissenting viewpoint is appropriate any time or place. Defamation of another in framing the argument for your point of view is *never* appropriate. In fact, it could be a violation of the Uniform Code of Military Justice (counter to the good order and discipline of the naval service and conduct unbecoming).

A junior should be mindful of the setting. It is one thing to speak personally and privately to a senior and offer a dissenting voice; it is quite another to speak up in a large group with subordinates present. If your view is not accepted, it will be much harder to carry your direction "as if it were your own" when some or all of your subordinates heard your counterargument. You must also be mindful of the chain of command. You might even be surprised to find allies and advocates as you go up the chain of command with your well thought out and carefully articulated position. You go around the chain of command *at your peril.*

There could be a time when you believe your conscience requires you to dissent or even not carry out an order. You must carefully examine both the requirement levied on you and your conscience. Be sure you fully understand the order or direction: Perhaps you have misunderstood, and clarification will shed a new light and a different understanding. It may even be prudent to seek legal counsel or the advice of a trusted mentor or spiritual counselor. If you cannot reconcile your conscience with your orders, you *must* address it with your chain of command.

An individual can change the course of events by dissenting from the convenient, easy, popular unethical path. The right course of action may not be the popular course, and it may be a difficult choice for you to make, but you will be able to live with yourself and know you did the right thing. You could be the person who sets the example and inspires others who may not have had the courage to take the right path.

Commitment. You cannot be less than fully committed to your profession. As a naval officer, you are voluntarily choosing a way of life, a life that gives you the opportunity and indeed the privilege to serve the nation and your fellow citizens. No one forces you to make this choice of service, but now that you have made that choice, much is expected. You must always do your best: People's lives could be hanging in the balance. You must constantly strive to improve yourself in all dimensions—body, mind, and spirit. As a leader of men and women, not only are you responsible for yourself; the nation's mothers and fathers, wives and husbands have entrusted the lives of their loved ones to you. It is a solemn and sacred obligation.

If you cannot be fully committed, you must make a different choice, choose a different career path, for there is no room in the naval service for the partially committed.

I have always looked forward to enlistment, reenlistment, commissioning, advancement, and promotion ceremonies as opportunities to bring special focus on commitment as a way of life for serving military members. A common feature of each ceremony is the administration of the oath of office. When I was the presiding officer, as a prelude to administering the oath to the honoree, I would always ask each military attendee to contemplate the relevance of the oath in their own lives and reaffirm their own commitment to service. I believe it made the ceremony more relevant to—and more interesting for—everyone attending.

Every day you will have the opportunity to demonstrate to others —and most especially reaffirm to yourself—that your commitment in the service of the nation and to your fellow citizens is steadfast and strong. Confidence that our own moral and ethical values are strong and integrated is liberating. They are touchstones for the decisions we make daily. They help us calibrate and correct our course if we should stray.

Case 59: Training

This is another case in which training records are falsified. The junior officer must weigh her future career objectives against loyalty to her commanding officer, her unit, and her country.

First Lieutenant Grimes just joined a unit and was assigned to be the training officer. She was well briefed about the importance of her duties, and she understood the concept that "we fight like we train."

After inspecting the unit training records, the first lieutenant was pleased to see that all departments and divisions of the command were training on a weekly basis and properly completing the training critique form.

Grimes had been there about a week when she decided that her position also required her to observe some of the training so that she could make suggestions for possible improvement. She watched one of the teams training and noticed that they didn't go through all of the evolutions required by the training plan. She wondered about the incomplete training but assumed that the unit would probably complete the missing parts in the next few days.

Later, though, when she reviewed the training critique form, she realized that the unit had taken credit for having completed all of the required evolutions. She knew that wasn't true.

Training is done to enhance the crew's knowledge. Grimes realized that the unit was probably less well trained than the completed reports indicated to a higher authority. As can happen with any documentation scheme, the completion of the form, rather than the training, had become the objective. This type of thinking leads to what is sometimes referred to as "gundecking" and the mistaken principle that "training well documented is training well done."

The first lieutenant recognized that training must be accomplished as prescribed first, and then, only after that step was completed, the critique form should be completed. She understood that documenting incomplete training as completed leads to a breakdown of the training process. In turn, this leads to a degradation of mission readiness and a general breakdown of unit cohesion.

As she investigated further, she found that there were a few other units that were also "gundecking" their training records. Those units were led by officers who had been with the command longer than she had. They were also senior to her.

If Grimes went along with the system, she would eventually move on to another job. But if she made waves, her career might be hurt by the comments and actions taken by the other officers.

Turn to page 211 to find out what happened.

Case 60: Inflated Readiness Levels

This case examines the false reporting of aircrew readiness levels, based on training. The reporting was done to make the squadron readiness look better. Is it harder to do the right thing when the command climate is to let it go?

Lieutenant Andrews was an O-3, newly assigned to a squadron. She found out that the more senior officers were exaggerating individual aircrew readiness levels to make the whole squadron look more ready. No one was getting adequate training and completing all the required events.

The squadron was suffering both short- and long-term effects. Its performance levels were low, which wasn't surprising considering people weren't getting the training they needed. The ethical climate of the command allowed everyone to think "that's the way it is" when it came to the practice of inflating crew readiness levels.

Andrews knew there had to be written instructions somewhere that documented what the required training was. She wondered whether it was worth talking to the CO.

Turn to page 212 to find out what happened.

The measure of life is not length, but honesty.

—John Lyly

Case 61: A Friend

This case study highlights two significant issues in the lives of military officers: the necessity of a strong team spirit and the friendship that emerges from that bond, and the tension that arises when the call to professional duty wars with the bonds of friendship.

The Naval Aviation Training and Procedures Standardization rule for pilots was that they should not drink within twelve hours of flying. This rule, known informally as "from bottle to throttle," was revised several years ago to include the two-hour period of flight briefs that occur before launch time. The "bottle to brief" rule still maintained the twelve-hour prohibition against drinking but in effect added another two hours to the period of required abstinence.

Lieutenant Hagen was the friend of a pilot who had just flown. The previous night he had witnessed his friend having a drink at a party held eight hours before the flight brief. The lieutenant had known this pilot for many years. Both of them knew the "bottle to brief" rule.

Lieutenant Hagen debated what to do. While it was legally the right thing to report his friend—and he realized that the rule was based on extensive experience with aviation mishaps—he was torn between friendship and doing what he knew was ethically correct.

He realized that if he reported the incident, it would adversely affect his friend's career. On the other hand, the safety of others, as well as of government property, might be at stake.

He wondered if he knew what he had seen. He had come to the party late and noticed that his friend had eaten a lot at the barbecue spread. He was drinking a beer but didn't seem intoxicated.

Hagen also had to consider the challenge of leadership—to be proactive. Many of his squadron mates were at the party. Didn't they also have responsibility? It was, after all, no secret as to who would be flying the next day. And what about the commanding officer? What sort of tone should he set to prevent transgressions?

The lieutenant knew his friend had committed an obvious violation of a clearly stated rule. His options in response were fairly limited. He could ignore the violation, turn his friend in, or counsel his friend about the risks of his behavior.

Hagen continued to ponder his dilemma. He knew that he would want a friend to cover for him if the shoe were on the other foot. He knew also that his friend knew the rules and had a good record. Was it his job to play informer and damage his friend's career?

Turn to page 213 to find out what happened.

Case 62: The Rifle Company

This case examines what happens to a unit when one officer behaves badly and finds ways to manipulate others. A newly arrived junior officer has to decide whether to take a stand and put an end to this behavior.

First Lieutenant Riley was newly promoted in the Marine Corps and recently had been assigned to Alpha Company, an infantry unit. He was given orders to deploy overseas on a Navy ship with a small complement of Navy and Marine officers who had been working with one another during routine training events over the past six months. Because Riley was the newest member of this well-established team, the other officers watched him closely at first.

The CO of Alpha Company, a Marine captain, was well intentioned but didn't have rapport with his subordinates. This may have been because the company XO, a Marine first lieutenant, lacked confidence in his own leadership abilities. The XO was influenced too much by his desire for the respect and liking of his peers and subordinates. Over time, the XO lost the ability to discipline the other lieutenants. In order to counter the common gripes and complaints of his peers, he began to badmouth the CO.

Second Lieutenant Jordan was the first platoon commander in Alpha Company. He was a picture-perfect Marine who was big, athletic, and imposing. Jordan had an impressive presence and bearing that made an immediate good first impression. However, those who knew him realized his fundamental professional knowledge was weak at best. Nevertheless, he managed to manipulate the XO in a variety of ways to suit himself.

As the deployment continued, Jordan continued to tell stories of "college pranks," which were actually criminal episodes. He also took advantage of women. His behavior split the Marines into three groups: (1) those who opposed him, (2) those who condoned him, and (3) those who found it easier not to get involved.

Finally, Jordan confided to some officers, including Riley, that when he stood duty in the garrison, he would sort through the CO's personal files and belongings in order to see what the captain was "up to." He had found the personal notebook that the CO used to track subordinates' performance.

Now he knew every decision the captain was likely to make regarding fitness reports.

Riley was appalled but unsure of the best action to take. He decided to wait for awhile.

One of the other officers approached Jordan and confronted him. Jordan wouldn't listen to any criticism and instead tried to verbally and physically intimidate the other lieutenant. He also tried to wreck the other officer's reputation and credibility by making snide remarks at opportune times.

Riley watched what happened to the other lieutenant and continued to agonize over his decision. If you were Riley, what would you do?

Turn to page 215 to find out what happened.

Not always right in all men's eyes, but faithful to the light within.

—Oliver Wendell Homes

ETHICS FOR THE JUNIOR OFFICER

Case 63: Grievance Hearing

A junior officer is asked to make a statement against her CO for an Article 38 grievance hearing. There are many implications to consider in testifying, including the effect on her career.

Lieutenant Saunders was asked by the unit's XO to make statements against the unit's CO during an Article 38 grievance hearing. Before the investigation began, this CO had assembled his officers and asked for their loyalty. He reminded them he would eventually find out who spoke against him.

Saunders felt that her CO was by far the worst she had ever served with. He fell short of the many qualities she had learned a leader should possess and try to exhibit. In fact, she felt that part of the reason morale was so low was because of his negative, unfriendly, and condescending treatment of unit members.

On the other hand, Saunders thought, the CO was technically proficient and the unit always accomplished the mission. In addition, she felt that testifying against the CO would (1) be an act of disloyalty, (2) probably result in an unfavorable fitness report, (3) possibly bring unflattering attention to her unit, (4) create an unfavorable work environment if the CO saw her statement, and (5) possibly result in her being labeled an outcast and untrustworthy. After all, the JO thought, maybe my perceptions of the CO are incorrect.

If she didn't testify, she knew she would feel guilty. She would feel that in not demonstrating the moral courage to stand up and be heard, for taking a careerist approach to her responsibilities, she had let down her country, the military, and her family.

Second, she would be contributing to a bad situation. If the charges couldn't be substantiated, the case would be lost. The CO could continue his unethical behavior. Not only would the current unit suffer from this lack of leadership, but so would the CO's future units. Her failure to testify would be an endorsement of the CO.

Third, she might damage the XO. If his allegations were correct, and no one supported him, it could affect his career and reputation. If you were this junior officer, what would you do?

Turn to page 216 to find out what happened.

Case 64: The Car Cover

In this case study, a CO asks one of his junior officer's subordinates to work on something that isn't appropriate or part of that person's job. Does the junior officer have a responsibility to protect his subordinates?

Lieutenant Christopher was the division officer for a group of parachute riggers (PR) in a medium-sized unit. He learned that one of his parachute riggers was called into the CO's office and presented with a torn car cover, made from a parachute. The CO wanted the car cover repaired.

Due to the age of the material, every attempt to fix one tear caused two new ones. Christopher kept his eye on how the job was going. When the PR determined that he couldn't repair the cover, Christopher told him to return it to the CO.

The PR came back after seeing the CO and told Lieutenant Christopher that the CO was furious. He had accused the PR of "ruining" the car cover. The CO also demanded that the PR make a new car cover out of the material used to make helmet bags and oxygen mask covers. More important, the CO told the PR to use off-duty time to complete this task.

Christopher realized that it wasn't the PR's fault that the old car cover was irreparable. Still, the CO was in charge. Christopher told the PR to finish the job.

The lieutenant had some qualms about what had happened and wondered how the CO had a car cover made from a parachute in the first place. As he thought more about the matter, he wondered about the propriety of making a private car cover out of government material.

After awhile, the CO asked Christopher how the job was going. He let the CO know that the PR wasn't happy about the task and that he had grumbled to Christopher about doing a job that was not in the PR's position description.

Turn to page 217 to find out what happened.

Turn to page 217 to find out what happened.

Leaders are the custodians of a nation's ideals, of the beliefs it cherishes, or its permanent hopes, of the faith which makes a nation out of a mere aggregation of individuals.

—Walter Lippmann

ETHICS FOR THE JUNIOR OFFICER

Case 65: The NATOPS Test

This case examines a NATOPS officer who has to decide whether to follow the rules and pay the consequences for disobeying the CO or obey and know that the rules, as well as the JO's own code of ethics, are being broken.

A junior officer held the position of NATOPS officer. His CO told him to take the annual NATOPS test in the place of a senior officer.

The test is a required part of the annual currency qualifications in naval aviation. Each person is required by NATOPS to take both an open- and closed-book test each year to remain current in a specific type of aircraft.

NATOPS requires each person to complete his or her own test, ensuring that everyone has the book knowledge to understand the aircraft and its systems. It is a Navy order and a matter of flight safety. Everyone is bound by this rule, regardless of rank.

The junior officer was afraid of what would happen if he didn't do what the CO wanted. The ethical climate of the command could be summed up by a phrase the CO used with his officers: "A little apple polishing goes a long way."

The junior officer knew that the CO wanted to please higher authority. As the NATOPS officer, if the junior didn't complete the test, the CO would most likely relieve him, punish him with a poor fitness report, assign him to another job, and then get another JO to take the NATOPS job. That new officer would be faced with the same decision.

The junior officer understood that taking the test for someone else was patently against the rules, regulations, and procedures, not to mention downright unethical. The NATOPS officer had the legal right and responsibility to refuse to falsify the test. But the JO perceived that officers in higher pay grades felt that the rules didn't apply to them and they often decided to ignore the rules and advice of their subordinates. They pressured and coerced juniors into going along with their wishes.

The JO felt his options were limited because he was deployed and those involved were in the CO's direct chain of command. If he got into trouble with this CO, it would probably result in reassignment. His career could be ruined by a negative comment on his fitness report.

On the other hand, taking a stand would make him feel better, because he knew he would be doing the right thing.

He was very troubled and talked to many friends and peers. Everyone felt he shouldn't take the test, but everyone knew what the punishment might be for disobeying the CO. The JO talked with an immediate boss, who then talked with the CO. The word came back loud and clear that the CO expected his orders to be carried out—that was the bottom line, end of discussion. If you were this junior officer, what would you do?

Turn to page 218 to find out what happened.

I prefer to do right and get no thanks, rather than do wrong and get no punishment.

—Marcus Cato

ETHICS FOR THE JUNIOR OFFICER

Case 66: Selecting Candidates

In this case study, a CO asks that special consideration be given to minorities. Is this just reverse discrimination? Or does the CO have something more in mind?

A command had just undergone a division inspector investigation for perceived racial prejudice. Afterward, the Marine battalion commander called in the subordinate commanders and told them "off the record" to give special consideration to minorities during the upcoming screening for a select program.

All of the commanders thought that special consideration undermined the purpose of the whole program, which was to find the best qualified person, regardless of race or ethnic background.

One subordinate commander saw the CO's actions as a way to counteract the effects of the recent investigation. He realized that any special consideration could hurt the command; in some cases, people who were the most qualified might not be selected. That could cause a backlash among the better-qualified Marines, also hurting the unit.

Turn to page 219 to find out what happened.

Case 67: Standing Watch

This case highlights how loyalty to a shipmate and loyalty to the ship can sometimes be in conflict.

Nearing the end of his watch, Lieutenant (jg) Bailey was waiting for the relieving officer to show up. When his relief had neither appeared nor contacted Bailey to explain his absence, Bailey worried that his relief was not only seriously late, but he might fail to show up at all. Bailey knew that in these kinds of instances the standard procedure in his unit was to notify the command duty officer. Bailey hesitated to do this, however, because if he reported it, the relieving officer who failed to show would be reprimanded and all of Bailey's peers would know he was the one who blew the whistle on the tardiness.

Bailey knew that, as an officer, he had a responsibility to report all unusual events, such as the failure of an officer to report for an assigned watch. He worried that the missing officer might have been in an accident. He also worried that if he failed to report the relieving officer's absence, he would be in trouble for violating standard operating procedure.

But Bailey was also concerned about what his peers would think if he reported another officer. He knew that they might shun him for failing to keep the faith with a comrade. They might also take out their annoyance with him by making his work life unbearable, reporting any and all small mistakes he might make to his senior.

Turn to page 220 to find out what happened.

When duty comes a-knocking at your gate, welcome him in;
for if you bid him wait, he will depart only to come once more
and bring seven other duties to your door.

—Edwin Markham

ETHICS FOR THE JUNIOR OFFICER

Case 68: Sanitaries

In this case, a young officer takes on too much responsibility, and what he considered initiative, his CO considered insubordination.

Lieutenant Griffiths, the officer of the day (OOD) on a submarine was approached by one of the enlisted who requested permission to pump sanitaries overboard. Since this procedure involved the safety of ship, the CO had issued standing orders that the pumping of sanitaries required his approval. Griffiths knew about the standing order but hesitated to disturb the CO (who was in the rack) to ask permission. Griffiths felt certain that the CO would approve the dumping since it was midwatch on the day before the submarine's return to port and the procedure needed to be completed within the next eight hours. And, he reasoned, if he authorized the dumping without disturbing the CO, he would be showing good judgment by anticipating an order the CO would probably have given if awakened and asked. Griffiths believed that since the CO was obviously the busiest person on the submarine, he needed his rest.

Turn to page 221 to find out what happened.

Boldness, without the rules of propriety, becomes insubordination.

—Confucius

Case 69: Passing Inspection

In this case, a young ensign bows to pressure and falsifies records.

Prior to an inspection, particularly an operational propulsion plant exam, the stress level in the engineering department always began to rise. It was during this period—a week or less away from the start of the inspection—that someone discovered that a page entry in someone else's service record was not there as required. But by then it was too late to qualify the individual properly and correctly in the needed billet. The engineering division officer was tempted to qualify that one individual by just typing *qual* in the service record and not making the person in question perform the actual PQS for the watch station.

The division officer pressured an ensign to make sure everything was in proper order rather than pressuring him to be sure everything was done properly. The division officer told him, "Just fix it so we pass." The ensign was left with two choices: either gundeck the quals for certain individuals or take a failing grade on the inspection.

Turn to page 223 to find out what happened.

ETHICS FOR THE JUNIOR OFFICER

Case 70: Sealed Orders

This case focuses on the difficulties of knowing how to react when a senior officer violates direct orders. It also shows how one wrong decision can sometimes haunt a person for years after the event.

In late spring 1945, an officer was serving as communications officer and operations officer (ComO/OpsO) aboard a ship that had been designated to play a key role in the amphibious landings on the Japanese home islands. To everyone assigned in the Pacific theater that spring, it seemed the war might well go on a few more years.

When he was ashore one day, the ComO/OpsO was given a set of sealed orders to take to the ship. The orders were not to be opened until the ship had left port and was en route to the invasion. As he brought the packet aboard, his captain saw the envelope and asked him to open it in his cabin and read the message.

The ComO/OpsO refused to open the sealed orders. The captain grabbed the packet from his hand and ripped open the envelope. He read the orders aloud as the ComO/OpsO tried to cover his ears to avoid listening. When the captain had finished and returned the orders, the ComO/OpsO left the room to consider his options. He knew if he didn't report the matter, and someone asked to see the sealed orders before they sailed, it would look like he had opened them. On the other hand, if the ComO/OpsO reported the incident to the agency that had issued the orders, the captain might deny he even knew the orders had been opened. If that happened, the ComO/OpsO would be in deep, career-ending trouble that could also land him jail.

Turn to page 224 to find out what happened.

Case 71: The Mine

This case highlights the importance of good communication between junior and senior officers and how that lack of communication can have repercussions far outside the immediate command.

A few days after World War II ended, the OOD of an escort carrier on a great circle route adjacent to the Aleutian Islands sighted a floating mine. He felt he had three options. He could have the 20-millimeter gun crew explode it, he could chart it and broadcast the location, or, citing a SEA 5 condition, he could simply avoid it and take no further action.

The officer knew that since the war had just ended, there was the question whether the surrender agreement allowed the destruction of a former enemy's military materiel. But he was also concerned that if the position of the mine were simply charted and broadcast, ships that missed the transmission would be in danger. The officer also thought that with the war over, his ship had a responsibility to all other ships that might be sailing these waters. He decided that the best course of action was to explode the mine, and he requested permission from the captain to do so.

Turn to page 225 to find out what happened.

Advice is seldom welcome; and those who want it the most always like it the least.

—Earl of Chesterfield

Moral Leadership

ADM Hank Chiles, USN (Ret.)
Distinguished Professor of Leadership, U.S. Naval Academy

In addition to all the advice herein, I've been asked to roll my internal clock back thirty-five to thirty-nine years and provide thoughts on moral leadership from the perspective of the junior officer.

First, it's worth noting that the world is changing fast. When I was commissioned, we thought Vietnam was a French problem. No one predicted the Berlin Wall would fall, that Russians and Americans would share a spacecraft and stand watch together in Europe, that Martin Luther King would have a dream that would change our lives and the way we see other people forever. No one told me that women would do superb work as line officers on our ships and in the air, that you could put ten warheads on a missile, or that the slide rule would disappear. Even twenty years ago, who would have believed that CNN could flash news instantly around the world, that we would be "netted" largely by glass fiber and with a constellation of satellite communications relays, and that the Soviet Union would fade quietly into the night? Furthermore, the pace of change seems to be accelerating.

Yet constants remain. Our standard of living depends on people outside our borders. Your life needs balance: work, play, rest, exercise, reflection. Family support remains a great blessing. International surprise happens (Pearl Harbor, the invasion of Kuwait, Barbarossa, etc.), and surprises in the future should not be too surprising. The world's sole superpower could be the world's prime target. Our country is likely to be challenged as every generation of Americans has been challenged, so in peace we should prepare for war. (In fact I believe our armed forces have a moral obligation to be prepared for potential conflicts.)

Leadership has constants also. Leadership doesn't equal showmanship. You must develop knowledge of your profession, detailed technical knowledge. It takes hard work. Further, you should analyze your organization and yourself. That's not easy, but it helps to develop your self-confidence. Your vision is essential. If you don't know where you want to take your unit, you'll surely go somewhere else. It's important that you develop a working command philosophy and priorities while you're a junior officer, so you're ready for more responsibility. In fact, I would argue, if you aspire to command you have a moral obligation to your people and your country to become as knowledgeable of your profession as possible, become adept at analysis in a changing environment, become self-confident without arrogance, and to develop a sense of essential priorities.

Be yourself; your troops will smell a rat if you try to be someone else. Stay calm, so you can think straight. Use your temper sparingly, preferably never, but your emotion can be a valuable tool. Share the credit, openly and quickly, and take responsibility for mistakes. And don't forget that optimism really is a force multiplier; you provide hope and inspiration. Personal recognition is crucial and has many forms. "Thank you" are two powerful words. Sun Tzu wrote, "The wise leader doesn't worry about people knowing him; he worries about knowing his people." Personal relationships count. But you won't get to know your people unless you get out and work with them. Become a problem solver. Competence comes with knowledge and practice. Get involved, know your commitments, and honor them. Personally train your people, teach them skills, share insights, and foster a creative atmosphere. Develop many sources of information and ask for feedback. You gain respect from your juniors just by caring enough to ask their opinion. Learn to listen; you don't know it all. Develop the ability to communicate your desires, concerns, and intent concisely and clearly. Without communications skills, your priorities and goals get lost. Remember you don't have a monopoly on all the good ideas; develop the habit of talking to your contemporaries at other ships or squadrons to see what they're doing. (Hopefully, your leaders are practicing the above. If not, that's a lesson in itself.)

Dignity means treating all your subordinates the same as you treat your seniors—no favorites, no prejudice. You should live this as an ethical truth. You have good people, and they want to do a good job. Plain and simple, they succeed in direct proportion to how well you lead. (I guess I didn't believe that as a junior officer. I'm certain of it now.)

Judgment is a precious commodity; it comes with careful thought and technical competence. Don't worry, everyone occasionally separates the wheat from the chaff and concentrates on the chaff. The trick is not to let that happen too often and to learn from your mistakes. Working long hours will not make you a more effective leader, and in fact, may leave you too tired to think through the crisis. Laziness doesn't work, either. Prioritize your day; save time to think.

Analysis counts. Generally, no decision is better than a bad decision, but indecision cannot be your hallmark. Expect problems, but remember that first reports of a problem, especially a shipboard material problem, are usually wrong. You know generally what's wrong, you may not know why it happened or the right thing to do. Take initial corrective action, don't kill the messenger, establish long-term, corrective action when you know the facts. Learn when fast decisions are necessary. Be thoughtful when you have time. (Successful leaders learn to handle this well; all of us had to learn the balance.) Let subordinates make appropriate decisions. Train them to think.

Your integrity, honesty, and straightforward demeanor are the absolute keys to your success. Talk is cheap; your actions are telling. Most importantly, trust is vital. You need to be able to trust your people; they want to trust their leadership. Trust depends on integrity. Without trust, expect poor morale and poor performance. Especially in crises your true character will show, just when you have the least time to think about it. Think about the integrity as well as the knowledge, self-confidence, communications skills, and judgment you need to do your job before crises occur. Consider that mental exercise the moral imperative of an effective military leader.

Sound like a lot? No one said leadership would be easy. Without question, you're going to be challenged in this profession. There will be times when you may be tempted to give a favored subordinate a break not accorded a peer, to shade a report your way, to hide the magnitude of a problem from your boss, to take a nap instead of giving the qualification check out to the subordinate who made an appointment. Fairness, total honesty, and living up to your obligations may seem difficult in the short term, but if you develop the habit of absolute adherence to strict interpretations of your moral obligation as an officer, in the long run it's easier. Your boss and subordinates will appreciate your candor, and you'll be more effective. The case studies should drive home that lesson.

One other thing before you read on. Humor is a powerful tool, especially self-deprecating humor. You're not paid enough to not have fun. Besides, as a junior officer keep in mind that if you're not enjoying your job, no one working for you is either. Your enthusiasm is contagious to your troops. Use it well. And as you slide down the bannister of life, may all the splinters be in the right direction.

Case 72: Command Responsibility

This case highlights two important values: carrying out the mission as ordered and following proper procedures. At times, however, as seen in the following case, trying to do one may preclude doing the other.

An aircraft embarked on a carrier received orders to conduct task-group night sea-air operations. The admiral's preparation brief stressed the importance of the exercise going well in order to demonstrate the task group's accomplishments and present level of capability.

Shortly prior to aircraft launch, the squadron commanding officer learned that several things were wrong. The copilot in the lead aircraft had failed to attend the previous night's operations brief. The lead pilot and copilot had not flown together, nor had they time to brief each other planeside. As the CO was considering these developments, a message arrived from the admiral telling him to ensure that his part of the operation started on time.

The CO realized that executing the mission on time and as ordered would reflect well on his squadron and on him personally. Accomplishing the mission is basic to every military professional. Further, he believed from his own experience that once the planes were in the air, the crews would have time to brief one another, as experienced crews have done in the past. And since the individual pilots in this situation had never been involved in a mishap during their thousands of flight hours, the risk of one occurring on this operation was minimal. After all, he reasoned, the only way to be sure of never having a mishap is to keep aircraft on the ground at all times.

On the other hand, he knew that aircraft and human lives are important and that military commanders are charged with preserving both if at all possible. Aircraft and lives should never be risked unnecessarily, and the current situation was peacetime training, not wartime operations. One of the reasons for training is to minimize uncertainty, mishaps, and accidents.

As he considered his options, the CO knew he could either go ahead as ordered and scheduled or he could delay flight operations in order to ensure that proper procedures were followed. He couldn't do both.

Turn to page 226 to find out what happened.

Case 73: Request for Transfer

This case focuses on the difficulties of confronting a senior officer.

As the officer in charge of a Family Service Center, Lieutenant Commander McPhail reported directly to the XO and CO of the naval station. He had been at his post for two years, but because of conflict with the XO, McPhail struggled in the position and requested an early transfer to a new assignment. The XO verbally agreed to the transfer, but BUPERS (Bureau of Personnel) delayed issuing the transfer orders.

When McPhail contacted his detailer about the delay, he discovered that the XO had misrepresented the scope of McPhail's position at the Family Service Center. According to the XO, McPhail did not deserve department head credit for the job.

McPhail debated whether he should take the issue straight to the CO, confront the XO, notify the base inspector, or just write off the tour as a bad learning experience.

Turn to page 228 to find out what happened.

Case 74: Equal Treatment

This case focuses on the importance of providing a safe working environment for all members of a unit. It also points out how juniors should approach their seniors with concerns.

Following consecutive sea tours, Lieutenant Harrison reported for duty at a small naval base. With a reputation as a "hard charger," Harrison had enjoyed his sea duty but was looking forward to the challenges of his new shore tour. While he was still getting a feel for his new job and new command, he began to notice things that made him uncomfortable. As administrative officer to the CO, Harrison had gained some insight into how the command operated, and he was concerned about a trend he was seeing.

He overheard a few conversations that were not very flattering to women. Having just come from a long tour aboard ship, Harrison was accustomed to some of the remarks, but they still made him uneasy. He also noticed that a few of his male counterparts were playing inappropriate jokes on the female lieutenants. Most worrisome of all, the CO had recently closed the only female lavatory in the building.

Harrison knew he had to do something, so he tactfully approached the CO and voiced his concerns about the treatment the women in the command were receiving. Harrison also raised the issue that some of the incidents could be seen as grounds for harassment charges against the CO.

Turn to page 229 to find out what happened.

Professional courtesy and good manners should be carefully integrated parts of your command and leadership principles, both up and down.

—MajGen Aubrey "Red" Newman, USA

Case 75: Standards

In this case, an officer works hard to recover his integrity and his self-respect after participating in behavior he believed to be unethical.

Lieutenant Hallman, the legal officer for an aviation squadron, was due to transfer in four months. His job had been frustrating and tedious, presenting many challenges and obstacles. Hallman found many of the XO's policies questionable, and he had been involved in an inordinate number of cases of administrative separations of enlisted personnel. In other commands, he felt sure the cases would not have resulted in administrative separation of the service member.

Over the course of his assignment, Hallman had noticed a pattern in the squadron: minority members were administratively separated more often than nonminorities. He was aware of the pattern because he had been involved in processing most of the separations.

His replacement, a female minority ensign fresh out of legal officer school, had recently reported to the squadron, and Hallman was very concerned by a few things that had happened after her arrival. On several occasions, the XO had verbally abused her. Hallman also knew the XO was trying to send another pilot to legal officer school to act as Hallman's replacement instead of the female minority. Hallman felt guilty about the way he had ignored past injustices and resolved that he was going to do something about the injustice this time.

Though he had compromised his own integrity to the point where he began to question his purpose and usefulness to the Navy, he considered tactfully approaching the XO to urge him to stop the harassment. He knew his own past actions had been cowardly and unethical, and so, after much thought, he decided to confront the XO about the present injustices as well as the past injustices to which, he felt, they had both been party. Resolved to make amends for his ethical lapses, he prepared a written statement concerning all those events and submitted it to the XO.

Lieutenant Hallman was ready to see justice done, even if it cost him his own career.

Turn to page 230 to find out what happened.

Case 76: Humor

In this case, an XO makes a difficult choice to live up to his responsibilities to his unit, his subordinates, and his CO.

Commander Martin had been the XO at a remote command for almost two years. He found his job challenging and enjoyed the station, though he thought the previous CO had been rather demanding. A new, less demanding CO had recently taken over command, and Martin welcomed the change in leadership, but now a few incidents were causing him concern.

The new CO was easygoing and likable, but at times his humor could be inappropriate and almost embarrassing. Commander Martin was even present on a few occasions when the new CO made inappropriate statements to newly reporting female lieutenants. The command master chief also told Martin that several female enlisted had told him they were uncomfortable working around the new CO.

The command master chief was not specific about what made the enlisted uncomfortable; he merely said he felt obligated to mention it to Martin as XO. One of the chief's top performers—a yeoman first class—was disturbed by a recent incident in the CO's office. But there had been no written complaints of wrongdoing, and Martin thought the matter might blow over. From personal experience, he knew that comments could sometimes be misinterpreted, and the women might be oversensitive to issues concerning gender.

After more thought, though, Commander Martin decided that all service members must be treated fairly. This meant that the CO's integrity was to be assumed to be above reproach until proven otherwise, as was the integrity of the females who were complaining about the CO's actions.

To get to the bottom of the matter, Martin started a full investigation to determine exactly what had been happening between the CO and the women. He respectfully advised the CO that he felt the need to investigate the matter and report his findings. Martin indicated that if the CO ordered him to drop the matter, he would be forced to report it up the chain of command.

Through conversations and interviews with many people in the command—the CO, the chaplain, the command master chief, and other male and female members—Martin determined that the CO had been engaging in inappropriate conversations with the female members of the command. The CO had commented on how form-fitting their clothes were and how they made an attractive addition to the office. These and other remarks with sexual overtones were disturbing to the women.

Turn to page 231 to find out what happened.

Case 77: Standards

The dangers of double standards and special treatment are at the heart of this case.

A student who was having considerable trouble with the syllabus during flight training had flown five unsatisfactory graded flights, two beyond the allowable limit. Another officer was debriefing a flight he had flown with the training squadron's CO when an instructor entered to tell the CO that the troubled student was marginal on the latest flight.

"And that," said the instructor, "is after two refresher simulator training sessions."

The CO, who was concerned with graduating enough pilots, told the instructor, "Give that student anything but another down."

The officer decided against pointing out to the CO the negative effect this action might have on all the other students and instructors, who would certainly know what had been done. The others were well aware of how many flight failures the troubled student had, and that he was past the limit and apparently receiving special treatment.

Turn to page 231 to find out what happened.

That which among men is called favor is the relaxing of strictness in time of need.

—Favorimus

Case 78: Cowardice

This case addresses the difficulty of confronting a senior officer about his bad behavior and the negative effect looking the other way can have on morale and performance.

Commander Quigley, the squadron XO, was carrying on an intimate relationship with a subordinate officer within his squadron, and most of the other squadron officers knew about it. They disapproved of his actions and believed he was taking unfair advantage of his rank and position. Though they spoke of the matter among themselves, no one said anything to Commander Quigley or the skipper of the squadron.

Lieutenant Ebbitt, a junior officer in the squadron, was disturbed by the extremely negative effect the XO's behavior had on morale, and he briefly considered choosing a time to say something to him. But when he talked his idea over with some of the other officers, they reminded him that Commander Quigley had a reputation for vindictiveness and could ruin Ebbitt's career without blinking an eye. So like the others, Lieutenant Ebbitt bit his tongue, looked the other way, and said nothing.

Turn to page 232 to find out what happened.

Duty—Honor—Country. Those three hallowed words reverently dictate what you ought to be, what you can be, what you will be. They are your rallying points: to build courage when courage seems to fail; to regain faith when there seems to be little cause for faith; to create hope when hope becomes forlorn.

—Gen Douglas MacArthur, USA

ETHICS FOR THE JUNIOR OFFICER

Case 79: The Accomplice

In this case, a junior officer struggles with his desire to please his commanding officer at the cost of his conscience.

An O-3 fleet squadron pilot who served as senior landing signal officer (LSO) and pilot training officer (PTO) worked for a commanding officer who believed very strongly that pilots who are aggressive, competent, intelligent, and spend most of their time thinking about aviation are most likely to become career aviators.

As the squadron prepared for deployment, the CO noticed that one of the junior pilots was having trouble. He was not doing well with carrier landings and was also not very aggressive in the performance of his ground assignments. The O-3 believed the junior pilot was slightly below average and seemed to be showing signs of stress and fatigue. The O-3 also thought the junior pilot was bringing his domestic problems (new home, new spouse, predeployment concerns) to work and it was hurting his flying, but that with a little timely help, the junior pilot's flight status could be saved.

The CO asked the O-3 to collect information and prepare the documentation to permit the removal of the junior pilot from flight status so that another pilot could be brought in by deployment. As LSO, the O-3 was in a position to disagree with the CO's recommendation. In addition, the O-3 knew that the CO respected his opinion. If the O-3 he told him that additional training was a better option than dismissal, the CO would likely retain the junior pilot. The O-3 doubted that the junior pilot would ever be better than average but still felt he was worth the time, effort, and money the Navy had spent on his flight training. The O-3 believed that though there were standards in place to purge average performers if their skills did not improve, average performance from a junior officer was acceptable if there was potential for improvement.

But the O-3 also knew the junior pilot just didn't measure up to the CO's personal standards for career aviators. He watched the junior pilot begin to fall apart as the CO increased his workload.

A Field Naval Aviator Evaluation Board (FNAEB) was convened, and the members of the board, chosen by the CO, shared the CO's views on career aviators. The CO told the O-3 he thought he was a "great pilot, LSO, and officer" and asked him to sit on the board. Though the O-3 was pleased and flattered, he also believed he was selected because the CO thought he could be influenced by the other officers on the board. He also felt the junior pilot's fate was sealed before the board ever heard from the first witness.

Turn to page 233 to find out what happened.

Case 80: The Investigation

How far should an officer go to protect his or her own career?

Several spouses sent letters of complaint accusing a junior officer of numerous liaisons with enlisted personnel. No one was surprised by the accusations because the previous year the officer had been seen openly drinking and dancing with many enlisted personnel. In confidence, one of the command's chief petty officers told the investigating officer of having had relations with the officer as had most of the personnel named in the letters of complaint.

The investigating officer completed all interviews and submitted a draft report to a senior officer. The senior made changes to the report, effectively whitewashing the entire issue, and recommended that the investigating officer formalize the changes and submit the final report. After reviewing the suggested changes, the investigating officer noted that statements had been changed and all statements of a negative nature had disappeared. Many of the witnesses also reported that they had been threatened with disciplinary action if they commented upon the results of the investigation.

By changing the report, the senior officer clearly intended to smooth things over rather than face the questions that would come up if the junior officer went to Mast and was then administratively separated from the service. In addition, so many CPOs and senior petty officers were involved that the senior officer felt it would be extremely damaging to the command and detrimental to the service to end all of those careers over the actions of one JO.

The investigating officer had to consider the desires of the senior officer as well as the requirements and responsibilities of an investigator's official duties. The investigating officer realized that his career may well be at stake because the senior officer had the ability to put negative comments in a report and was likely to express displeasure in the investigating officer's fitness report.

Turn to page 235 to find out what happened.

Case 81: Speaking Up

When, if ever, should a junior officer confront a senior about dangerous behavior?

On cruise, Lieutenant (jg) Carlton, a junior pilot who had previously been involved in a class "A" mishap, was assigned as copilot to a squadron's commanding officer who had a reputation as a "hot dog" pilot. On flights with other officers, Commander Buchanan had exceeded NATOPS altitude, radius-of-turn, and angle-of-flight limits.

As soon as the two pilots launched, Commander Buchanan let Carlton know that he would demonstrate the capabilities of the aircraft and the skills required of a pilot. Carlton, knowing exactly what was going to happen, was extremely uncomfortable. He had already experienced one mishap in which a life was lost, and he carefully considered how he should react to Commander Buchanan.

Carlton knew that if he didn't say anything, his silence would be taken as approval of Buchanan's actions. The CO might then feel a license and possibly even an obligation to show off to all the other junior pilots. But Carlton was also concerned that if he spoke up about his reservations, Buchanan would view him as weak and timid, less than a "warrior."

Carlton knew, however, that the CO had never pressured other junior officers into hot-dogging it. If I speak up now, Carlton reasoned, Commander Buchanan might not put the aircraft into an inappropriate altitude. If I don't speak up, he thought, he'll never know how I really feel.

Turn to page 236 to find out what happened.

One manner of consent is, when a man is still and telleth not.

—John Wycliffe

Case 82: The Classified Inventory

This case study focuses on why it's important to do the job right every time, not just when someone is looking.

Major Kovarik, a department head, was the officer who monitored two individuals conducting a classified material inventory. Although it usually took only fifteen minutes to conduct the inventory, she conducted the check while doing other paperwork and did not pay full attention to all the details.

Later that afternoon, a document from the inventory was discovered missing. It was eventually found in a two-person-controlled safe that had been opened once that day though nothing had been placed in it. Though monitoring of the daily inventories was required by the command, it happened only occasionally. Kovarik was the officer responsible for the inventories, and the program had not been running the way it should.

Turn to page 237 to find out what happened.

To be persuasive, we must be believable; to be believable, we must be credible; to be credible, we must be truthful.

—Edward R. Murrow

Case 83: The Air Show

This case emphasizes the importance of personal responsibility and the importance of speaking up.

An experienced pilot, who was also a NATOPS evaluator, was scheduled to perform short-field runway landings at an air show. Before the day of the show, he briefed his copilot on how the mission would be flown, including the steepness of the approach to the runway. Though the copilot had serious reservations about the approach, he did not voice them to the pilot.

The day of the show, the pilot made an extremely steep approach to the runway, possibly in an attempt to impress other pilots as to just how short a landing could be made.

Turn to page 239 to find out what happened.

An officer should make it a cardinal principle of life that by no act of commission or omission on his part will he permit his immediate superior to make a mistake.

—Gen Malin Craig, USA

Case 84: NATOPS Check Flight

In this case, two pilots pay a terrible price for failing to appreciate the inherently hazardous nature of their jobs.

A flight was arranged to evaluate a pilot's proficiency in a particular aircraft. The evaluating senior instructor, who knew the other pilot socially, approached the check flight as a "pilot appreciation hop" between friends as opposed to the scheduled NATOPS flight it was intended to be.

Turn to page 240 to find out what happened.

The military profession is more than an occupation; it is a style of life.

—Morris Janowitz

Case 85: Lack of Courage

This case focuses on several related issues, including how an unprofessional leader can damage his command and how officers who fail to challenge a lack of professionalism can lose their self-respect and their effectiveness.

The CO of a certain command was usually a very likable, dynamic person, though he had an unfortunate history of failed marriages, womanizing, excessive drinking, and fraternization with both female enlisted personnel and junior officers. He was technically proficient, but his personal behavior on deployment often caused him to be late to morning briefs. Occasionally he missed them entirely, even though the briefs represented long hours of work by his personnel.

Over time, the CO's behavior, especially his fraternization, created serious morale problems and permanently damaged camaraderie in the wardroom. The command had once enjoyed an enviable operational record and had distinguished itself during deployment in support of wartime operations, but now some of the other officers were following the CO's example. Those who did not participate felt particularly in the middle. They were torn between their loyalty to their skipper and their obligation to their troops.

With every passing incident, morale dropped lower. Officers who did not carouse with the CO and his friends feared their fitness reports would be affected. Male enlisted personnel felt threatened because some of their female counterparts were having sexual liaisons with men they were sworn to obey. A few officers who normally would have curbed their own behavior felt no compunction about following the attitudes and actions of their commanding officer.

Several of the concerned officers discussed the matter amongst themselves and felt that if the problem was reported, the ensuing headhunt and the likely recriminations of a full-scale investigation would hurt the command even more. At least, that was the consensus of the officers who felt caught in the middle. Though they talked about the problem at length, they were always careful to avoid any actions that might smack of disloyalty.

One O-3 worried constantly about his CO's behavior because he knew it was a reflection on the entire officer corps. He felt powerless to do anything to change the situation and restore the morale of the troops and he began to consider his options. He thought about talking to the XO since the intervening department head was also involved with the CO's more questionable activities, but the O-3 worried that the XO would be too concerned about his own career to act. The situation was made even more difficult because though the CO's behavior was often highly questionable, the CO himself was a very likable man.

Turn to page 241 to find out what happened.

The higher in rank you go, the more people look to you to set examples.

—Gen Maxwell D. Taylor, USA

Case 86: Ecstasy

In this case, the right thing is not always the easiest thing. How far does an officer's loyalty to his friends go?

One Friday night, four junior officers were on their way to a dance club for a night of entertainment. On the way, Ensign Pacy, one of the officers, was short of money and asked the driver to stop at an ATM. After getting his money, Pacy returned to the car to find the three junior officers picking up small pills from the floor of the car. He soon found out that they had dropped a bottle of Ecstasy pills. All partook of the favors except Pacy, who declined the offer.

Pacy was so surprised he didn't know what to do, so he told the others he'd decided not to go out that evening after all. The next day Pacy consulted Lieutenant Graden, a more senior JO, about the incident, and Graden reported it to the chain of command. The problem was taken out of Pacy's hands and an investigation resulted.

Turn to page 242 to find out what happened.

Laws are not masters, but servants, and he rules them who obeys them.

—Henry Ward Beecher

Case 87: The Munitions Case

In this case, a senior officer pressures a junior to change an honest belief. Does the junior stand by that belief?

During the 1980–88 war between Iran and Iraq, Major Conrad, a military officer, advised against delivering a certain munitions package to Iraq. An agency of the American government, intent on helping Iraq defeat Iran, pressured Major Conrad to change his recommendation, but Conrad refused. He stood by his initial opinion that providing the munitions package to Iraq would enable Iraqi aircraft to possess the same capabilities as U.S. aircraft.

When the agency couldn't persuade Conrad to change his written recommendation, they pressured his boss to force him to change it. The boss spoke to Conrad about his refusal to change and said, "Conrad, as a military officer, you don't know all the facts and you are acting on a principle that doesn't apply in this case."

Major Conrad continued to stand by his belief that the munitions package should not be delivered to Iraq. When his boss again directed him to modify the recommendation because of pressure from the agency, Conrad again refused to back down from his position.

Conrad's boss eventually rewrote the recommendation himself and sent it up the chain for approval.

Turn to page 243 to find out what happened.

Case 88: The Friend

In this case, the nature of friendship is called into question, as are notions of loyalty and faithfulness.

A married junior officer was having marital problems. He confided his difficulties to a more senior officer with whom he had become friends during earlier tours. Out of friendship for the JO, the other officer (who was unmarried) agreed to speak to his spouse privately.

During the talk, the unmarried officer recognized that the spouse was extremely attractive. She came on to him in a very sexual fashion, and he realized that, if given a little encouragement, she could be very aggressive. She seemed confident an intimate relationship would help everyone involved in the difficult situation.

The unmarried officer knew, however, that even a one-night stand with the spouse, if it were discovered, would likely be the end of his otherwise successful career. But he also realized that he had some romantic interest for the JO's wife. He even considered helping her get a divorce so he could act on his impulses.

Turn to page 245 to find out what happened.

Something between a hindrance and a help.

—William Wordsworth

Case 89: Tailhook '91

During Tailhook '91, several lieutenants seem to have had a chance to stop the "gauntlet." Their missed opportunity had repercussions none of them ever could have imagined.

Several lieutenants from a branch of carrier aviation they felt was underrated and ridiculed attended Tailhook '91 with the idea that their presence might improve the image of their community. Although none of them were involved in the infamous "gauntlet," they were in a room nearby and could see and hear much of what went on. In considering what to do, they reasoned that if they tried to stop the gauntlet, they would reinforce the negative opinions about their community.

The lieutenants considered their options. They first thought about asking the people involved in the gauntlet to stop. They rejected this idea because it seemed the gauntlet was some sort of tradition and they thought the mob mentality in the hall, coupled with alcohol, would make asking them to stop unworkable. They considered asking hotel security to intervene but soon discovered that hotel security was already there and was doing nothing. Their last idea was to find a flag officer and ask that officer to stop the gauntlet, but no flag officers were around. Furthermore, the lieutenants had already seen several midgrade officers there who seemed content to let everything continue.

The lieutenants argued among themselves about what to do. Some felt that if they intervened, they would be stopping something that was obviously wrong. The other lieutenants listed their arguments and said they didn't want to get involved because (1) they would be further ostracized as an aviation community, (2) they were outnumbered by about ten to one in the hall, (3) they didn't want to be branded as snitches, (4) they were newcomers to the convention and wondered, "Who are we to tell them how to run their party?" and (5) if the senior officers wanted it to stop, it would stop. It seemed to the lieutenants that they were the only ones who thought anything was wrong.

Turn to page 246 to find out what happened.

Case 90: The Prank

This case focuses on the difficulty of knowing how far is "too far" when it comes to practical jokes.

Bender and Armstrong, two newly winged O-2s with orders to fleet squadrons, were invited by several O-3 instructor pilots to participate in a prank against the jet training command's chief of staff. The prank, in honor of the training squadron's out-going CO, was to take place at the change of command ceremony.

The CO was a superb officer and had earned the enduring loyalty and respect of his squadron. Many of the O-3s, however, considered the chief of staff to be something less than an outstanding officer. And though nothing was ever said or done in public, many of the junior officers perceived personality differences and genuine dislike between their CO and the chief of staff.

A few days before the change of command ceremony, several pilots from the training squadron "temporarily removed" (stole) a large picture of the chief of staff from the Officer's Club. As Bender and Armstrong arrived on the morning of the ceremony, they were approached by several O-3 instructor pilots who asked, not forced, them to consider joining in the prank. If they wanted to participate, they would have to retrieve the "borrowed" picture from its hiding place, take it to the Officer's Club, bolt it in a toilet stall in the men's room, and hang a sign on the stall that said, in effect, that the only appropriate place for the chief of staff was in the toilet.

This was the first that Bender and Armstrong had heard of the prank, and they were caught off guard when the O-3s asked if they wanted to participate. As Bender and Armstrong saw it, they had four choices: (1) they could decline to participate, advise the O-3s that the prank was unethical, and then inform the proper authorities; (2) they could tell the O-3s they thought the prank was a bad idea, but not tell anyone else about the plot; (3) they could decline to participate, say nothing to the O-3s about their ethical concerns, and just forget they ever heard about the prank; or (4) they could join in the prank with the O-3s.

They thought their chances of getting caught were slim. They also thought that even if they were caught, the would probably only receive a verbal reprimand and a weekend's duty. And after all, they said to themselves, "that would be a small price to pay for such a great prank."

Turn to page 248 to find out what happened.

Tact in audacity is knowing how far to go without going too far.

—Jean Cocteau

Case 91: The Stories

In this case, a young junior officer struggles with how to react to activities that may or may not constitute harassment to members of a highly rated maintenance crew.

A maintenance crew of eighteen men and two women had earned a reputation for outstanding performance. Five of the men enjoyed reputations as "lady killers," and they delighted in sharing their exploits with the other members of the crew during work breaks. The women didn't ask the men to stop telling their stories, but they always looked disgusted when the men had finished their tales.

Lieutenant (jg) Hannifin had recently been placed in charge of the maintenance crew. After witnessing the first storytelling session, he considered the feelings of the female members of the crew and was concerned about the disregard for them that the men seemed to be showing. The team worked so well together, though, in spite of the stories, that he was hesitant to step in and make any changes since the tales didn't seem to be affecting work. He carefully considered his options and their ramifications.

If Hannifin stepped in and halted the storytelling, he worried that he might upset the camaraderie of the team and affect the quality of their work. He also recognized, however, that if he stopped the inappropriate storytelling, their production might well increase in both quality and quantity. By ending the stories, he would likely remove some of the irritants between the men and women, and the overall quality of work might improve upon its already high standards. He also considered the possibility that the storytellers hadn't really considered the feelings of the women and when the inappropriateness of their behavior was pointed out, they might apologize and work harder themselves to make the team stronger.

Hannifin also worried about the possibility that by drawing attention to the storytelling, he could cause a rift in the team and hurt work quality because the men would likely blame the women for ending their "fun." It was possible, he reasoned, that the women might not want him to do anything at all because the male members of the team might ostracize them as a result.

Turn to page 249 to find out what happened.

Case 92: Rescue Mission

When his report is altered for reasons he doesn't entirely understand, an officer struggles with the proper response.

Commander McPherson was the CO of an aircraft squadron embarked aboard a carrier stationed off the coast of a country that had illegally imprisoned several American citizens. He was notified that his squadron had been chosen to fly cover for a rescue mission that would begin in forty-eight hours. His report on the status of his unit's readiness must be filed within two hours via the chain of command.

When Commander McPherson reviewed the status of his aircraft, he learned that all requisitioned repair parts hadn't been received. Some of the missing parts were critical to meeting the mission readiness required for the task. The ship's supply officer determined that the parts wouldn't be delivered for at least seventy-two hours, and McPherson sent a readiness report stating that his unit would not be fully ready because of the delayed parts.

Within minutes, he received a call, over a secure line, from the admiral who was the task force commander. "Commander McPherson," he said, "a few aircraft one way or another will not have a significant effect on the mission. Revise your report to state that your aircraft are ready."

McPherson refused to change his report, but an hour later he discovered that the report had been changed to say that his aircraft were ready and had been submitted to headquarters over his signature. Commander McPherson was concerned because he knew the task force commander had been handpicked by the area commander and that the area commander showed great trust and confidence in him.

Commander McPherson decided to say nothing about the falsified report and to take no action to have it changed. He reasoned that by letting the report go and making no effort to have it reversed, he was doing the right thing by supporting his senior officer.

Turn to page 251 to find out what happened.

Case 93: Training Supervision

This case focuses on what can happen when a young pilot is too eager for a dangerous mission and a CO fails to recognize his inexperience.

A squadron in desperate need of a pilot for a special mission assigned Lieutenant Erickson, one of its newest members, to the task. He had come to the squadron with an excellent reputation and had shown great willingness to participate in all evolutions. The training officer's records on the new pilot were incomplete, but Erickson assured everyone that he could handle the mission without difficulty, and he was eager to help meet the squadron's operational needs.

After considering other pilots who were qualified to fly the mission, the training officer, under the pressure of chronic manpower shortages and a high operational tempo, approved the flight. Erickson again assured him that he had all the necessary training and experience for the mission, and the training officer asked the CO for the authority to send Erickson on the mission. Based on Erickson's affirmations and the training officer's recommendation, the CO okayed the flight.

Turn to page 252 to find out what happened.

Case 94: The Submarine Inventory

In the pressure to get ready for a full deployment, a CO *directly orders an O-3 to skip one step required by regulations. Does the junior officer obey the order?*

The supply officer (O-3) of a *Los Angeles*–class nuclear-powered, fast-attack submarine received orders to detach from submarine duty and transfer to a new command. Although excited about the new orders, the lieutenant knew that executing them would be difficult because the sub was scheduled to commence an extended deployment on the same day as his detachment.

In addition, due to the rigorous underway schedule, the new supply officer would be unable to report aboard until just five days prior to the lieutenant's departure. This demanding schedule allowed only four days for the new officer to relieve the out-going lieutenant of all accountability and assume all duties and responsibilities as supply officer.

This problem was further exacerbated by the fact that the four-day relieving window overlapped a holiday weekend. The major portion of the relief process was the required inventory of all subsistence items for which the out-going lieutenant was accountable. Normally, this process was a relatively simple one, but in this case, because of a number of extenuating circumstances, it would be arduous.

In preparation for the upcoming extended deployment, a full load of food had been delivered, bringing the sub's subsistence inventory to just above the required ninety-day endurance load. As a result, it would take the full four days to complete the inventory and the reconciliation of stock records. Anticipating the situation, the out-going lieutenant prepared an inventory plan and presented it to his CO for approval. The CO later called the lieutenant to his stateroom and told him not to conduct the inventory.

The lieutenant asked him why, and the CO advised him that, first, it would be too difficult and would take too long with the full deployment load on board. Second, in order to support both the required pre-underway ship's maintenance and the inventory and reconciliation, a "port and starboard" (two-section watch bill) would be required.

The lieutenant told the CO that government regulations required a full inventory during the relief, since the supply officer is held personally accountable for all provisions. The CO was not persuaded at all by the legal argument and said that conducting the interview would require him to "hydro-test" his crew on a predeployment holiday weekend and he simply refused to do that.

The CO ended the conversation by giving the supply officer a direct order specifically forbidding him to perform the inventory. After much thought, the lieutenant decided that the CO had issued an illegal order. He met with the relieving officer and the two of them mulled over their options. The lieutenant, feeling that most of the burden was his, thought it through carefully and decided he had only three viable alternatives: (1) proceed with the inventory as required (which was certain to attract the full wrath of the CO), (2) force his relief to sign a "paper inventory" based on the current stock-record card balances, or (3) notify the submarine squadron supply officer of the problem and seek his advice and assistance.

After long deliberation, the lieutenant decided that his best option was to consult with the squadron supply officer. After the lieutenant discussed the matter with him in his office, the squadron supply officer immediately briefed the commodore. The commodore called the submarine commander and ordered him to ensure that a full inventory of all subsistence items was conducted prior to the relief's arrival, as required by Navy regulations.

Turn to page 253 to find out what happened.

The man who does something under orders is not unhappy; he is unhappy who does something against his will.

—Seneca

ETHICS FOR THE JUNIOR OFFICER

Case 95: Billet Assignments

This case study points out how insidious and unconscious discrimination can be, as a new XO has to assign two new crew members to working billets.

Commander Jacobs, the ship's new executive officer, had only been aboard two weeks when two new seamen reported aboard for duty. One was a member of a minority, the other was not, and the XO's job was to assign each to a working billet. Commander Jacobs knew that most of the minorities on board were assigned in the supply department and most non-minority personnel were assigned in operations.

Knowing that a decision needed to be made fairly quickly, Jacobs considered assigning the minority member to supply and the nonminority to operations, in keeping with the current racial makeup of the ship's crew. Jacobs thought that perhaps by assigning the sailors in this way, he could help them be more comfortable on the ship.

Turn to page 254 to find out what happened.

We hold these Truths to be self-evident, that all Men are created equal, that they are endowed by their Creator with certain unalienable Rights, that among these are Life, Liberty, and the Pursuit of Happiness.

—Declaration of Independence

Case 96: Systems Acceptance

This case focuses on the importance of following your conscience and always telling the truth to the best of your ability.

An O-6 project manager who had recently visited a contractor's plant for an update on performance testing, directed the project engineer, a subordinate military officer named Captain Nathan, to travel to the same facility and sign the acceptance papers for the system. But after he arrived at the plant and conducted the evaluation, Captain Nathan found he had thirty-six typewritten pages of serious discrepancies.

Nathan knew he faced a serious dilemma. If he rejected the system outright, he would be defying his boss, the O-6 project manager, and implying that the man didn't know what he was doing when he sent Nathan to the plant to accept the system in the first place. Nathan considered accepting the system against his own better judgment because he knew that was what his boss wanted. But, Nathan wondered, what if his boss hadn't really done his job thoroughly and would be pleased that Nathan had saved him from embarrassment by discovering the discrepancies?

Captain Nathan did not believe that his boss would direct him to sign an acceptance form if, in fact, the system was not ready for military delivery. And Nathan didn't want to impugn the integrity of his senior officer since he didn't know all the facts of the O-6's previous visit. Conditions at the plant may have changed since the visit, or the contractor may have intentionally misled the O-6. It also occurred to Nathan that the whole situation might be a test of his own integrity to see how he would respond under such pressure.

Turn to page 255 to find out what happened.

Sensible initiative is based upon an understanding of the commander's intentions.

—Soviet army's *Field Service Regulations,* 1936

ETHICS FOR THE JUNIOR OFFICER

Case 97: Communication

In this case, a lack of communication leads to leadership breakdowns within a command and has other, far-reaching effects that none of the participants could foresee.

Lieutenant Johnson and ADCS Whitman had a serious communication problem that bordered on out-and-out hatred. Because of their poor relationship, and the fact that the lieutenant was the immediate superior of the senior enlisted E-8, it was difficult for their subordinates to use the chain of command. Lieutenant Johnson knew the situation between them was very serious, but he did little to ease the tension, and, in fact, on a few occasions he deliberately made it worse. Since Johnson took no steps to resolve the difficulties, it was easy for Whitman to do nothing as well. The lack of communication between the two regularly caused problems and ultimately a loss of control.

In this situation, neither participant was leading by good example, and leadership by example is a critical component for all successful military units. The commanding officer realized what was going on between them, and he was concerned about the message their relationship was sending to officer candidates who were training with the unit.

Turn to page 256 to find out what happened.

Case 98: The Competition

This case focuses on the point that although winning is important, it isn't everything.

[*Editor's note:* In the aviation community, tactical air training and competitions often take on a life of their own as the aviators try to train like they fight and live by the axiom that war is not a game. The aviators take winning very seriously, and winning a competition often depends on eliminating something called "first time–itis" by ensuring that all aircraft systems are fully operational and by understanding as much as possible about the planned target.]

Just before an annual bombing derby, the squadron CO and the operations officer of an A-6 crew launched on a functional check flight (an authorized evolution) to ensure the aircraft was ready for competition. Winning was very important to them, and in an attempt to give themselves every possible advantage and eliminate one element of first time–itis, the CO and the OpsO violated air competition rules by taking target area photographs.

Turn to page 258 to find out what happened.

Nobody can acquire honor by doing what is wrong.

—Thomas Jefferson

Case 99: Fraternization

In this case, a young officer's seemingly good intentions combine with poor judgment to ruin a career.

A junior officer was sent to a Safety Officer School for five weeks of temporary duty and assigned a BOQ room for the length of the training. At the same time, an enlisted person of the opposite sex was on leave near the school. They met one day by chance, and the enlisted person told the JO details of a serious personal problem that had caused the enlisted's spouse to force the enlisted out of the house that very afternoon.

Although there was an excellent command master chief and Family Service Center at the home base, the JO failed to seek their help after initial contact with the enlisted person's problems. Instead, the JO offered to share the BOQ room and help the enlisted talk through the problems. Between sharing the room and all of the free time the JO had while at Safety School, the two developed a mutual emotional attraction.

Turn to page 259 to find out what happened.

Am I my brother's keeper?

—Genesis

Case 100: Video Harassment

In this case, a junior officer is confronted with a senior who is unconcerned about harassment and discrimination within the command.

Lieutenant Kerry, stationed aboard a destroyer in the Mediterranean, had been on the ship for almost two years and was nearing the end of his tour. A few days earlier, the electronics division had used a camcorder to record a skit that made fun of the only African American in the division. Lieutenant Kerry saw the video and considered it not only distasteful but also a direct contradiction of the Navy's policy on equal opportunity. Kerry took his concerns to the XO, but the XO dismissed the whole incident as a matter that did not deserve disciplinary action.

The XO's lack of concern troubled Kerry. He felt that because of the authority entrusted to him as an officer, he couldn't simply let the matter go, and he submitted a formal grievance through the chain of command.

Turn to page 260 to find out what happened.

A prejudice is a vagrant opinion without visible means of support.

—Ambrose Bierce

Case 101: Designation

This case focuses on the problems and issues that arise when certain people are not held to the same standards as everyone else.

Lieutenant Lupo, a fully qualified pilot, was appalled when the squadron allowed some of its personnel to achieve their final designations as PPC (patrol plane commander) or TACO (tactical aircraft coordinator) even though they did not demonstrate the abilities to fulfill these duties effectively. Yet regardless of opposition from Lupo and other key personnel, the command granted the designations.

In all cases, the individuals had completed the required training events, but their performance had been below standard. One of the individuals was even designated an instructor. By granting the designations to marginally qualified personnel, Lupo's squadron took the path of least resistance and avoided confronting those individuals with their poor performance.

Lieutenant Lupo considered his options: (1) make waves to insist that the squadron make the hard, right decision and reconsider the designations or (2) just let it go because one individual really can't make a difference.

Turn to page 261 to find out what happened.

A failure is a man who has blundered, but is unable to cash in the experience.

—Elbert Hubbard

Case 102: The Complaint

How should an officer react to complaints of harassment against a well-respected colleague?

A junior enlisted member approached an officer who was not within the enlisted's chain of command and complained of harassment from another officer of the same rank who was held in high esteem at the command. Concerned by the complaint, the officer considered the various options for dealing with the situation: (1) forward it up the chain of command, (2) report it to the officer in question, or (3) do nothing.

The officer reasoned that forwarding the complaint up the chain of command could hurt the accused officer's career and family. The officer also thought that doing nothing might be appropriate because the matter was outside that officer's particular chain of command and, honestly, what officer could be expected to know everything that goes on in the military? The accused officer was well respected in the command, and reporting the complaint could possibly alienate the other officers. For the officer who received the complaint, doing nothing began to look like the most attractive option because it would help maintain a greater degree of harmony in the unit.

The last option was to bring the complaint to the accused officer's attention. This course of action would likely avoid alienating the other officers, but it would fail the chain of command by not allowing seniors to know of a potentially serious problem.

Turn to page 262 to find out what happened.

Many free countries have lost their liberty, and ours may lose hers; but if she shall, be it my proudest plume, not that I was the last to desert, but that I never deserted her.

—Abraham Lincoln

Case 103: The Haircut

This case focuses on the dangers of double standards.

Ensign Fiske was a newly qualified ensign standing his first OOD watch on the quarter deck. A few days earlier, the ship's XO had put the word out that all hands leaving the ship must be in proper uniform or civilian attire. During his watch, Ensign Fiske sent back several junior crew members who tried to cross the quarter deck with improper haircuts and shaves. Eventually, after all junior crew who were going ashore had left, a highly respected and hardworking chief approached. He was obviously in need of a haircut.

Several members of the crew were working on deck, and they all watched Fiske to see what he would do. Ensign Fiske knew the chief was leaving late on liberty because he had been helping one of the new personnel learn their assignment. He also knew the chief would have been well within his rights if he had left earlier, but helping new people was one of the senior chief petty officer's main strengths.

The ensign reasoned that since the chief's poor military appearance was a minor infraction and liberty hours would soon be over, he would talk to the chief and explain that he was carrying out the XO's orders about proper appearance. Fiske considered letting the chief go with a small warning that he trusted "all appearance standards will be met in the future."

Turn to page 264 to find out what happened.

What is shown by example, men think they may justly do.

—Marcus Tullius Cicero

Case 104: Discipline

This case focuses on the importance of the chain of command and of balancing personal concerns with the larger concerns of maintaining good order and discipline.

A petty officer second class had been placing inappropriate anonymous notes on a chief petty's car while it was parked in base housing. The PO2 was harassing the chief this way because he felt the chief had taken advantage of his higher rank to park improperly on property normally assigned to lower-ranking enlisted.

Lieutenant Wilkins, the junior officer who supervised both individuals, carried out an investigation and discovered that the junior PO2 was in the wrong. As he considered what action to take, Wilkins was concerned because he knew that his decision would affect not only the junior PO2 but also his family. He knew a bad mark on the junior PO2's service record could have very serious repercussions for that junior's career.

Turn to page 265 to find out what happened.

ETHICS FOR THE JUNIOR OFFICER

Case 1: Canteen Tops

(From page 11)

What Happened

The CG surprised the company commander with the question, "You borrowed them in anticipation of my inspection, didn't you?"

The company commander admitted he had.

The CG continued. "When I'm inspecting, I'm not just looking at an individual unit. I'm inspecting the entire division. If you willfully cover up how inept the supply system is, you're not demonstrating loyalty. In fact, your cover-up is worse than just a simple lack of canteen tops. I know the problems in the supply system. I realize that not having canteen tops is not a reflection on you or your unit. However, your attempt to grandstand and look good is a problem. You could have contributed, either knowingly or unknowingly, to my making a bad decision based on the faulty information that you gave me."

The CG finished by telling the company commander: "You may have a great future in front of you. But I don't think it's in the Marine Corps."

The company commander later resigned.

Discussion

The company commander intentionally took measures to leave the CG with a false impression. He focused on "looking good" rather than on "being good." Instead of trying to look good, the commander should have channeled all that effort into making sure his company, and the entire division, was prepared to go into the field. If he had tried to get the chain of command's help in resolving the issue of tops for the canteens, it would have improved the readiness of the whole division and no doubt would have been appreciated by the CG.

There is no such thing as legitimate lying, misrepresenting, or omitting information to one's senior or one's country. This concept is inherent in the commission you accept as an officer. By implying that all the canteen tops in the unit that day *belonged* to his unit, this company commander was omitting key facts, thus misleading the CG. This was, as the CG made clear, unacceptable behavior.

Questions for Consideration

Do you think the company commander understood all of the purposes of
the inspection before it happened?

Did the company commander show initiative, albeit misguided?

Were the results of the incident (with the company commander separating
from the service) appropriate?

Case 2: Travel Orders

(From page 12)

What Happened

Commander James was caught when the clerk at the terminal tried to issue
him a commercial ticket on the fraudulent orders. His criminal actions
caught everyone by surprise. He was arrested at the military terminal by security personnel and was later convicted in a court-martial.

Discussion

In many such cases, an individual rationalizes that a minor ethical violation is justified, either because it won't be detected or because the good outweighs any possible harm to anyone else. Once you buy into the "end justifies the means" rationale, you are trapped into evaluating every decision
according to whether it will or will not hurt more people than it helps.

Officers of the U.S. armed forces must set the example. They cannot decide to obey only those rules they think are worthwhile. If an officer thinks
a rule is wrong, he or she should work through the chain of command to
make changes to it.

In this case, the officer needed help. He didn't trust the organization for
which he worked, nor did he discuss the matter with peers or senior officers. All personnel have a senior to whom they can go and appeal for help.
While this situation eventually may have needed the area commander to resolve it, that would have at least been a workable, ethical solution.

It's important to do the right thing because it's the proper thing to do, not
because you're afraid of being caught. Officers and subordinates alike must
understand the rule of law and obeying the rules.

Questions for Consideration

Did the commander have other options (for example, buying a commercial ticket)?

Who could Commander James have contacted for advice before he decided to act?

If a fear of being caught drives an officer to behave ethically, why is that wrong?

In this case, does the end justify the means? Why or why not?

Case 3: The Fitness Report

(From page 13)

What Happened

Commander Whitley, the commanding officer, chose to cheat the system, and he got away with it. All five department heads from year group A were selected for promotion.

(*Editor's note:* In 1996, the Bureau of Naval Personnel, now the Naval Personnel Command, overhauled the fitness report system so that this kind of cheating is no longer possible.)

Discussion

Within that squadron, the commanding officer was a hero to the department heads, and the XO learned that it was okay to take care of the department heads by cheating if necessary. For the service, Whitley's decision meant that other, more qualified officers—whose commanding officers did the right and ethical thing—were not selected.

Because the military generally operates under a reduced-manning basis, the *best* officers are needed at every level to handle flash incidents around the world, to work effectively and efficiently. Also, when there are larger conflicts, there must be an outstanding cadre of officers on active duty when and if reserve and National Guard units have to be mobilized.

This commanding officer disregarded the oath he took to "obey the orders of the President of the United States and the officers appointed over me." Deciding which rules should be obeyed and which should not is not only illegal but bad in the long run for the armed forces of the United States.

Loyalty to one's subordinates is commendable, but officers owe a greater degree of loyalty to their service and their nation.

The concept that cheating the system is alright as long as you don't get caught is not acceptable. America is a nation governed by rules and laws. If each of us determines which laws we will obey and which ones we will not, anarchy will result.

Questions for Consideration

If you were the XO in this unit, what lesson might you have learned from your commanding officer's actions?

What do you think about this commanding officer? Would you want to be like him?

What might happen to the morale of a unit whose commanding officer followed the ranking and reporting rules?

How do you balance loyalty to your subordinates against loyalty to your service and nation?

Case 4: Certification

(From page 15)

What Happened

Lieutenant Thomas didn't want to compromise his credibility as the mission commander and a naval officer, so he reported the incident. He earned the respect of his crew, peers, and senior officers. Also, the department head was wrong about no one being able to detect the error; the divers who recover the practice mines would have seen what happened.

Discussion

Moral courage is an integral requirement for an officer, and the lieutenant's actions assured his commanding officer that he was both well informed and able to achieve overall command readiness.

It is important to do things because they are the right thing to do. Sometimes, a senior may be testing a subordinate to see if he or she will do the wrong thing under pressure. Doing things wrong usually catches up to you, as would have been the case here if a "new" radar had observed what had happened.

Questions for Consideration

If you were the commanding officer in this unit, how would you feel about
the lieutenant's action?

How would lying about the test run's results have affected command
readiness?

Is it possible that the department head was testing Lieutenant Thomas to
see what he would do under pressure?

Case 5: Takeoff Time

(From page 16)

What Happened

Captain Storace felt the colonel's pressure and decided that although the
order seemed illegal, surely a senior officer wouldn't give improper instructions. He then radioed that the takeoff time was 0602, and the colonel
thanked him.

Two days later, Storace was called into command headquarters to explain why he had falsified the takeoff time. The investigating officer, a
major, had reviewed the flight logs and the radio message and came to the
conclusion that Storace had reported the time wrong so that his unit would
appear to be operating perfectly. Storace was going to lose his flight examiner status and right to fly because his integrity had been compromised.

Storace explained his conversation with the colonel, and the major
played the recorded radio conversation. It had indeed taken place as Storace
had said, but he nevertheless was wrong in what he did. The colonel was
on the IG's staff, and the captain had failed the test.

Discussion

Captain Storace had given in to the pressure put on him by a senior officer. Rather than standing on principle, he obeyed an illegal order. The officer corps depends on the complete trust and honesty of its officers. Those
who obey illegal orders risk not only their careers but also, potentially, the
lives of others.

Did Captain Storace have any other options? What else could he have done?

How do you feel about the colonel? Was it ethical to do what he did to the junior officer?

Case 6: Reporting Ready Status
(From page 17)

What Happened

Lieutenant Commander Lee let the practice go on without fighting it further. Several months later, in a joint NATO operation, Lee's fighter wing was called upon for a maximum effort at 0500. It reported, as it had done in the past, that it was fully operational.

Even though this was a training exercise, Lieutenant Commander Lee's wing wasn't able to put enough aircraft in the air. The commander, U.S. Forces Europe, was very embarrassed and investigated the matter.

As a result of the investigation, the wing commander was relieved, as was the maintenance officer. Lieutenant Commander Lee was retained long enough for a new maintenance officer to be appointed and moved into place, then he was allowed to resign. A promising career had ended.

Discussion

It's important to maintain your integrity at all times, even when—perhaps especially when—the people around you are not.

Questions for Consideration

What other options did Lieutenant Commander Lee have? What else could he have done?

Were there other people Lee could have asked for advice?

Given the situation described above, what would you have done?

Case 7: Missile Test Firing

(From page 18)

What Happened

The illegal backdating was never needed because the shot did take place at 1623 on 30 September, just seven minutes before the range closed.

Discussion

The fact was, though, that if they had shot on 1 October, many people would have known, including nine officers and forty-five civilians, and they would all have had to keep quiet.

Even if only one person knew that something illegal was going to happen, that person would have taken the first step to compromising his own integrity, as Admiral Burke's article in appendix A points out.

Again the message is one of trust, integrity, and ethical behavior. When one person considers doing something illegal, it says to everyone else that they, too, may unilaterally decide which rules they will break. The military is a team operation. One person or more doing something wrong begs the question as to how many others are also doing things wrong.

In swearing our oath, we're also agreeing to obey laws, rules, and regulations as long as we retain our commissions.

Questions for Consideration

Does postdating expenses really matter? What's unethical about it?

What if one person had disagreed with the group's decision? What options did that person have?

What consequences could be expected if you disagreed with the group's decision?

Case 8: The Exam

(From page 19)

What Happened

In this case, Ensign Peterson didn't even try to ask for leave, which the command might have approved. He left town and flew home, taking along classified material to study on the flight. When Peterson returned, he falsified the logs. Because classified documents were involved, Peterson is no longer in the service. He was caught, taken to Mast, and given an administrative discharge.

Discussion

Peterson was in trouble from the minute the first rule was broken. The following quote from ADM Burke's essay applies:

> Finding no way out, you begin to rationalize, and then you are hooked.
> The important fact is, the men who travel the path outlined above have misused the very basic quality and characteristic expected of a professional military man, or any other professional man, for that matter; they have compromised their integrity.

On top of everything else, Ensign Peterson took the chance that classified material wouldn't get lost on the trip. That loss could have jeopardized national security and affected the entire service.

Questions for Consideration

If Ensign Peterson was going to study anyway, what's the problem with filling out the logs to say that he studied all weekend?
Was there anyone that he could have contacted for advice?
Do the consequences to this student seem fair?

Case 9: The Lone Ranger

(From page 20)

What Happened

Lieutenant Salamon refused to falsify records and consequently was taken off the list for "prime" orders. Because Salamon wouldn't cooperate, the command had to fly numerous sorties to gain qualifications that normally would have taken one flight. By not letting a senior officer influence his decision and by refusing to accept less-than-honest qualifications, the JO helped the command ultimately attain legitimate qualifications.

Discussion

Evaluating the situation more carefully is always a good start. Whenever you are assuming that everyone else is wrong, take time to consider carefully what to do. That said, this is another example of a JO sticking to time-honored naval principles. Certainly everyone involved wanted the squadron to look good, but Lieutenant Salamon wanted its reputation to be achieved honestly.

Two centuries ago, Edmund Burke said that "for evil to triumph, all that is necessary is for enough good men to do nothing." An officer takes an oath to defend the Constitution and thereby swears to uphold the laws of this country. This includes obeying the rules.

Lieutenant Salamon made the right ethical decision in spite of any pressure from peers or senior officers to do otherwise. Officers are expected to do the right thing, and thinking through what you would do in a situation like this helps you to make the proper decision when it actually happens.

Officers should be selfless in their service to the nation. Part of the reason that Salamon made this decision was that he knew his stand would force the squadron to be much better prepared in the future.

When an officer does something wrong, it's nearly inevitable that others will find out. That contributes to a climate of distrust. In the military, we want our bosses to look good, but not if what we do gives no substance to the achievement. It just hurts the very people we're trying to help.

There may be unfavorable consequences to an ethical decision. In Salamon's case, he was taken off the list for good orders. Still, there's a concept known as "psychic income," which means that even if you don't get real dollars or recognition for doing your best, you'll have the knowledge that you did right and that you made a difference.

Questions for Consideration

Do you agree with what this JO decided to do? Why or why not?
What factors would you consider in deciding whether to take action in this
    situation?

How much does the idea of doing the right thing for its own sake, or "psychic income" motivate you?

Case 10: The Parking Pass

(From page 21)

What Happened

Lieutenant (jg) O'Neill decided to listen to his friends and not to use the fake parking pass. Another officer—who saw how easy it was to make a fake pass and who was unimpressed by their friends' warnings—tried using a fake parking pass and was caught.

During interrogation, the officer implicated O'Neill as the one who had come up with the idea. The officer who was caught was disciplined severely and O'Neil was censored. Both of them lost the trust of their peers and seniors because they didn't seem to understand that college-type pranks have no place in the officer community. Because O'Neill didn't destroy all the copies of the fake pass, however, he made it possible for his friend to be caught.

Discussion

In this case, other officers didn't stand by while a friend did something foolish. They risked losing the friendship to make sure their fellow officer didn't commit an unethical act.

When this incident happened, the command had a poor ethical climate. Other people were doing questionable things without command repercussions. That climate made it all the more difficult for those officers to speak up and refuse to accept Lieutenant (jg) O'Neill's behavior.

Forging a parking pass is stealing. If an officer doesn't understand when something is stealing, that officer's friends have a duty to educate that officer. Again, think of ship-shipmate-self, and you'll never bring discredit to other members of the command.

Most colleges have some form of honor code or precept that regulates everyone's conduct. In the military, lying to fellow officers, enlisted personnel, or government officials is never permissible. Don't try to find the exception to the rule. It could lead to your dismissal, your friend's dismissal, disgrace to the military—or all three.

Is a concern about what others would think of your actions the same as being ethical?

What do you think of Lieutenant (jg) O'Neill? Would you want a friend like him?

Do you think the officers should have turned O'Neill in?

How do you balance loyalty to your friends against loyalty to your command?

Case 11: Lost Documents

(From page 22)

What Happened

Although Lieutenant (jg) Shane felt that Walker was trustworthy, she refused to sign the destruction record. Walker asked other friends and the answer was the same. They felt their integrity would be compromised. Finally, Lieutenant (jg) Walker decided that without a destruction record, he would have to tell the truth.

The material was eventually found. It had been brought up for destruction with a larger pile of material. While the other material was being destroyed, the papers in question fell off the table, behind some equipment. No one noticed, and it was assumed later that these papers had been destroyed along with the larger pile. Because they were not destroyed, however, no record of destruction existed.

Discussion

Reproducing a destruction record is not an ethical choice because signatures verify that the material was destroyed by the individuals present at the time of destruction.

Although it's possible that Walker's intentions were good because he honestly believed that the material had been destroyed, he was an attempting to compromise someone else's integrity by asking them to falsify destruction for the sake of continuity of paperwork.

Questions for Consideration

What do you think of Lieutenant (jg) Walker?

Is it possible that the only reason Walker didn't commit a crime was because he couldn't persuade anyone to cooperate?

Do you think Walker had tried before to get his friends to cover for him?

What do you think of Lieutenant (jg) Shane's actions? Should Shane and the other officers have reported Walker?

Case 12: To Fail Oneself

(From page 23)

What Happened

The ensign lied about using marijuana. That wasn't the end of the story. A JO—either the candidate himself or someone who knew the story—reported this incident to previous editors of this book. The person who submitted the story noted that (1) "to this day, this information has not come out, and [it] could damage the individual's career due to a lack of integrity" and (2) "an ethical decision would be made by coming clean; however, the career would be ended, thus making an ethical conclusion the wrong answer."

Discussion

Is an ethical conclusion the wrong answer? This individual knows that a mistake was made. If this is the candidate himself, then he knows he lied. If it is someone who knows the story, then he or she failed too for not reporting the matter. Officers have a responsibility to report the illegal actions of others.

The person who submitted this story concluded that "due to the factor of time, it is best not to divulge info." He or she went on to write, "Final decision: forget about it."

Everyone makes mistakes, and we're likely to make more earlier in our lives. Ethical mistakes, however, tend to stay with us. They fester, reminding us of our failures. If you make an ethical mistake, having a privileged conversation with the command chaplain is an option. The chaplain's counsel may help you determine a course of action. Keep in mind, too, that senior officers were juniors once, so try their counsel as well. They may surprise you by how much they understand.

The person who said "forget about it" really hasn't; he or she is still bothered by what happened. If the ethical decision had been made, it's likely that this person's mind would be clear. No one ever said being ethical is easy—it's just what the American people expect of their military officers.

Questions for Consideration

Do you agree with the assessment that acting ethically was the wrong answer in this situation? Why or why not?

What do you think of the ensign? Is he someone you admire?

Do you think the person who submitted this incident really has forgotten about it?

Case 13: Training

(From page 24)

What Happened

The officer continued to falsify data and no one questioned his reports, which were approved through the chain of command for submission. Because of the data he submitted, his unit won the award.

As time went on, falsifying data bothered this officer so much that he wrote to the editors of this volume about this matter, hoping that others would be dissuaded from doing the same thing.

Discussion

In this case, the focus wasn't on how you played the game but on whether you won the award. This officer was caught up in a "win at all cost" syndrome.

Commanding officers at every level must recognize that it's possible for officers to lose sight of the end objective—in this case improving training. These officers may do unethical things, without the commanding officer knowing, in the hopes of making the commanding officer and the unit look good.

All JOs need to remember that everyone trusts them to always do the right thing.

An officer who acts improperly may never be caught, other than by his or her own conscience. Working on this book has made it clear to the editors that those officers who have done wrong know they have, are ashamed, and wish they could turn the clock back.

The impetus for avoiding something unethical has nothing to do with whether or not you'll be caught. Instead, it has everything to do with a sense of loyalty to other officers, the service, and the nation. Either we all do the best job we can, as ethically as we can, or chaos will result as each officer tries to outsmart all other competing officers.

As Admiral Bulkeley has pointed out, we are in an honorable profession, and to each of us falls the task of seeing that we are honorable and that others are as well. In this case, the JO should have told the commanding officer immediately what was going on. From that point forward, he should have reported correct numbers. A unit can cope with the discovery of a cheat in their ranks far better than having to face all the other units after improperly winning an award.

Questions for Consideration

What do you think of the officer's actions?

Do you agree that the officer should have told the commanding officer immediately what was going on? Did he have other options?

Case 14: Travel Claim

(From page 25)

What Happened

Major Trevor took his wife along with him. When he returned home, he submitted a false claim for reimbursement that said he had upgraded to other accommodations, which hadn't happened. The officer hoped that he would get enough money back to cover his actual expenses.

Reimbursement was only authorized at the lower rate, so the officer complained to the Personnel Support Detachment about not having been reimbursed for the fictional upgraded accommodations.

The officer's complaint came to the attention of the chain of command, which was chagrined and amazed! However, the decision was that public embarrassment for the command wasn't in the best interests of the service. The officer was reprimanded for his fraudulent claim, and he opted to accept the PSD check for the lesser amount.

Discussion

An officer should always be able to come up with a variety of approaches to solve a particular problem. The challenge is not so much in coming up with a solution but in coming up with a legal and ethical solution that doesn't send a negative message to others—a solution that sets an example of how future operations should be conducted.

If it was important enough to have his wife along, and there would in fact be time for them to take liberty together, the officer could have considered applying for a loan from the credit union or charging the trip to a credit card.

Officers are expected to be not just problem solvers but also problem preventers. If this wasn't going to be the last trip this officer would make, another option was to start saving for the next time and planning to bring his wife along on that trip.

This officer's actions were blatantly wrong. Keep in mind that the officer corps will be able to maintain its good reputation only if people like this are weeded out. Through his irresponsible actions, this officer brought discredit to his unit and ran the risk of making taxpaying civilians suspect that there are many more such officers in the armed forces.

Questions for Consideration

Do you agree with the chain's decision to spare the command public embarrassment?

Can you think of other situations in which an officer might think the military "owes" him or her something extra? Is that kind of thinking valid?

Case 15: Specifications

(From page 26)

What Happened

Lieutenant Commander Hyatt decided not to report the out-of-specification reading. He wanted to protect the image of a work center that was operating properly. Unfortunately for him, the problem was discovered, and the work center gained the reputation for hiding problems. In addition, Hyatt lost his reputation for trustworthiness, along with the respect of peers, juniors, and senior officers.

Discussion

This case seems to be relatively straightforward. One would expect that an officer who's entrusted with personnel and materiel could be counted upon to reaffirm the trust and confidence placed in him.

Hyatt's life wasn't at risk, nor would anyone hold an officer responsible for a piece of equipment malfunctioning, as long as it had been properly maintained. In fact, that's the purpose of inspections—to check if any equipment has failed before its expected time.

The military services are dependent on equipment, and it's critical to know how that equipment is operating. That way, needed modifications can be made in both current items and those produced in the future.

Hyatt's decision to withhold information was an immature one. He hadn't learned to accept responsibility as an adult and an officer. The service is no place for the game of hide-and-seek. An officer who tries to see how much information can be withheld is a danger to everyone.

Questions for Consideration

Do the officer's concerns about reporting the out-of-spec readings seem to be valid ones? Why or why not?

What would you do in this situation?

Case 16: The Fall

(From page 27)

What Happened

The ensign disclosed the head injury on the questionnaire. The matter was submitted to a medical board for a decision. The officer waited two anxious years for the final determination.

The medical board was impressed by the ensign's truthfulness. Considering his integrity and the fact that he had remained symptom-free and passed another EEG, the medical board decided that the officer should be allowed to enter the flight pipeline.

Discussion

The medical board's decision was influenced by lessons learned over a long period of time. They considered the possibility that the officer might have other medical problems if allowed to fly under conditions that might increase the chance of blackouts, due to the high G forces inherent in air operations.

This wasn't an easy decision for the board because they had to consider both the officer and anyone who would be flying with him or in the same air space.

If he hadn't told the truth, the ensign would have always worried that his career would end if anyone found out he had lied. The officer corps has no place for people who abuse the trust and confidence placed in them.

It's important to understand that if this officer had been denied and forced to pursue a nonflying career, his very strength of character that led to him speaking up would have also enhanced the rest of his career and his life.

Officers must understand that their job is to serve the nation first. Ship, shipmate, and self are important, in that order. While flying, pilots risk not only their lives but also the lives of others. We expect pilots to ground themselves when they're not fit to fly. This is an extension of the ethical principle that requires an officer to come forward when anything happens that would cause regulations to be broken or other people to be harmed if the truth weren't told.

We are pleased to report that this officer successfully completed flight school, graduating number one in his class.

Questions for Consideration

What do you think of this officer? Would you want to be like him?

Do you think he made the right decision?

What if the medical board had turned him down? Would your opinion of his decision change at all?

Case 17: Zeroing the Truth

(From page 29)

What Happened

Lieutenant (jg) Tallarico, the JO, disliked the idea of turning in a fellow pilot yet finally acted according to the dictates of his conscience. He reported the overstress and the reason for it to Maintenance Control and other senior officers. A Field Naval Aviator Evaluation Board was convened for both pilots. After that, both Tallarico and Gage were severely disciplined.

Discussion

It's always easy to sit back after the fact and analyze other people's dilemmas with a critical eye. It's easy to wonder why they couldn't bring themselves to do what was so obviously correct.

In both our personal and professional lives, we've all endured our own forms of personal pressure. The situation is usually much less dramatic than ones that put someone else's life, or our own career, on the line.

This incident was that dramatic, and Tallarico had made the wrong decision initially in not reporting it. He made up for his mistake, though, by making the hard, smart, and correct decision to report the violation. He surmounted his inner turmoil and any exterior peer pressure in order to prevent lives being lost and damage to government property.

Regardless of his initial decision, this incident taught Tallarico to be a better leader, willing to make tough decisions without compromising his sense of ethics. He realized that concern about others' safety has a higher priority than allegiance to friends or to himself.

Of course, the whole incident could have been avoided if both pilots had shown more respect for the regulations and trusted that certain maneuvers have been prohibited for very good reasons. The fun they might have had doing the loop was certainly not enough to justify the consequences.

Questions for Consideration

Do you feel that Lieutenant Gage ignoring the prohibition in the NATOPS manual was an ethical lapse?

Do you think Lieutenant (jg) Tallarico made the right decision? Which one? Why or why not?

Does the fact that the aircraft was apparently flying fine after the incident affect the decision you would make if you were in this situation? Why or why not?

Case 18: Letter from Home

(From page 35)

What Happened

The flight went ahead as scheduled. However, the copilot's lack of sleep and inattentiveness at the briefing led to disaster. There was an accident during the formation flight that resulted in four deaths and the destruction of two aircraft.

Discussion

Clearly, the copilot was irresponsible when he didn't admit that he hadn't had enough sleep to perform his duties safely. In addition to that, he didn't pay attention during a crucial briefing because he was reading a letter from home. Normally, in the day-to-day world, being tired and absorbed by personal matters aren't serious ethical breaches. However, when you accept a duty that puts others' lives in your hands, you must be held to a higher standard of responsibility and accountability.

The copilot's behavior can be described as gross moral negligence. He may have rationalized his behavior by saying to himself, "So I'm a little tired, big deal" or "It's just a routine briefing. I'll be fine if I listen with half an ear while I read my letter." What he should have said was, "I'm tired, and I could be putting all of our lives at risk" and "If I read my letter during a briefing, I'll be committing the double fault of disobeying regulations and putting my own interests ahead of the crew's."

The copilot is not the only irresponsible person in this situation. Every person in that briefing who watched him read his letter had an obligation to insist that he pay attention. It's never easy to step in and correct a peer's behavior. It requires moral courage. However, when the faults of others can have such grave consequences, having the moral courage to make them do the right thing becomes a life-and-death necessity. It may be uncomfortable to act as an "ethics enforcer," but it's certainly better than allowing unchecked actions to result in tragedies.

Not every tired copilot causes an accident. And it may not be the case that every time an officer reads a personal letter during a briefing, people die. Whether or not small mistakes lead to large disasters is often a matter of moral luck. If you consistently act responsibly and have the moral courage to hold others accountable for their actions, you can reduce unnecessary danger to yourself and others. Do what you're supposed to do, always pay attention, and if you see that another officer isn't prepared to do a job as spelled out in regulations, advise your senior, so that someone else can be assigned that task.

Questions for Consideration

Is a violation of the rules or regulations *always* an ethical violation?
Does the fact that the violation was or was not intentional have a bearing on the answer?
Is failure to enforce rules or regulations an ethical lapse?
Does the outcome of the episode change the answer?

Case 19: Computers

(From page 36)

What Happened

The co-worker's report was investigated. During the hot-line investigation, it was determined that the officer had taken leave to conduct personal business, as opposed to family affairs. The officer was discharged and required to pay the value of the personal services he had received, that is, computer and telephone usage.

Discussion

This officer made a number of ethical mistakes, including lying to his senior officer. The use of government equipment, services, and facilities for other than official government purposes is a violation of the Standards of Conduct. Frankly, it is also a waste of finite government resources.

One of the reasons these rules were made was to avoid putting those business people in the civilian world at a disadvantage. If Lieutenant Cunat's assignment wasn't requiring his full-time performance, he should have told his senior officer so that the senior could have combined the job with some other assignment.

Some shore-based officers may enjoy an eight-hour day and have the time to supplement their income with other jobs with their commanding officer's approval. However, the general rule is that an officer is available for duty twenty-four hours a day. Not many officers can complete their duties in an eight-hour day, and most officers find themselves with ever-increasing responsibilities.

When officers consider secondary employment, the first consideration has to be whether their extra time should really be devoted to their military job, so that they can more effectively and efficiently serve the service and the country.

The concept that we are in the service twenty-four hours a day is partly based on the belief that ours is a profession rather than just a job. At sea, an officer may work eighteen hours a day, and sometimes longer. In an increasingly complex world, the responsibilities of the military can be expected to grow. The work will have to be done with less people, requiring more of us to work longer. The same is true for the civilian world.

Questions for Consideration

Do you think it's possible to have a second job and not short the military?
  What would some of the guidelines be?
What are some other options, rather than working a second job, for supplementing income?

Case 20: The Thief

(From page 37)

What Happened

Second Lieutenant Roland did not confront Second Lieutenant Keller about the other thefts. Because Keller was such a good friend, the lieutenant didn't want to find out the truth. She wanted to remember Keller as a good, dear friend, not as a potential thief.

Keller was later kicked out of the military. Roland continued to write to Keller, but the replies she received were from Keller's husband, not Keller herself. After a while, Roland was forced to give up on both Keller and their friendship.

Discussion

When the officer decided not to confront Second Lieutenant Keller, it didn't preserve their friendship. All she lost was the possibility of finding out who was behind the other thefts. Roland worried more about her friend's feelings than about the welfare of her fellow officers. Because the matter was handled so quietly, Keller seemed to be leaving only for another assignment. Thus the officers who remained in the unit were still under suspicion.

Questions for Consideration

Do you agree with the decision Second Lieutenant Roland made? Why or why not?

Did she have options other than confronting Second Lieutenant Keller directly (for example, talking to the commanding officer, requesting that Keller's effects be searched, etc.)?

What would you have done in this situation?

Case 21: Private Information

(From page 38)

What Happened

Lieutenant (jg) Schultz realized the ethical thing to do was for McCullough to have kept that information to himself and not to have shared it with others. He decided that doing nothing would condone what McCullough had done. He felt uncomfortable with bringing the matter to the commanding officer but realized that unit morale, cohesion, and performance could all be affected if personal information was leaking out at parties. Schultz went to see the commanding officer about what had happened.

The commanding officer investigated privately. When he discovered the accusation was true, he relieved the personnel officer and made the appropriate career-ending remarks in McCullough's fitness report. While the commanding officer praised Schultz for his actions, Schultz himself didn't feel very good about them.

Discussion

The concept of "need to know" applies to all information that officers hold. In effect, it says that what you need to know can only be divulged to others who also have a need to know, based on their position or the requirements of their jobs.

Of course, this includes security information. Secret information cannot be shared with another individual, even if that person holds a "secret" clearance, unless they have a legitimate need to know certain information in order to help them perform their duties.

In the course of our work, we all learn something of personal nature about others. The concept of trust implies that what we learn, if it has no bearing on the person's job, should not be repeated to a third party. The exceptions are in unusual circumstances, such as criminal behavior or self-destructive behavior. If, on the other hand, we feel that what we know will affect the person's performance, we have a military obligation to relay the information to the chain of command, so that they can determine what if anything should be done.

Remember, as part of your military duties, you may be expected to face an enemy or your own death. Losing a career is not a fate worse than death. It's reasonable to expect that officers will act according to their oath to uphold the Constitution and the principles of trust that we all share.

When we raise our hands and take the oaths of office, we swear to uphold the special trust and confidence placed in all officers. In time, Schultz realized that he had done the right thing, even if it was a painful experience for him.

As officers, most of our assignments and service lives are full of positive experiences. There will be times, however, when the hard, right decision is the only choice to take, versus the easy, wrong decision of doing nothing. If you want to be a professional military officer, you have to act like one, assuming all the responsibilities expected of commissioned officers.

Questions for Consideration

Do you agree with the decision that Lieutenant (jg) Schultz made?
Do you think that Schultz should have confronted McCullough privately?
What other options did Schultz have besides taking the matter to the commanding officer?

Case 22: The Notepapers

(From page 39)

What Happened

After agonizing over his decision for months, Ensign Rivers decided that because the information was old and outdated, and he didn't want to lose his career, he should burn the papers.

Discussion

While the security of the United States may or may not have been at stake, Rivers's main consideration was the impact his actions would have on his career.

His actions were inappropriate and unethical. This officer failed to meet the standards of trust and confidence to which we must all adhere. In the competitive environment of a career military officer, ethical dilemmas occur daily. As we move through this period of uncertainty, ethics, morality, integrity, and character must be the hallmarks of successful officers. These officers must avoid the temptations that go along with success as they march through their military careers.

Officers must be total professionals. The hot line shouldn't be the basis for an officer being ethical, but it's worth remembering that a number of the cases in this volume were first brought to the attention of the inspector general because of hot lines.

In this case, Rivers thought no one else would know of his mistake, so no one else would be affected. But he knows, and none of us escapes, even though our punishment may be more psychological or physiological.

Also, Rivers didn't realize how many people he affected. The enlisted personnel who handled classified papers on that first tour suspected that something was wrong, since he conducted affairs differently from all the other new officers. The message was clearly sent to these enlisted that some officers make up their own minds about which rules they would obey. This set a poor example for the enlisted.

Questions for Consideration

What do you think of Rivers as an officer? Would you want to be like him? Should the relative success or failure of one's career have any bearing on the decision made in this situation?

Case 23: Sleeping on Watch

(From page 41)

What Happened

The EDO, who was extremely tired that morning and felt that telling the CO would result in more hours of work, decided not to mention the incident to the CO or anyone else.

Discussion

The officer who reported this issue put it like this: "You fear for your career. The SRO is a good watch stander. No one else knows. You feel that even if you do come forward, no changes would be made to allow for more rest."

The fact that this officer reported this case indicates that he knew his actions were ethically wrong. But he wanted to save his career.

He knew about the lost submarines *Thresher* and *Scorpion* and was ready for life-risking duty, yet when it came time to act ethically, he didn't have the courage to do that.

If we're driving our equipment and crews past their endurance limits, someone who knows this must speak up. The use of Blue and Gold crews to operate nuclear submarines recognizes that equipment is actually more capable of extended operating hours than is its human crew. Safety is, of course, the watchword all the time, although we're in an inherently dangerous profession. In a peacetime environment, a ship's schedule will usually avoid placing its crew in this position, especially when conducting critical and complex testing. But there may be times where this is done to ready crews for combat conditions.

The EDO was impressed by the commanding officer and felt that the commanding officer was fair. Commanding officers trust their subordinates to speak up, and they show confidence in their crews by risking their lives diving with them. The EDO's career was important, but if each officer fails to report his or her own human failures, how will the people who design submarines know where to make changes to accommodate human crews?

As a junior officer, if you speak privately and confidentially to a senior, you can be reasonably certain that the trust you're showing your senior will be reciprocated. You expect your seniors to place their trust and confidence in you. Is it too much to expect you to do the same in them?

Questions for Consideration

Who created this situation? The CO for fostering this environment or the
   JO for abdicating his responsibilities?
Should the fact that the SRO was a good watch stander and a good sailor
   have any bearing on the decision?
Should the fact that no one else knew have any bearing on the decision?
Should the length of time asleep have any bearing on the decision?

Case 24: The Party
(From page 43)

What Happened

Both the senior and the subordinate lived to regret their mutual lack of communication.

Discussion

The first issue to be considered is, Who is responsible for one person receiving a communication from the other? Usually, the sender is responsible for seeing that the message is sent in terms that the receiver will understand, and the sender should look for feedback that the message was in fact received as intended.

In a military organization, the completeness and accuracy of communications are the responsibilities of the seniors and their subordinates. On one hand, the seniors must create a climate where everyone feels free to speak. It's the responsibility of the senior to make sure that all juniors know they won't be held accountable for bringing bad news.

Conversely, juniors have to be sure that the seniors understand. They must recognize that a busy senior officer isn't always paying full attention to their remarks. If the senior is extremely busy, it's the junior's responsibility to find an alternate way to inform the senior. The junior must make sure the senior understands what he or she is being told, along with the expectations and implications that derive from that knowledge. When a JO thinks something is wrong, it's the responsibility of the JO to ensure that the senior is made aware of it in a timely fashion. It is, of course, also the senior's responsibility to listen. The JO must apply as much bravery and directness in dealing with his or her commanding officer as you would do in dealing with an enemy.

A senior is expected to be responsible and reasonably prudent enough to recognize the significance of violations of the UCMJ. In addition, the senior should attempt to draw details from the junior and not become distracted with other issues.

The SECNAVINST 5520.3 series require immediate reporting of major criminal offenses to the Naval Criminal Investigative Service. Officers need to consult the JAG to define, identify the nature of, and determine the degree of the offense so that the next steps can be determined.

When a junior is trying to reach a senior and is put off, she or he should demand to get through if the situation is critical enough.

Communication is also an ethical responsibility of both seniors and subordinates. Seniors create the command climate, while juniors insist, as necessary, to be heard.

Who created the situation? The senior or the junior?

What kind of critical conditions would make you demand to talk to your senior officer?

Case 25: Government Equipment and Services

(From page 44)

What Happened

The O-3 pointed out to the commanding officer that the help being given a civilian friend was improper. The commanding officer decided not to let his friend use the office printer.

Discussion

The issue is who is authorized to use government equipment. Since Congress hasn't authorized access to everyone, it's not fair to give one person special access. For example, an air show gives all of the public equal access. They can come on the base and enjoy activities as part of a public affairs program.

Since only one person benefited from the use of government equipment in this case, that use wasn't ethical.

The relationship between a base and the civilian community is a close one. Sometimes, it's hard to tell which activities improve that relationship and which ones are unethical. Before entering into any kind of arrangement with a civilian, check with the local Judge Advocate, who can advise about the legality of what's being considered.

Questions for Consideration

Do you agree with the O-3's actions?

If you were the commanding officer, how would you feel about the O-3's actions?

Case 26: Motivation Isn't Everything

(From page 45)

What Happened

On one flight, Danton wasn't able to recognize the aircraft's approaching stall, likely because he was distracted and hadn't had refresher training in a while. He couldn't recover the aircraft in time and had to eject. A very expensive aircraft was destroyed.

Discussion

Officers must be able to handle multiple tasks under stress. Part of a senior officer's job is to recognize when a subordinate is having trouble with concentration or multitasking.

In this case, the senior officer relied on his judgment and experience. He couldn't quantify all his experience of knowing Lieutenant Danton. The question is whether an officer should rely on his own judgment or allow the thoughts and records of others to play a role.

In this case, all the signs of a pilot who had other things on his mind were there. If the commanding officer, who was probably extremely busy, had investigated the situation further, Danton's lack of refresher training and experience would have shown up. He wouldn't have been allowed to fly.

This situation could have been worse; at least the pilot wasn't lost. However, the loss of this one aircraft equaled half the operating budget of the entire U.S. Naval Academy for a year.

Scrutinize your own judgments about other people's capabilities. Refusing to face the possibility that you might be wrong is an ethical failure. Look for the truth. If all of the information and other opinions you can find confirm your judgment, go with your decision. Even if you find out later that other factors were involved, at least you tried to get all the information you needed in order to make the best decision.

Questions for Consideration

How could the commanding officer have found out more about Danton's situation? Were there other people he might have talked to? Documents he could have checked (for example, flight surgeon, the XO, recent performance records, etc.)?

Do you agree that refusing to examine your own judgment is an ethical failure? Why or why not?

Senior officers are extremely busy. How do you balance getting the job done against taking the time to investigate further? How would you make that decision?

Case 27: The Drug Test

(From page 46)

What Happened

The division officer counseled Edwards but didn't report the problem. Edwards has performed well since, without any reported drug problems.

Discussion

Edwards was a good performer, and certainly the division officer recognized that we all make mistakes. It could be that Edwards was scared enough by this close call to avoid drugs in the future. However, no matter what kind of sailor Edwards is or how scared he was this time, his behavior can't be tolerated. The Navy's policy is zero tolerance.

This case challenged both the ethics and the compassion of the division officer. Unfortunately, he didn't have the authority to decide not to take action, that the zero-tolerance policy didn't apply in this case.

Some kind of action must be taken. First, because the division officer only had the petty officer's word that he had used drugs, and because that word was prior to the petty officer being advised of his rights and was therefore inadmissible in any court-martial proceedings, perhaps counseling, documentation, and removing Edwards from the Personnel Reliability Program would have been appropriate.

Second, the division officer should have reported Edwards for further investigation, which might have determined that this wasn't the first time he had used cocaine. Of course, even a one-time use of cocaine has been shown to be addictive, so the situation was a disaster waiting to happen. If the division officer had reported Edwards, he could have also testified on his behalf about his performance.

The point is that officers must support the rules. By not doing so this time, the division officer in effect put his crew in danger, because Edwards had demonstrated weakness under stress. The officer's inaction may also affect his division's morale. Most people don't want to serve with someone who's irresponsible and unreliable.

Questions for Consideration

Do you agree with the division officer's actions? Why or why not?

Would Edwards's negative urinalysis results affect your decision? Why or why not?

Can you think of any reasons why Edwards may have lied about using drugs (for example, maybe he just wants out of the Navy)?

Edwards has continued to perform well. Does the outcome of the case affect your evaluation of the division officer's actions?

Case 28: Drinking Contest

(From page 47)

What Happened

The officers hadn't asked for permission from their command in order to operate the bar during their off-duty hours, so they were censured for that dereliction. They were also admonished for their poor judgment in allowing the drinking contest.

Discussion

[*Editor's note:* Off-duty work should only be undertaken after consulting SECNAVINST 1700.11 and discussing the venture with the base JAG officer. You also need the approval of your commanding officer.]

As an officer in the American military you are—in addition to any other specialty—a public affairs officer representing your particular branch of the service. The civilian community will judge the entire military by your appearance and conduct. When you accept a commission, you also tacitly accept a position as a role model. You have a responsibility to maintain good order and discipline, as well as to obey the laws of the state and nation.

Alcohol problems are a great concern to the military community, as they are to the civilian one. Accidents both on and off the job are often caused by excessive alcohol consumption.

To address that concern, establishments often have breath-alcohol analyzers available so that people can determine whether they have exceeded the legal limit of alcohol ingestion.

The concern, which is a matter of law in a number of states, is that if a customer becomes legally intoxicated, torts or crimes committed by the inebriated person may be traceable to the operators of the establishment that served the liquor that caused the patron to go over the legal limit. In that event, the operators of the bar can be held liable for damage resulting from the action of the customer who became intoxicated in their bar.

Questions for Consideration

If you were the reporting senior for these officers, would you hit them on their fitness report for lack of judgment?

Do you think career progression is based more on your past achievements or your seniors' assessment of your good judgment?

The officers' actions may have been illegal. Do you think they were also unethical? Why or why not?

Case 29: Interaircraft Communications
(From page 48)

What Happened

An after-accident report revealed that the pilots hadn't discussed NATOPS emergency procedures before the flight. Also, weight and balance had been calculated incorrectly, and the cargo wasn't secured properly. The cargo shifted in flight, causing the aircraft's center of gravity to change. In addition, communications and cockpit coordination between cargo air control and the two aircraft were inadequate.

Discussion

Attention to detail is a matter of ethics. Both pilots forgot that every day they train to be better officers as well as pilots. They forgot that they were officers first, pilots second. They failed themselves, their squadron mates, their seniors, and the taxpayers.

This mishap could have been prevented. The pilots disregarded the rules that govern being a good pilot and a good officer. As officers, we have a special trust and confidence placed in us, and we must not abuse that.

Questions for Consideration

Do you agree that attention to detail is an ethical requirement? Why or why not?

What if you worked with these pilots and saw their behavior? Would you do anything?

Case 30: Transportation

(From page 49)

What Happened

Commander Jay asked his junior officers to help his friend move. The officers were happy to do that for their senior, because they felt he had treated them well. The officers helped with the move and then had their night out with the van.

Unfortunately, someone in the motor pool placed a hot-line complaint, feeling it was inappropriate for officers to commandeer a van for their own entertainment. It was actually more than just inappropriate. The final finding was that it was illegal for both the senior officer and the juniors to use government equipment in that way. The senior officer received a letter of reprimand and was fined. The junior officers received letters of caution.

Discussion

In this case, Commander Jay made three mistakes: (1) arranging government transportation for the civilian friend, (2) arranging for the juniors to have government transportation, and (3) asking the juniors for help. The junior officers were also responsible for misusing the government van, since they, like Commander Jay, could be reasonably expected to know that government equipment cannot be used for private purposes.

The commander's request may have seemed more like a demand to his junior officers, because of his position. A senior officer's actions help to strengthen or weaken the juniors' value system and their faith and confidence in the senior.

Civilians often approach the armed forces for help in everything from flood relief to collecting Toys for Tots at Christmas. Rules and regulations about what's legal and what isn't are constantly changing. Before taking part in a nontraditional operation, check with your base legal officer. Avoid even the appearance of wrongdoing. If you're still not sure whether something is authorized, ask permission from higher headquarters.

Questions for Consideration

Assuming that the junior officers were truly volunteers, was there a legal way to help their senior officer's friend with his move?

If you had been in the same position as the junior officers, what would you have done?

How could Commander Jay have handled the matter differently?

Case 31: The Bus to Liberty

(From page 50)

What Happened

The senior officer was impatient because of the delay, so Lieutenant Commander Boyle asked both families and the driver to board the bus. The trip to the family theme park went well; everyone had a good time.

Several weeks later, an investigator from the IG's office called Boyle. The investigator was responding to a hot-line call about the extravagant waste of taxpayer money that resulted from such a long bus trip for so few people. The complaint also asked why an enlisted driver spent the day ferrying two officers and their families around the countryside. The two officers involved were admonished for their lack of good judgment, which probably didn't help their careers.

Discussion

When you're using equipment and supplies that are purchased by taxpayers, consider how you as a taxpayer feel about the expense. Would you be pleased to see the story on the evening news or read about it in the paper? If not, then you have the answer: don't do it. Use common sense and spend the dollars allocated to you wisely.

Questions for Consideration

If you were Boyle, would the fact that you liked the senior officer have influenced your decision?

What do you think would have been the consequences had Boyle canceled the trip?

Case 32: Crew Assignments

(From page 51)

What Happened

After interviewing each officer, the XO discovered that the female ensign had majored in mechanical engineering and sincerely wanted to be involved with shipboard propulsion. The male ensign had majored in political science and aspired to do graduate work in the public affairs area.

Commander Berben assigned the female ensign to the DCA billet and the male ensign to the administrative billet, where he could begin establishing a public affairs office.

Discussion

Commander Berben was able to assign both candidates to billets for which they had the most potential, as well as send a message to the command that assignments are based on merit and expertise. This dispelled any misconception that women are better suited for less technical assignments.

Questions for Consideration

What if their talents had been switched? If you were the XO, what kind of assignment would you have made?

Discuss the ethical implications of the XO's actions. Why is this considered to be an ethics case study?

Case 33: The Combination

(From page 52)

What Happened

The junior officer reported the incident to the CO. As a result, Lieutenant Falk and Lieutenant (jg) Lawson were both reprimanded by the wing commander. That left a permanent mark in their fitness reports. The command paid more attention to educating officers in CMS (classified material security) procedures, resulting in improved training that was given more frequently.

Discussion

This case study is about the ethics involved in safeguarding classified material. The choices are supposed to be clear. On one side are the rules and regulations that govern COMSEC material. On the other side is the belief that, as long as no one knows, it's alright to bend the rules now and then.

These officers very deliberately chose to ignore rules and regulations. To memorize a combination and use it, one has to make a conscious effort. It doesn't happen by accident.

One of the factors that contributed to this incident was the substandard COMSEC training and the lack of any refresher training. This may have led to an overall lax atmosphere when it came to dealing with COMSEC material.

However, even if the training was faulty, these officers betrayed the special trust and confidence the president and senate places in each of us when we accept a commission. When an officer does something wrong, it reflects badly on all officers.

As an officer, not only are you expected to do the right thing, but you have also an obligation to report any wrongdoing, so that a thorough and impartial investigation can be made. Complacency, particularly with classified materials, is harmful to national security. The Walker and Pollard spy cases are both examples of how failing to react to impropriety can lead to disaster.

Questions for Consideration

If you were the junior officer who saw what was going on, would you feel obligated to report it?

If Falk and Lawson were both honorable individuals, who had no intention of misusing the COMSEC material, what's the harm in them both having combinations to the container?

Who or what is ultimately more responsible for this incident? The junior officers? Or the failure to provide proper COMSEC training?

Case 34: The Performer

(From page 53)

What Happened

Lieutenant (jg) Naville made the decision to send the PO2 to the CO's Mast. His decision sent a strong message to the work center about responsibility and discipline. After Mast, it was made plain to the PO2 that he must improve his work performance and obey work center policies. Unfortunately, the PO2 continued to violate policies and went UA again. He received an administrative separation from the service.

Discussion

There are two things to consider in this case study. The first is the petty officer himself, and the second is the effect of the petty's officer's actions on the people in the work center and the rest of the crew.

If Naville had given the petty officer another chance, perhaps he would have learned his lesson and saved his career. On the other hand, if the petty officer's performance had stayed the same, the work center's morale, and the rest of the crew's, would have been badly damaged. Lieutenant (jg) Naville met the ethical responsibility of his position, to take a stand and pursue the action he thought was necessary.

The petty officer started out as a good performer, but for some reason he lost motivation. Could something more have been done? What if the junior officer had looked for the root causes beneath the petty officer's behavior? If the petty officer had been counseled skillfully, perhaps by a trained Medical Service Corps psychologist, maybe he would have returned to the ship and continued what had been a promising career.

Remember that the individual is the basis for all accomplishments. Sometimes we have to admit to ourselves that we don't have the counseling skills or the ability to solve the problem. It's then good ethical conduct on our part to admit we need help to address the problem.

Questions for Consideration

Should you take someone's upbringing into consideration in making a decision about discipline?

How much counseling is enough? Where would you draw that line?

Do you think the question about whether more could have been done for this sailor is a valid one? Why or why not?

Case 35: Off-Duty Employment

(From page 54)

What Happened

Lieutenant Colonel Snyder pointed out to Major Gale that even if there were other violations at the post, that wouldn't justify continuing to break the rules. Snyder talked to Gale about the Standards of Conduct, focusing on Gale's compromising the Army by wearing his uniform when doing business.

Next, Snyder talked to the two antique dealers in town and assured them that the post commander was taking their complaints very seriously. He explained the major's financial problems and said that the post commander would tell the major to disassociate himself from the business. Snyder left, sure that the antique dealers understood that the post commander was committed to doing the right thing.

Snyder's personal approach was successful. The town antique dealers agreed that it was acceptable for the major's wife to handle all the business arrangements.

Discussion

The military is very much a part of every community in which it's located. Since the community and the military are both concerned with the welfare of the same nation, it's important that they work together. Consider in advance anything and everything an officer does to make sure it has only positive effects on the community. If the very nature of the military's mission causes a negative effect, that must be discussed with the community so affected. Military personnel must remain sensitive to the perceptions others have of them.

Questions for Consideration

Do you agree with the steps Snyder took? Why or why not?
Does the reason Gale needed the money affect your perception of the case?
    Why or why not?

Case 36: Flying a Scheduled Mission
(From page 55)

What Happened

Commander Harlan landed safely, but the aircraft was destroyed on impact. The flight data recorder, electronics, and tape were unrecoverable because of the fire and impact damage.

A mishap review board determined that the ejection sequence had been normal. The aircraft departed flight due to slow air speed, high nose attitude, and high angle of attack, with the stall warning signs disguised by a destabilizing configuration of external fuel tanks. Harlan took off in a flight configuration that exceeded the center of gravity for air combat maneuvering, because it was known to aggravate high angle of attack hang-up situations. It also disguised stall warnings. This particular situation could be deduced by the rocking of the wings and aggravate a hang-up situation.

The investigation also revealed that Commander Harlan wasn't current in air combat maneuvering, because he hadn't flown for eighteen days prior to the mishap. NATOPS requires flight within seven days for this particular aircraft.

In addition, Harlan had briefed and flown an unauthorized flight. When the board questioned him, he contended that he wasn't familiar with the full definition of ACM. He felt that basic fighter maneuvering, consisting of missile breaks and guns defense, was separate from ACM and thus not subject to the same rule.

Discussion

The basic question in this situation has to do with who schedules a mission and whether a pilot has the authority to change the mission once it has been scheduled by the commanding officer.

Had the rules been followed and ACM not flown, the mishap would not have occurred. However, Harlan's wingman was the flight leader and didn't question the mission changes. When an officer perceives that something wrong is going to happen, he's under the obligation to question that order even if it's given by a senior.

It's also been suggested that having seniors flying in junior supporting roles may need to be reconsidered. When training demands this kind of arrangement, the two officers must understand that they need to reverse their normal senior/subordinate rules.

Since the commanding officer had specifically scheduled a mission that *everyone* was authorized to fly, and current instructions clearly spell out ACM definitions, maneuvers, and restrictions—it was the flight crew's responsibility to understand the rules and restrictions as they applied to their aircraft and mission.

Rules in the military, especially those relating to aircraft, have been developed based on the experience gained through mishaps, injuries, and deaths. They're there for a reason. When officers don't live up to the trust placed in them to follow these rules, they fail themselves, their teammates, and their country.

Questions for Consideration

Why do you think it was so difficult for the wingman to speak up?
Who's most at fault in this situation? Commander Harlan? The wingman?
The rest of the flight crew? Why?

Case 37: The Missing Item

(From page 56)

What Happened

The JO consulted a senior enlisted member in the unit who suggested working out a plan with one of the civilians working on the base. The civilian agreed to trade the missing part for two foul-weather jackets. The JO was jacket custodian and made the trade. With the missing part, the unit passed inspection.

Discussion

The common word for this kind of trade is "cumshaw," but in reality it's just stealing. It not only steals from taxpayer funds meant for a particular purpose but also withholds information from senior personnel. Cumshaw denies them a realistic picture of supply requirements. Cumshaw is neither officially sanctioned, nor is it honest.

It's important that junior officers realize that their seniors were once juniors, too. A junior officer shouldn't make assumptions about how seniors will react when they hear about a problem.

Here's one way the situation could have been handled. When the junior officer had exhausted every legitimate option, he should have gone to his senior. At that point, the senior could have taken charge and either come up with a workable plan or changed the checklist.

It's a rare senior officer who will hold a subordinate responsible for failing to complete a task when the junior has given the senior notice about the problem in enough time to work out a solution or change the objective.

In this instance, maybe the checklist should have been changed. However, by covering up the matter, the JO made sure that others would still have to inventory a part that might not be needed anymore. The JO also encouraged the enlisted personnel to disregard rules and procedures if it would make accomplishing the mission easier.

When we decide which rules we'll obey and which ones we won't, we send a strong message to subordinates. This JO may have won a very small and insignificant battle but contributed to the loss of the supply war by resorting to and accepting unethical conduct.

Questions for Consideration

Who could the junior officer have asked for advice about this problem?
Do the junior officer's fears about telling his CO seem justified?
In this situation, how would you balance your need to accomplish the mission against the ethical approach of telling the CO what happened?

Case 38: Civilian Attire

(From page 57)

What Happened

The JO spoke to the two enlisted about their attire. There were no repercussions from the command.

Discussion

While it's reasonable to want to be liked, that's not a good motivation for any action. Officers are entrusted with enforcing regulations rather than waiving them.

When an officer enforces only certain rules, the enlisted or other junior officers might think they can also determine which rules to obey. When enlisted personnel are off-duty on liberty, they are still subject to the UCMJ, and so it's the duty of the officer to rectify the situation on the spot—politely—and then report the matter to the enlisted person's chain of command upon return to the base. The immediate senior of the two enlisted personnel may also speak to them and prevent this situation from happening again.

As professionals, it's crucial for us to realize that we are obligated to enforce the rules. A commissioned officer can never escape or hide from this responsibility. Using tact and courtesy, an officer can make sure that respect and discipline exist within the military.

Since the enlisted personnel may have changed into civilian attire after they left the base, it may not be the fault of those who inspected them at the base. Also, the time and distance of applicability for regulations is, for the most part, the same everywhere.

Junior officers who want to become seniors will obey the rules themselves and ensure that others do so as well. Their seniors trust the juniors to do that enforcement. Finally, subordinates do not respect seniors who let them break the rules. They may be happy to get away with something, but they lose respect and confidence in the senior.

Questions for Consideration

Is it possible that enforcing the rules during liberty hours could actually make an officer unpopular with his or her seniors? If so, should that matter?

Is wearing inappropriate civilian attire an offense worth reporting?

Case 39: The Valve

(From page 58)

What Happened

Lieutenant Dunn called the appropriate personnel and a critique was held. The critique addressed the equipment problem and criticized Dunn for not reporting the first valve's position.

Discussion

By not disclosing the first valve condition, Dunn ran the risk that if he was incapacitated, the replacement EDO wouldn't recognize the trend when he came across the second valve.

Failing to report the first valve sent a terrible message to the enlisted, who knew the procedure and what should have been done. Leading by example simply means that what you do will be taken as a example for your subordinates to follow.

The correct course would have been to report the first valve incident immediately. Not reporting it may have saved time, but it could have led to bigger problems if there was an epidemic of mispositioned equipment.

Officers are to be trusted, and through this incident Dunn lost his credibility. He was willing to jeopardize expensive equipment and the entire crew by not reporting what was a series of engineering installation mistakes. The military runs on trust; if you cannot or will not accept that premise, you should resign for the good of your fellow officers and the enlisted. There's enough danger in both training and operational evolutions to suggest that your staying on active duty is a danger to everyone with whom you come into contact.

Safety procedures developed as a result of small and large mishaps. No officer has the authority to set aside any regulation, without first discussing it with senior officers. If you don't agree with a requirement, discuss that with your immediate senior or consult the assigned legal officer.

Questions for Consideration

What's the problem with Lieutenant Dunn just fixing the valves himself?
   Is that being proactive?
If you were Dunn's senior officer, what would be your opinion of him?

Case 40: First-Time Use

(From page 59)

What Happened

The government didn't dispute that Jengeleski was doing an excellent job and had potential, but any drug abuse is intolerable. The policy, the procedures to get help, and the repercussions all should be well known, particularly to an E-8.

Without substantial evidence to the contrary, drug abuse equals OTH separation. The chain of custody, collection procedures, and lab work were strictly in accordance with legal standards. The CO and E-8's chain of command reluctantly agreed. The board found misconduct due to drug use by a vote of three to zero.

The use of cocaine wasn't in dispute, and separation from the service was clearly appropriate. The type of discharge was an agonizing decision. Jengeleski could lose his Veterans Administration benefits and be unemployed. The board considered his sixteen years of good performance.

OTH was considered too severe, yet the military requires absolute commitment to earn an honorable discharge. It was important to send a message about drug use, but Jengeleski's service had to be weighed against that. Jengeleski's family would also suffer for his mistakes.

A general discharge was considered the most appropriate. It penalized the E-8 but left some benefits intact. The message of zero tolerance was clearly delivered to the command.

Discussion

Drug abuse isn't honorable service. Outstanding performance does not excuse or even mitigate drug abuse. What example was this setting for subordinates and peers? Jengeleski knew the consequences, weighed the risk involved, and decided to use cocaine.

This story has been told many times. If you want to avoid making the difficult decision these officers did, don't treat drug education lightly. Drug education isn't just something that you go through once or twice a year. Remind your personnel about drug education. Share with them the medical effects and legal consequences of drug abuse. If some day you have to terminate someone's career, you'll be able to do that knowing that you delivered a fair warning first.

Questions for Consideration

Would you have voted differently? Why or why not?

How would you imagine the crew would have reacted to the news if Jengeleski had received an honorable discharge? What if he had received an OTH discharge?

In this situation, how much weight should you give a person's past experience and performance?

Are there other factors you would consider in determining the type of discharge?

Case 41: Software

(From page 60)

What Happened

The JO decided to go forward and suggest alternative software. The JO became the duty expert for the system even though he was only the assistant project officer.

In the meantime, the contractor proceeded with work on software development. The JO continued to point out the bugs in the proposed software package the contractor was going to deliver.

The JO found some government-owned alternate software packages that had proven results but was ordered to stop all further attempts to look for existing software because, he was told, the research was disruptive to the contractor.

The contractor went ahead with their software package development, which cost the government an inordinate amount of money. The JO was removed from the project and given a lukewarm fitness report. As a result, the JO wasn't advanced to the next higher rank.

The JO, however, never questioned the decision to go forward. The junior said later, "A person has to do some real soul searching in order to make any decisions that may affect his life and the lives of others."

Discussion

The JO did the right thing because of loyalty, integrity, honesty, and dedication to accomplishing the mission. This particular case doesn't have a happy ending, but we in the military must nevertheless always choose the ethical and proper course of action.

As shown by this case, there's more than one kind of combat. This JO showed the courage expected from all officers of all ranks. Fortunately, this was an isolated story. If officers in general remember this JO's principles, they will be able to emulate them both in and out of combat.

Questions for Consideration

Do you agree with the JO's decision to continue to look for alternate software? Why or why not?

Why do you think the project officer was so adamant about stopping the JO?

> *Do the right thing, even if it means dying like a dog without the esteem of anybody you value knowing what it cost you.*
>
> —ADM James B. Stockdale

Case 42: Dealing with a Vendor

(From page 62)

What Happened

Someone placed a hot-line complaint, sparking an investigation. The commissary officer advised Larry Masters that the matter was under investigation. She also told Masters that he had the right to remain silent, to have union representation if desired, and to choose an attorney. The officer pointed out to him that government employees are not allowed to accept gratuities, a regulation spelled out in the Standards of Conduct.

The officer also told him that it was his position as a purchasing agent that had triggered the gift, and so it appeared that Masters was using his position for personal gain, making him suspect. While there was no loss to the government, the appearance of wrongdoing did exist. The investigation continued, and Masters returned the baby food.

Discussion

The basic guideline is that government employees may not accept gratuities from contractors or businesses that are engaged in (or desire to engage in) financial dealings with the government.

When Masters took the free baby food, that constituted acceptance of a "gratuity"—something for which the government didn't pay fair retail market value.

It was the responsibility of the commissary officer to emphasize to Masters the intent and provisions of the Standards of Conduct. The incident might have been avoided altogether if annual training had been done as required. The lack of annual training raised questions during the investigation about the commissary officer's competence.

Questions for Consideration

Who's more responsible for this situation—Larry Masters or the commissary officer? Why?

Do civilians working for the military have any responsibility for finding out about the applicable rules and regulations themselves?

Case 43: Component Parts

(From page 63)

What Happened

In this case, there was no violation. As it turned out, one of the component parts was needed urgently before the others.

Discussion

It is not enough to be a good problem solver. While the investigation cleared the contracting officer, it drew his time away from other activities.

If the contracting officer had just informed everyone concerned about what was being done, that would have taken far less time than clearing up the whole hot-line complaint.

Hot-line complaints are usually made by those who are trying to ensure that the government and the people of the United States are treated fairly. The first step in making sure that command personnel don't misunderstand any action taken is to explain in advance why a particular action was taken.

In this case, since equipment normally can't be broken down into component parts to avoid competitive bidding, it would have been smart to make sure everyone connected with the transaction understood why it was being handled that way.

Second, since the action could also be misinterpreted by noncommand personnel, it would have been a good idea to check with the JAG and base supply personnel to ensure that everything was being done properly.

Finally, to avoid vendor misunderstanding, it would have been effective to tell the vendors what was being done, so that they knew they were still actively being considered for all procurements. This extra step might have revealed a second supplier who could have been relied on in the future. In any case, we must never forget that we are agents of our government and represent what the people have determined to be proper behavior.

In a related issue, many hot-line complaints can be avoided if the so-called whistle blower had checked with the chain of command. Those who perceive some sort of impropriety are obligated to tell their chain of command instead of immediately picking up the phone to call a hot line. Just asking may result in a satisfactory explanation and save everyone a lot of time and effort.

Every action by an officer should be the result of prior planning, education, and training. Just as a pilot thinks about and practices combat maneuvers—considering what the enemy might do—so must an officer consider how others will view the action and its results.

Questions for Consideration

Do you think that disseminating information about why decisions are made will reduce hot-line complaints? Why or why not?

Why do you think people don't consult the command before making a hot-line complaint?

Case 44: Fund Raising

(From page 64)

What Happened

After the ride had been auctioned to a bidder for several hundred dollars, someone in town filed a hot-line complaint that special treatment was being given to someone for a fee. The average taxpayer could not take advantage of the service.

Although the conclusion of the JAG's memo said the decision was the CO's, the main body, when carefully read, indicated that Captain Bloom would probably be in violation of written instructions if he permitted the donation of a ride on a vehicle to an auction.

The service chief felt that this violation of the Standards of Conduct showed poor judgment in a CO, who by virtue of his rank and years of experience should have known better.

Bloom was directed to return the money and he made restitution out of his own pocket.

Discussion

The basic principle is that officers may use government equipment in the performance of their jobs. They are not the owners of that equipment, even though they are responsible for its care and maintenance and may be held liable if something happens to it.

Our actions are always subject to review and censure because we are servants of the people. While we choose to work for less than we might make in the civilian sector, and accept the risk of death without reservation, we must meet standards.

Recipient of the Medal of Honor, ADM John Bulkeley, USN, was also awarded France's highest medal, the Legion d'Honneur, for spearheading the Normandy invasion and the liberation of France. In his dedication to the book *Naval Leadership: Voices of Experience,* the admiral wrote:

> For in my mind there is but one honorable profession. It requires the daily attention of all faculties, the persistence of a bulldog, the compassion of a man of the cloth, foresight entrenched in previously learned lessons, the willingness to sacrifice for the good of the service all that has been personally gained or earned, and unyielding belief that it is better to serve peace than to wage war, the self force-feeding of knowledge and new technology, and the unyielding conviction that it is far greater to serve one's country rather than oneself. These requirements demand a foundation, and that foundation is, inescapably, experience.
>
> The naval officer is truly unique, for he must have the capacity to simultaneously love his country, his service, his family, his shipmates, and the sea. He needs each of them unquestionably as each of them needs him. And the demands that each place on him never diminish, they only grow.
>
> Beyond all the words and phrases of a naval officer's dedicated service, honor and professionalism must remain his past, present, and future. That, sir, is why it is "The Honorable Profession."

Questions for Consideration

Did the JAG officer do anything wrong?

Do you have any obligation to make sure that the senior officer understands what you've communicated to him or her?

Who was more responsible for this ethical violation, the JAG or the CO?

Case 45: Overpayment

(From page 65)

What Happened

The CO issued this officer a nonpunitive letter of caution because the CO believed the officer hadn't taken timely steps to repay the money and resolve the matter.

Discussion

Two mistakes were made in this case. First, the unauthorized flow of money wasn't stopped, and second, the funds weren't promptly repaid. The officer's excuse that there were other, higher priorities was a poor one.

Officers are paid for the duties they carry out in their official capacity. They're expected to know to the penny their pay entitlement, allowances, and travel expenses.

An excess payment is basically an unauthorized transfer of funds from the government to an individual. While an agent of the government may have made an administrative mistake in issuing the excess money, the officer is expected to realize that the money is not his or hers. Consequently, as with finding someone's wallet, the officer should see that the money is immediately returned.

A related issue falls under the responsibility of personnel officers. They have a duty to expedite travel claims so that military members are not experiencing hardship while waiting to be reimbursed.

Questions for Consideration

Have you used pressing priorities at work as an excuse to avoid administrative paperwork? At what point does that become unethical?

If you were this officer's CO, would you trust this officer after this experience?

Case 46: The Christmas Gift

(From page 66)

What Happened

The command leadership in this case was committed to doing the right thing. The command was also pragmatic in its approach, making allowances for the different traditions and cultural mores in this overseas location. Given all this, the officer in this case was confident that all parties could be satisfied while still conforming to the spirit of the Standards of Conduct.

The officer's experiences had also taught him that only when someone tried to go it alone or cover up something did that person suffer. He informed the proper person in his organization about the situation and let the legal experts help him to resolve it. The legal counsel decided that it was proper not to return the gift, but rather to have the officer anonymously donate its contents to the command's Christmas party.

Discussion

This solution maintained the professional relationship between the contractor and the government while avoiding the appearance that the contractor had influence over government affairs. In these matters, it's always wise to contact legal counsel. They will know what's proper in order to spare both the individual officer and the U.S. government any embarrassment.

Questions for Consideration

What do you think of this officer? Would you want to emulate him?

The traditions and norms of Italian culture affected the decision the legal counsel made. Can you think of other situations in which cultural norms might affect a decision about ethics?

Case 47: The Gift

(From page 67)

What Happened

Three months later, the command inspector general, acting on a hot-line tip, investigated the case. A few months after the party, the contractor fired the company's project manager for poor performance. The PM agreed with this decision.

After being dismissed, the former employee called the hot line and told them about the practice of giving gifts. The IG brought charges against both the FM and the PM for coercing a contractor to provide a gratuity, accepting the gratuity, and conduct unbecoming an officer.

The case was dealt with at Admiral's Mast. The two officers voluntarily reimbursed the contractor for the cost of the art work.

Discussion

Contractors are in the business of landing and keeping contracts. For that reason alone, the government should not accept gifts from contractors. Even if it doesn't influence contract awards, companies and the public may presume that it did have influence, if only by creating an image of a corrupt government operation. Perception can be all-important in some situations. Even "the appearance of impropriety" can be construed as illegal or ethically questionable.

As soon as an officer learns that something unethical is going on, immediate steps should be taken to stop the practice and notify the staff judge advocate—through a senior—to find out what remedial acts need to happen.

Every military and civilian employee of the Federal Government has access to the military's fraud and abuse hot line, which has been established to identify and prosecute wrongdoers who aren't stopped within their organizations.

Questions for Consideration

What do you think of the PM?
Why would the FM agree to one more gift?

ANSWERS

Is morale a valid consideration when making a decision about unethical actions?

Case 48: Working with a Contractor

(From page 69)

What Happened

The contractor persuaded First Lieutenant Ames to accept overnight lodgings without cost to the government. Ames could then file for and keep his housing reimbursement, which was illegal. The contractor also provided Ames with free meals.

Ames was also involved in several extramarital affairs that further damaged his reputation. The result was a court-martial conviction, a fine, and a less than honorable discharge.

Discussion

Remember that the livelihood of the people doing business with the government depends on their abilities to please their customers—in this case, the military—and so they extend every effort to provide the government with a good product and good service.

Several companies are usually capable of providing different goods and services. Because of this, a company may try to go the extra mile not only to please the customer on the current contract, but also to help them to secure other contracts.

If you represent the government in negotiations with civilian companies, don't engage in any action that might confer any special benefit to the contractor or compromise the government's position.

Our country expects us to meet higher ethical standards than the average person. When we don't, we let our country down and make it more difficult for others to trust the officer corps. All of us must protect and defend the good name of the officer corps.

Questions for Consideration

What other options did Ames have?
Did it surprise you to learn that Ames was also cheating on his wife?

Case 49: The Disbursing Officer

(From page 70)

What Happened

One last time, Ensign Colbert went through every bill separately (about $400,000). She went slowly and stayed calm, as she was already resigned to having to report the shortage. Somehow, this time, her safe balanced with her books.

Discussion

The problem worked itself out, but Ensign Colbert's actions reveal three interesting points. First, although she believed she had let her boss down, she realized it was much better to identify the problem than to cover it up. Even the appearance of a cover-up, in an accountable position, can hurt one's reputation and career. Your seniors will look at the fact of the cover-up, not how much or how little you tried to hide. Second, a good litmus test for your actions is whether you can go home at night and feel good about what you've said and done. Third, when she made up for losses from her own money, she may have been unintentionally hiding someone else's thefts. Also, by covering up the small shortages, Colbert didn't let her procedures come under scrutiny. There may have been a minor, easily corrected procedural problem that was causing the shortages.

Generally speaking, the military trusts those who act in a trustworthy manner. In the final analysis, officers are supposed to obey rules and file adverse reports on themselves as necessary. They owe their allegiance to ship, shipmates, and self—in that order. Trying to look good rather than being good is both unethical and incompatible with being a good officer.

Questions for Consideration

Why do you think Ensign Colbert was afraid to report the problem? Do you think such fears are justified?

Colbert encouraged her cashiers to report problems and not to worry. Why do you think she was harder on herself than she was on them?

Can you think of other situations in which people are afraid to report problems?

Case 50: The Flight

(From page 72)

What Happened

The senior officer was reprimanded and had to pay for the cost of the flight.

Discussion

Using a flight to take the flag officer to a private function was wrong. Both the subordinate and the pilot who made the trip were at fault.

Government funds are allocated in order to meet mission requirements. There also are regulations to "avoid flights open to misinterpretation by the public." The pilot and the subordinate clearly violated this regulation.

The senior was at fault, too, for not taking into account what it means to be an officer and the power that officers have. Seniors are expected to know all the regulations that govern their behavior, so not knowing about this specific instruction is not a valid excuse. In addition, the more senior you become, the more sensitivity you need. Both your behavior and your use of government funds are constantly under review.

The last factor is the power that seniors have. They must be aware that just asking a junior a question sometimes leads the junior officer to assume that the senior wants him or her to "make it so." All officers have a desire to please their seniors. It's important for seniors to remember how they felt and acted as junior officers.

Questions for Consideration

Making the flag officer feel good might help the morale in the command.
   Is this a valid reason for using a government aircraft to make the trip?
Do you think the flag officer realized what the junior had done to make the flag's trip possible?
If you were the flag officer, how could you have avoided this situation?
   How would you have acted differently?

Case 51: The Hotel

(From page 73)

What Happened

Second Lieutenant Meister accepted his brother's offer and took the additional discount at motels as he and his family went across country.

One of the motel's staff made a hot-line complaint, because he knew that the motel chain was losing money because of the double discount. He was loyal to his company and wanted what was best for it.

Meister received a letter of caution, and his brother was reprimanded by the motel chain.

Discussion

The issue here is whether the second lieutenant was given special treatment, more than he was entitled to as a military officer. The motel chain is in business to make a profit for its owners or stockholders. Their granting of a special military discount means a reduction in their level of profit and represents their awareness of the military's contribution to this country.

In addition, the motel chain tries, as do many other companies, to reward its own employees with discounts for using the company's own product or service. Since rooms are occupied and have to be cleaned the following day, this discount also reduces the motel's profit at the same time it shows the motel chain's gratitude to its employees. Given all this, it is not fair for Meister to take advantage of both discounts.

As officers, we will find ourselves given special privileges because of what we've done or may do. While officers are individuals with private lives, they must also recognize that they are in the public eye, in the same way that a mayor or a chief of police would be. What they do in their private lives may be looked at in a "public" way.

Officers are expected to set a higher example than the average citizen. It's unethical for an officer to accept special treatment unavailable to others. In this case, the officer's acceptance of the discount also might have been perceived as a sign that the officer would throw additional business to the motel chain. The perception, even if it's only a perception, that an officer is receiving or giving special favors is damaging.

Can you think of other examples in which people have felt entitled to receive extra benefits because of the work they were doing?

Was sending Meister a letter of caution enough of a reprimand? Was it too strict?

Case 52: Submarine Pictures

(From page 74)

What Happened

Ensign Michaels told the ship's superintendent that he wasn't going to trade shrimp for pictures. Michaels then told the CO what had happened. The CO had a talk with the superintendent, who had the pictures taken and printed.

Discussion

The CO's actions reinforced in the ensign's mind that the command's ethical climate was good. The chain of command can serve to strengthen the moral and ethical climate, as well as the behavior, of an organization.

This case shows a junior officer trying to please his CO, but managing to do so without compromising his integrity. The rest of the command was unaware of what happened. Making the right decision—even if it had resulted in not getting the pictures—was a good thing for this ensign. He made his CO aware of his integrity, and the CO appreciated that more than the pictures.

In this case, Ensign Michaels maintained his integrity and the crew got the bags of shrimp that were allocated to them. Even if no one else would have known had the ensign made the trade, he would still have had to live with himself.

Questions for Consideration

Do you agree with Ensign Michael's decision? Why or why not?

How do you balance your sense of ethics against your need to accomplish the mission?

Does where you draw that line depend in any way upon what the mission is?

Case 53: The Junior Officer

(From page 75)

What Happened

Lieutenant Ward chose the ethical approach. He focused on his future reputation as an officer, his future ability to lead and discipline, and his goal to clean up the aircrews and the command.

In this case, it worked. The command was cleaned up. Many personnel disliked the "new order" and shunned the lieutenant. His CO liked the outcome but didn't support him openly. However, Lieutenant Ward was rated highly on his fitness report.

Discussion

It's important to note that as the CO and other personnel changed, the command in question also changed—it became more ethical.

Lieutenant Ward saw the process through, met his personal goals, and felt that he had done the right thing for the command and the Department of the Navy. Eventually, Ward moved to better assignments.

Questions for Consideration

What do you think of the CO in this case? Would you want to emulate him? Why do you think the CO failed to support Lieutenant Ward openly?

Case 54: Extra Labor and Equipment

(From page 77)

What Happened

Purbaugh was fully aware that he was violating standards of ethics for his own personal gain, but there was no "adult" supervision of his activities. The foreign nationals became increasingly cynical about the American military because of what was happening.

Ultimately, a new CO–XO team arrived and put a stop to this improper use of employees. Purbaugh earned a reputation for his behavior and didn't receive any more promotions. The image of the military had been severely damaged in this location.

Discussion

In this case study, Purbaugh used the authority in his position to reap undeserved personal benefits. This case also implies that the rules of ethics might be different in the American armed forces when personnel serve overseas. This is, of course, false. If anything, Americans should be aware that their behavior will be especially scrutinized when overseas.

It's important to remember that the standards of ethics and integrity vary from one culture and country to another, but American service personnel must always meet the highest of standards of our country and the Naval service. In many countries, the only interaction that country's populace has with Americans is through their contact with members of the United States military. Our country is judged by the actions of our people. In past deployments, some service personnel have engaged in prohibited activities or outrageous behavior that brought shame to the country.

There's no valid excuse for this officer's actions. At whatever level an officer is, he or she will always have subordinates. These subordinates will take their guidance from the senior. The military runs on trust, and while a CO or XO may not be paying close attention to what's happening, that's no excuse for taking advantage of the situation. Even if the culture itself allows "shady dealings," by engaging in them, an officer sets an unsatisfactory example to his or her subordinates.

Questions for Consideration

How do you think this officer rationalized his decision?
Should the command climate share the blame for this situation?

Case 55: Cheat

(From page 78)

What Happened

By the time Montarelli finished her degree studies, she also was interested in investing. She remained stateside and was promoted to O-3.

Since she had already decided it was alright for her family to use the office copier, she continued to use it for personal investment purposes. She had even earned a real estate agent's license. She was very busy and sometimes went home early, leaving some of her work for the senior enlisted personnel, hoping that her seniors would think that she was delegating effectively.

Classes were full for the overseas rotation preparation, so she opted for another stateside tour. When she wasn't phoning the local stockbroker, she took time off during the day to sell real estate.

Montarelli rushed around town to make her appointments, and she received several speeding tickets. She received lower fitness reports, and tensions mounted as she tried to meet all of her commitments. She began to drink. Her drinking was followed by child abuse and divorce.

She couldn't meet her mounting expenses with only her income, so she started to hedge on government travel claims and income taxes, figuring all the while that the military and the country owed her that extra money because of the travel she had done and the sacrifices she made.

Finally, just to get through the day, she started using drugs. She lost her driver's license, and her life fell apart. The military's investigative service proved her travel claim fraud. She was picked up for drug abuse by the command's urinalysis program. Then the IRS filed felony charges for income-tax fraud.

Her brief military career was terminated by a court-martial, OTH discharge, and a federal prison sentence.

Discussion

While this is a horrendous case, and certainly represents the worst possible scenario, there are lessons to be learned from it. First, don't cut corners, and don't mix personal and military business. Second, let your actions give meaning to the words that are part of our commissioned officer corps' heritage: "special trust and confidence." Third, serve the military, not yourself. As officers, our ethical integrity should be a source of pride for us and an example to others.

Remember that there will be times when decisions about what is ethical and what is not are made in the context of the command's general ethical climate. Still, that may be a mistake if the command has an indifferent attitude. Officers are held to a strict standard of conduct, and the fact that others may not be meeting that standard is not a valid excuse for sinking to a lower level.

Questions for Consideration

What do you think the military's policy of taking care of service families means?

Do you find it believable that a seemingly small ethical lapse could have such large consequences?

Case 56: The Computer

(From page 79)

What Happened

The officer violated the standards of conduct because the purchase spanned a long period of time. If the officer wanted to sell the equipment to the enlisted member, he should not have financed the deal.

Two violations were actually committed. The second, more serious one, is that the officer was the enlisted's direct supervisor. If the officer hadn't been the enlisted's supervisor, it's possible that action wouldn't have been taken against the officer.

Discussion

As an officer, you are permitted a one-time sale within certain limits. Officers should be acutely aware of their relationships with enlisted personnel and should never enter into any type of open-ended or long-term business relationship with them.

The military standard of ethical conduct required of officers is much higher than for executives in either industry or government. Because of this, every action should be examined for its ethics.

This officer should have considered the problems that could result from selling a computer to a subordinate or how that action could be perceived by other personnel. Others might see the enlisted as being coerced into paying the officer's price for the equipment. Going through this thought process in advance might have avoided the whole situation.

Also, seek the guidance of other senior members of your command and discuss any questionable situation with a legal officer, especially if it involves dealing with an enlisted member. Sometimes, it's intuitively obvious that some actions by an officer may be illegal or unethical. Sometimes, it's not. Be sure to get advice.

Questions for Consideration

Is it possible that the officer thought he was doing a good thing, a favor even, for this enlisted member?

What do you think this officer's peers thought about his actions?

Case 57: The Dinner

(From page 80)

What Happened

First Lieutenant Jaso felt that all that was involved was a friendly dinner with no intention by the contractor to influence him. Still, he realized that more might be involved than he knew, so he consulted with his XO, who raised the question with both the CO and legal counsel.

In discussions, the point was made about the importance of not accepting—or giving the appearance of accepting—gratuities from contractors, no matter the amount. As a result of these talks, everyone agreed that Jaso should decline the invitation. The first lieutenant wrote back, tactfully explaining why he could not attend and thanking the senior executive from the company for his invitation.

Discussion

There were four factors in this decision:

(1) The very appearance of First Lieutenant Jaso at the dinner would give the impression that he was personal friends with the company executives.

(2) Even though another officer would be taking over the liaison work with the firm if a new contract was made, the perception would be that there was a continuous relationship between whoever held Jaso's position and the company.

(3) The appearance of impropriety must never exist. It may be perceived that the government is favoring one contractor over another. Such perceptions in the past have led to hot-line complaints and letters to Congress. These misconceptions have also

exacerbated relationships between the military and the community where the work is being done.

(4) Jaso could never be certain that one day, as a more senior officer, he wouldn't be assigned back to this area. He might possibly come into contact again with the same contractor.

An honest company will understand the refusal of such an invitation and not be insulted. It will continue to do its best work for the government because of its own pride in doing a good job.

Questions for Consideration

What factors have to be considered in trying to keep a balance between maintaining the contractor relationship and following the government's standards of conduct rules?

Do you agree with the decision not to attend the dinner?

Do you think there were other options that could have been explored?

Case 58: Repair Parts

(From page 81)

What Happened

With the backing of his CO, the officer kept pushing for justice. As a result of the continuing investigation, the contractor had to bring his prices into line, which was the reason the investigation began in the first place. The officer was transferred to another assignment on the base. Because the story had appeared in the newspapers, several investigative reporters asked the officer to go public with his side of the story, but he declined.

In the end, the officer wasn't hurt. He was promoted on time and at the end of his tour, he received a meritorious service medal. His fitness reports were all excellent. Despite his short-term reputation as a troublemaker, the officer gained the respect of his fellow officers within the command, as well as his CO.

In looking back on the incident, the officer who reported this case said, "Most importantly, I felt good about myself. I had maintained my integrity against terrific odds. I felt I did what was right and would probably do it again."

Discussion

This officer was not only willing to be in the military and to possibly face death to defend the principles of the Constitution, but he was also ready to sacrifice his career should that be necessary.

As a junior officer, you need to know that there are thousands of other officers who make the hard, right decisions rather than the easy, wrong ones. You will not be alone when you act responsibly, hold yourself and others accountable, and ensure that integrity and ethics are part of every day in your life.

Questions for Consideration

Can you think of some reasons why the contracting office didn't want to get involved in the investigation?

If you were the CO, what would your impression be of this junior officer?

Do you admire this junior officer? Why or why not?

Case 59: Training

(From page 88)

What Happened

First Lieutenant Grimes wasn't sure if the commanding officer knew what was going on in the unit, but she reasoned that it didn't really matter. She knew that something was wrong. Her loyalty to her CO, unit, and country demanded that she not tolerate the falsification of records.

She recognized that speaking up might alienate her fellow officers, but her ultimate loyalty wasn't to them. It was to her country, and she had sworn to do her job to the best of her ability.

The first lieutenant decided that from that day forward all training would be done completely and as prescribed. The first step was to take the falsified report and return it, with a short note, to the responsible officer. Grimes's note indicated what sections of the training hadn't been completed. She let the officer know that her assumption was that the missing training would be done before the next week's schedule and that she would be monitoring training from now on.

For the first month, the lieutenant monitored all training. Word quickly spread that all training had to be done correctly or there would be consequences. None of the officers who had skimped on training wanted the matter brought to the CO, so one junior officer was able to make a difference.

Discussion

We train so that we will always be ready, even though we may not be called into action for years. Our country depends on us to be ready—not just ready on paper, but ready to perform our mission according to requirements.

No matter what your rank, you can make a difference if you remember that your job is to be a professional, not just someone trying to have a long, uneventful career. All COs depend on their officers to ensure that requirements are met. We have an ethical obligation to meet that expectation or resign our commissions—there is no middle ground.

Questions for Consideration

Do you agree with what First Lieutenant Grimes decided to do? Why or why not?

What do you think about Grimes? Is she the kind of officer you would like to be?

Do you think the CO knows what's going on?

Can you think of other situations in which loyalty to your command will take precedence over your own career objectives?

Case 60: Inflated Readiness Levels

(From page 90)

What Happened

During meetings with more senior officers, Lieutenant Andrews brought up the issue and came into conflict with the O-4 department heads of Training and Operations. She gave up, deciding to do nothing. She succumbed to the influence of the senior officers, who were accepting the less-than-required training results.

Instead of bringing the aircrew up to standards through effective training, the command failed to provide basic training events while recording that they had indeed been completed. The most suitable course of action would have been to follow the required training according to instructions.

If Andrews had insisted on the specific requirements for training, it's likely her seniors would have felt pressured into doing the right thing. This is another instance of an officer who is willing to die for the nation but not willing to lose a career over what's right and appropriate.

Questions for Consideration

Why do you think Lieutenant Andrews and the other junior officers accepted the situation?

What's likely to happen when any members of the squadron leave to join new ones? How will their performance levels compare to those in the new squadrons?

Case 61: A Friend

(From page 91)

What Happened

Lieutenant Hagen decided to compromise by counseling his friend. He concluded that his friend had made a simple error in judgment by drinking a beer. In Hagen's estimation, there wasn't enough of a transgression to end a career. He avoided having to turn in his friend by assuring himself that the pilot had learned his lesson and would not repeat the mistake in the future.

Discussion

An important question immediately presents itself: Was the lieutenant being true to his friend at the expense of his oath as an officer? Friendship, clearly, is one of the great goods that human beings strive for in life, yet loyalty to one friend at the expense of loyalty to the Constitution and the code of military conduct is not in keeping with the standards of a military officer.

An officer is not at liberty to break rules at his or her own discretion. To do so violates the principles of accountability, responsibility, and trust placed in all officers. If an officer fails to obey the rules, that officer is setting a precedent for other military officers to follow their consciences as well, leading to a disruption of good order and discipline.

Military rules and regulations are the laws by which the armed forces operate. They are designed for the effective operation of an organization required to act precisely, swiftly, and competently. While the rules are, by necessity, written to enforce strict guidelines on behavior, they do allow for some flexibility.

In some commissioning sources, while the officer candidate is learning the system, counseling is permitted as a means of dealing with a minor infraction of the rules—but even in those situations, it is not meant as an alternative to reporting a serious breach of military discipline.

In this case, a serious breach has occurred that places a serious moral burden on the pilot who witnessed the event. His duty toward his friend is trumped by his duty to his military oath to uphold rules that are designed to ensure the safety and well-being of pilots and crew. Ending someone's career would be extremely difficult, but attending that person's funeral because you failed to care enough to stop an illegal and dangerous activity would be an even worse fate. An officer is bound to uphold a standard that is not dependent upon time, place, or person.

Questions for Consideration

How does the notion of overlooking a friend's transgression of rules or regulations because of that friendship square with your idea of what friends ask of each other?

What is expected or required of you in such a situation?

Do you think that counseling the friend—the option chosen in this case— was the right thing to do? Why or why not?

Case 62: The Rifle Company

(From page 93)

What Happened

First Lieutenant Riley began to believe that Second Lieutenant Jordan was endangering the unit's integrity, morale, and functioning. With that in mind, Riley went to the CO about Jordan. The CO was shocked by Riley's revelations and called in his officers for personal interviews.

The battle lines were drawn as some officers hoped to either distance themselves from the event out of cowardice or support Jordan out of misplaced loyalty. Other officers corroborated Riley's accusations about Jordan, which was the moral and ethical choice to make.

Finally, the CO called all his officers into the stateroom. Accusations were made, and officers nearly resorted to blows. One person began to cry, realizing the scope, severity, and ramifications of this behavior among officers.

There were painful consequences to Riley's delay in bringing the matter to the CO's attention. Some officers chose not to be in the same room with other officers for the rest of the deployment. In fear of Jordan's retribution, officers began to lock up all their personal belongings at all times.

What happened was well known throughout the rest of the Marine and Navy personnel aboard other vessels, and the Marine CO suffered as a result of this publicity. Officers requested transfers to other vessels to finish out their deployment, and an environment of suspicion permeated the small group of officers on the ship. Jordan was discharged from active duty.

Discussion

It's easy to see why Riley was reluctant to say anything about Jordan. Whenever you criticize anyone, you run the risk of having your own deficiencies exposed. Young officers often have an unwritten code by which they "stick together." This is a fine concept because it adds to morale, esprit de corps, and camaraderie.

In the Marine Corps, it's called the LPA (Lieutenants' Protective Association). It's a way of allowing young officers who are inexperienced to work together to help their fellow officers. This kind of system, though, should never be used to hide or condone poor judgment, performance, or behavior. Such actions make all the parties as guilty as the actual offender.

The lesson here is that we must police our own ranks, and simply because you are not perfect doesn't mean that you don't have the right and the duty to police your peers and subordinates. Small lapses in judgment or performance do not equate to someone else's criminal behavior.

Many young people in the military view friendship and loyalty as two of the most important values they can hold. You often hear people say, "He's my friend. I'd do anything for him." Or people may cover for a friend out of loyalty. There is no friendship or loyalty that outweighs someone's behavior or performance endangering the collective unit.

Questions for Consideration

What do you think of the CO in this case?
Was Riley's delay in acting justified? Why or why not?
Where does one draw the line in deciding to abandon friendship for the
    greater loyalty to the unit? How would you make that decision?

Case 63: Grievance Hearing
(From page 95)

What Happened

Lieutenant Saunders recognized that the XO was attempting to take the unpopular, but morally correct, course of action on behalf of his unit, and his decision might destroy his career. She realized that if she supported the XO's allegations and received an unjust fitness report as a result, she could petition the Board of Correction of Naval Records to have it removed. She knew very well this would be an uphill battle, but she wanted to take the honorable course of action, so that she never had second thoughts in the future when similar situations arose. She wanted to do what was right, so she made a statement.

After a review of all the preliminary statements, there was adequate proof of the XO's allegations to order an investigation. The CO was relieved from his command. Saunders was transferred to another unit within a few months. She received a commendatory fitness report and was promoted to lieutenant commander.

Discussion

Saunders faced a classic dilemma: whether or not to be disloyal to the CO for the greater good of the unit. She decided to do what was honorable and right and supported the XO. To fail to do so would be endorsing all the negative aspects of the CO's character. It would be taking the easy, weak, irresponsible approach to important leadership issues.

Questions for Consideration

Was it fair of the CO to ask his officers for their loyalty?
Do you think the junior officer had a responsibility to support the XO? Why or why not?
How do you think her peers felt about Saunders's decision?

Case 64: The Car Cover

(From page 96)

What Happened

Before the PR completed the new car cover, the CO rescinded his order. The CO moved up the ranks, becoming the XO of a much larger unit, and eventually made O-6.

Discussion

The military is not composed of perfect individuals, and we cannot have confidence that all officers will be trustworthy 100 percent of the time.

Lieutenant Christopher failed by (1) not returning the cover to the CO the moment the PR received his assignment, (2) sending the torn cover back with the PR, thus failing to take responsibility for the work of a subordinate (Christopher should have taken it back), (3) allowing the PR to make a new car cover, (4) permitting the use of government materials to repair or replace private property, and (5) reporting the grumbling of the subordinate while not personally speaking up as the officer in charge.

We don't know how many officers contributed to the CO's thinking that it was alright to mix personal and government property. We don't know how many officers taught the CO that it was alright to have enlisted do personal work. Christopher should have recognized that this CO was out of line. This officer failed to show any courage in dealing with the CO and protecting both enlisted personnel and government resources.

Years ago, officers use to put their shoes outside their doors in the evening, so that the enlisted personnel could shine them by morning. It was not unusual for the enlisted to pack an officer's belongings for a move or have the motor pool fix private cars for the officers. We recognize today that enlisted personnel are there to do a job for the unit and the nation, not individual officers. We recognize that the taxpayer expects every last dollar to go for its originally intended purpose.

The actions taken by this CO were improper. In the future, all officers will be held accountable for participating in such illegal and unethical activities, and future officers will find their careers limited and terminated by such activities.

Questions for Consideration

Would you want to serve with Lieutenant Christopher? Why or why not? How would you deal with this kind of behavior by the CO?

Case 65: The NATOPS Test

(From page 97)

What Happened

The NATOPS officer documented all his conversations with the people involved and put off doing the test for a short time. Eventually, the JO filled out the test and delivered it to the senior officer, leaving the name space blank. This way, at least the senior had to fill in his name to use the test, which spared the NATOPS officer from having participated in the falsification.

The practical result was that the NATOPS officer took the test for the senior officer. Without that help, the senior would have failed. The junior did, in fact, allow expediency to interfere with his ethical judgment.

Ultimately, no one was helped, but fortunately, no one died. By not having to personally take the test, the senior's cockpit knowledge suffered. Several officers protested by refusing to fly with the senior. The CO labeled everyone who protested as a "troublemaker." The JO kept his NATOPS assignment.

Eventually, the NATOPS officer was held responsible for following an illegal order from the CO. Later that year, the senior officer and the CO both came under investigation, and both were relieved of command.

Discussion

While there may be dire consequences in the future for those who act ethically, the desire to do so is increasing. The armed forces of the United States are continually improving in every area, especially the one that recognizes and rewards ethical actions.

It's important for junior officers to comply with ethical rules and requirements, so that progress can continue to be made.

Questions for Consideration

How do you think the CO would rationalize his actions?
Why did the senior officer agree to let someone else take his test?
What message did the senior's actions send to the rest of the junior officers?
Do you agree with what the junior officer did? Was not filling in a name
   on the test sufficient?

Case 66: Selecting Candidates

(From page 99)

What Happened

The subordinate commander asked for more discussions of the subject. During the meeting, all of the subordinates asked the CO to reconsider his decision and screen for the best-qualified applicants. The CO agreed, realizing that selecting the best Marine would allow the organization to do the best job and ultimately cause the command to achieve its mission.

Discussion

The subordinates could have simply defied the CO, but that would have destroyed the team concept of the battalion. There are many assignments for qualified military personnel, but in those rare cases when the best person is required, that person should be selected without regard to race or ethnic background.

All commanders have a responsibility to conduct training so that all personnel have a chance to become outstanding performers, and thus be eligible for selection to every program. It's also appropriate for every command to continually review equal opportunity goals, to ensure not only that equal training is provided but also that superior performance is recognized regardless of an individual's ethnic status.

Questions for Consideration

Do subordinate commanders have a responsibility to do what's ethically correct, even if that seems disloyal to their commander?

What if the commander had refused to change his decision? Would the subordinate commanders have other options?

Case 67: Standing Watch

(From page 100)

What Happened

Lieutenant (jg) Bailey decided to cover for the missing officer. Eventually the relieving officer showed up, and it was not necessary for Bailey to report him to the command duty officer (CDO).

Discussion

Though efforts were made to reach the missing officer, he could not be found. In covering for the relieving officer, Bailey was more concerned about what others would think of him than about his duty to the command.

It should be noted that if more than several hours had gone by before the missing officer arrived, Bailey intended to report the situation to the CDO. (OPNAV instructions require a report to BUPERS of any officer missing from appointed place of duty for one hour or more. A phone call early on may prevent this from becoming an issue. This is why most watches are scheduled to relieve fifteen minutes early.)

It is not always easy to be a junior officer. Though still young in many ways, junior officers are expected to act with the honor and integrity expected of professional military officers. It may help to remember that as a

JO, you don't make the rules, but you are expected to obey them. If regulations require you to report the lateness of another officer, two people are hurt if you ignore the rule.

The missing officer is hurt because he has failed to learn the importance of meeting responsibilities. If he continues the lax attitude toward his duties, he may well lose his career over repeated instances of dereliction and tardiness. Perhaps an outcome of that sort could be prevented if the officer had been disciplined for the first mistake before the habit could become ingrained and threaten his career.

It's important to remember that you can be hurt by covering for a friend because you give the impression that you can't be trusted to report even the simplest of matters. Your seniors will see that you allow protecting a friend to interfere with doing your job properly. If you don't think a regulation is appropriate, make an appeal for its modification through the chain of command. Don't establish a reputation as someone who makes his or her own decisions about when and whether to obey the rules.

It may also help to remember that a true friend does not take advantage of you and would never expect you to cover for them by disobeying orders they are supposed to uphold and enforce.

Questions for Consideration

Did Lieutenant (jg) Bailey have any other options besides covering for the missing officer or reporting him? If so, what were those options?

Do you think the rule about reporting an absence of one hour to BUPERS is fair? Why or why not?

Why is time so critical to good order and discipline in the military?

Case 68: Sanitaries

(From page 101)

What Happened

Lieutenant Commander Griffiths went ahead and authorized the dumping—in direct violation of the CO's standing order. Griffiths then compounded his error by failing to tell the CO about the dumping. He didn't want to admit that he had directly disobeyed a standing order, and he justified the cover-up to himself by reasoning that he had only done it because he had the best interests of the commanding officer at heart.

The CO found Griffiths's violation of a standing order and his attempted cover-up completely unacceptable. He felt it clearly indicated extremely poor judgment on Griffiths's part and this was subsequently made part of his fitness report.

Discussion

It is not unusual for a junior, out of a sense of loyalty to a senior, to take on certain authorities that have not been delegated. In taking the authorities, the junior is acting without all the knowledge that the senior would likely have brought to the decision-making process.

Standing orders exist because no CO can stay awake twenty-four hours a day. For that reason, there is an OOD who has, for the period of the watch, been delegated many of the authorities that normally rest with the CO. Because some procedures and evolutions require the intimate knowledge and judgment of the commanding officer, a CO may not delegate all authority.

The CO knows that his responsibilities often require that his sleep will be interrupted. That is one of the responsibilities and sacrifices of command.

In this case, Griffiths failed to understand that orders are just that—procedures to be followed and obeyed. Only in the case of inability through injury or nonavailability or death may a subordinate take over the command prerogatives of the CO. Officers are granted great discretion in the performance of their duties, and it is assumed that they will understand not only what they are authorized to do, but also what they are not authorized to do.

When a CO puts an order in a unit's standing orders, the CO must have complete confidence that subordinates will follow those orders. Officers who will lead must first learn to follow.

Questions for Consideration

What effect did Lieutenant Griffiths's actions have on the crew when they saw him directly disobey a standing order and assume authority that had not been delegated to him?

Why would Griffiths have wanted to avoid waking his CO?

Was it his place to decide whether or not to awaken the CO to ask for permission to dump sanitaries?

Case 69: Passing Inspection

(From page 102)

What Happened

The ensign decided to gundeck the quals and the division passed inspection.

Discussion

One of the problems, of course, with the gundeck approach is that there are not really qualified "qualified" personnel standing a particular watch station. Also, personnel lose motivation and respect for seniors when officers handle problems in unethical ways.

If this case had been handled in an ethical manner, the ship would have failed the inspection. Along the same lines, however, it's important to note that if the junior and senior officers had been doing their jobs properly from the start, there never would have been a problem. But we live in the real world and things do slip through the cracks.

It is relatively easy to explain why officers are tempted to cut corners in the manner described in this case. With advancement and screening boards becoming harder and harder in each cycle, the pressure to excel is high. And even one negative mark may ruin a career. An officer may well wonder whether it pays to be honest and ethical in the decision-making process.

But the picture doesn't have to be this bleak. Those officers who are looking so hard to beat the system could put that same effort into working within the system and excelling. It will take today's junior officers working with more senior officers to ensure that his happens. Every junior officer needs to know that doing the right thing will be respected, even if it isn't necessarily liked.

If you tell the truth, your seniors will always know they can count on you. You will avoid ulcers, even if it means losing your career, by not lying, not cheating, not gundecking, not failing to tell the entire story, and not falsifying records.

The ensign had another option for dealing with this situation, though apparently it didn't occur to him. He could have provided interim qualification letters—qualify the sailor on what he does know, not on what he should know. The inspecting officer would see that he was dealing with an honest ship and likely have a greater level of confidence when the officers say they are prepared in other areas.

America's armed forces are currently the best in the world because of our equipment, training, and commitment of personnel. Other nations, both large and small, are striving to catch up, but as long as integrity and ethical behavior—along with acceptance of responsibility and accountability—are our watchwords, we will prevail in future conflicts. It is up to today's junior officers to help make sure we are prepared to win.

Questions for Consideration

How would the falsification of qualification records effect readiness and morale?

What would likely happen to the ensign and the engineering division officer if the subterfuge were discovered by the inspector?

Case 70: Sealed Orders

(From page 103)

What Happened

The ComO/OpsO, who had experience in catastrophic combat, weighed the alternatives of loyalty to his captain and the chain of command and decided not to report the incident.

Discussion

In this case, it's important to remember that in 1945 communications were not as swift as they are now. Classified information was not likely to be revealed unless it was compromised by someone within a military organization. But occasionally, information did leak out because of security compromises, and so the ComO/OpsO faced a very difficult decision after his captain opened the sealed orders. It is a situation that many officers will have to face in one way or another, so it is appropriate to plan ahead about what to do.

The reasons for reporting and not reporting the incident seemed equally compelling to the ComO/OpsO. (In the end, he felt that the decision was ultimately taken out of his hands when President Truman approved the plan to drop the atomic bomb on Hiroshima and Nagasaki, ending the war.)

Now, more than fifty years after the incident, the ComO/OpsO is still bothered by his decision. He knows that he should have reported the captain, and he has contributed this case so that today's junior officers might be better prepared to make the right decision when they are faced with a similar dilemma. If we remember that we swear allegiance to the Constitution rather than to the president or the chain of command, decisions of this nature may be easier to act upon, even though they may end a career.

Questions for Consideration

Why does that one decision—made fifty years ago—still bother the ComO/OpsO?

Did the ComO/OpsO have options other than the two he considered?

Case 71: The Mine

(From page 104)

What Happened

The captain told the OOD to simply chart the location of the mine and broadcast its location. No reason for this decision was given, even though there was no doubt in the OOD's mind that in a SEA 5 condition they could have at least sunk the mine.

Discussion

It will be apparent to the reader that the captain made a decision that could have had terrible, catastrophic consequences. Two major questions spring immediately to mind. What if the next ship to come along had done so in the dark? And second, even if the next ship had been traveling during the day, would it have had a sharp-eyed lookout?

To blow up the mine in direct contradiction of the captain's order would break down the authority of the chain of command and present an example to the crew that each of them had the right to make the decisions they felt were correct, even though their actions might countermand the orders of their seniors. The OOD could have taken another consideration into account in this scenario. It was possible that because the captain had so many matters pressing on his mind, he did not fully consider the consequences of his decision.

A junior has an ethical responsibility to a senior to ensure, through further explanation and argument, that the senior fully understands the consequences of actions about to be taken. This is not to suggest that in the heat of battle every order of the CO should be questioned, but, where time permits, and especially where bad decisions could cost lives, the junior has a moral obligation to speak up and "tell the king he is wearing no clothes." The junior must also be prepared to fully explain his or her reasons for disagreement and provide an alternative solution.

However, for this type of communication to be successful, the senior must be approachable and willing to listen to the ideas and suggestions of subordinates. This does not mean that the captain has to accept the suggestions, but rather seniors must ensure that their subordinates feel they can be heard.

Questions for Consideration

What were the junior officer's responsibilities in this matter?
Having once pointed out to the captain the "right" course of action, was there any further action he could take?
Should he have taken it upon himself to blow up the mine? Why or why not?

Case 72: Command Responsibility
(From page 109)

What Happened

The CO chose to launch the planes on schedule. There was a mishap, and the aircraft in question and its crew chief were lost at sea.

Upon investigation, the accident appeared to be the result of confusion among the crew about what was to be done and how to do it correctly— confusion that may have been eliminated, or at least greatly reduced, by appropriate preflight briefings.

Discussion

While it is impossible to trace the causes of the accident back to one or more specific sources, there are nonetheless several possible contributing factors and several potentially responsible actors. Each of the actors made a choice, consciously or otherwise, that might have contributed to the mishap. The copilot chose not to attend the operations brief and chose not to inform his chain of command of his absence. The operations officer and the lead pilot either did not notice the copilot's absence or, if either one did, they chose not to report it or take other appropriate action. Both the pilot and the copilot failed to perform the required plane-side brief and both chose not to report that omission.

The squadron commander, learning of these omissions (admittedly at the last minute), nonetheless chose to launch the flight operations as scheduled. One way to interpret that decision is that he chose to please the admiral by following his orders to the letter and, by so doing, chose not to follow proper safety procedures.

Following or not following proper procedures in not merely box checking. Both have clear and important ethical content. All flight operations, particularly military flight operations, and most especially night time carrier operations, are inherently dangerous and threaten both expensive pieces of equipment and human lives. Procedures and checklists are designed to preserve both hardware and people while enabling the successful completion of the mission.

The pressures to accomplish the mission as directed can be enormous, but they must be measured—militarily and ethically—against the solemn responsibility of all military officers, especially commanders, for the safety and lives of their troops. The rules and procedures are guides developed from previous mishaps. Not following them is as much an ethical failure as not showing up for deployment.

In any military organization, the commanding officer is ultimately responsible, though subordinate personnel have varying degrees of responsibility depending upon their assignments. Subordinates not fully prepared are ethical failures and are disloyal to their superiors, whose objectives they should be trying to meet. It is important for all levels of the chain of command to realize that their mistakes affect not only themselves, but the mission, their superiors, their peers, and their subordinates.

Questions for Consideration

If the CO had made the same decision (to launch flight operations despite the problems) and no accident had happened, what lessons about his honor, his courage, and his commitment do you think his squadron mates and subordinates would have drawn from his actions?

Case 73: Request for Transfer

(From page 110)

What Happened

McPhail's first step was to document all incidents that related to his differences of opinion with the XO. Then, he approached the XO with a formal written complaint that was addressed to BUPERS through the chain of command. By facing the issue squarely and ethically, McPhail obtained the support of the CO and transfer orders were issued with department head credit.

Discussion

One principle of ethical conduct is for seniors to let juniors know where they stand. If a senior is recommending action against a junior, the latter should be advised so that he or she may provide any important amplifying information.

In this case, McPhail took an acceptable course of action. He could also have added an intervening step by scheduling a meeting with the XO to find out why he had taken those actions with BUPERS. If the meeting had been unsatisfactory, he could have taken his concerns directly to the CO.

McPhail would also have been within his rights to file a complaint directly with BUPERS without using the chain of command. This approach would create the least immediate disturbance in daily operations, but the long-term effects would be more disruptive. Filing a written complaint through the CO would keep the chain of command informed, reduce ambiguity, and increase the likelihood of justice being served.

Questions for Consideration

Were the XO's actions with BUPERS ethical? Why or why not?

Did McPhail have any other options to resolve the situation than the one he ultimately chose?

Do you think the decision to confront the XO and file a formal complaint was difficult for McPhail? Why or why not?

Should the CO have known about the difficult relationship between the XO and McPhail? If he should have known, should he have taken action to resolve it?

Case 74: Equal Treatment

(From page 111)

What Happened

Harrison's discreet approach brought all parties together and as a result of discussing grievances, the male lieutenants stopped the inappropriate treatment of the female officers in particular and the harassment of females in general at the command. The women's lavatory was also reopened.

Discussion

In addition to being responsible to the commanding officer and fellow shipmates, officers must ensure fair and equal treatment of all personnel. Harrison also could have considered handling the situation at the lowest level by raising his concerns with the male lieutenants and suggesting they stop the harassing comments and practical jokes. There is always the danger, though, that this approach might backfire and increase the harassment and sense of alienation for the female personnel.

Questions for Consideration

Did the harassing lieutenants know their behavior was inappropriate or could they have thought they were just engaging in harmless teasing?

Should the women have taken any action to stop the behavior even before Harrison arrived? Why or why not? If they had taken action, what could they have done?

Case 75: Standards

(From page 112)

What Happened

As a result of Lieutenant Hallman's aggressive action, the female ensign was allowed to assume the duties of legal officer. The XO finally realized that he had been too quick to order the administrative separation of minority personnel in previous cases. Due process was restored in the squadron, and attempts were made to rehabilitate, rather than automatically separate from the Navy, personnel who had strayed from standards.

Discussion

By taking a stand, Hallman saved his career. He also returned to the high road and ensured that justice was done in all his future dealings.

This case further highlights the message contained in the essay by ADM Arleigh Burke in appendix A. The possibility always exists that speaking up may end your career, but in not challenging your senior when he is acting unethically and not standing up for what is right, you become part of the problem rather than part of the solution.

The entire officer corps depends on trust. By pledging your oath to support the Constitution, you have placed yourself in a difficult, but not impossible, situation. Your obligation is also to all who observe you. The legal officer must set a standard. If he or she doesn't stand up for what is right, many others may come to believe that standing for justice and principle is almost impossible.

Questions for Consideration

Why did Lieutenant Hallman allow his integrity to be compromised during his tour of legal officer?

Why did Hallman change his mind and decide he could no longer live with his lack of integrity?

What would have happened if the XO had not responded favorably to Hallman's complaint?

Case 76: Humor

(From page 113)

What Happened

When Commander Martin presented the evidence to the CO, he immediately apologized to the individuals concerned. And he also thanked Commander Martin for his involvement.

Discussion

As XO, Martin's primary responsibility was to ensure mission accomplishment. But the job also involves fostering harmonious working relationships both up and down the chain of command.

It is important that naval personnel never lose confidence in either the chain of command or the Navy. It will be detrimental to morale if service members are denied the due process of investigation, and both male and female members of a command will become concerned if any member is mistreated.

It took courage for Commander Martin to say something to the CO and carry out the investigation, but it was the right thing to do. It resulted in a better operating command and a feeling among all personnel that everyone was being held to the same standard.

Questions for Consideration

Why was it important for Commander Martin to notify the CO that he was beginning an investigation?

What could have happened if Martin had ignored the women's concerns and let the matter go?

Why might the CO not realize how offensive and inappropriate his comments were?

Case 77: Standards

(From page 115)

What Happened

The instructor complied with the direction from the CO. Three months later, after the original class had graduated, the troubled student was winged.

Discussion

It is not possible to know if anything the instructor might have said would have changed the CO's mind about passing the troubled student. But the officer did fail his senior by not speaking up about his concern.

We expect our seniors to look out for us, but we must remember that it is a reciprocal arrangement. We must look out for them as well.

Passing a struggling student by repeatedly providing more opportunities to pass raises troubling questions in the minds of others. They often wonder if favoritism or undue influence are at work in a situation. Additionally, it is possible that a CO can set a struggling student up for a future aviation mishap by ignoring poor performance.

Since pilots generally work in teams, the passing of less-than-qualified students raises doubts in the minds of those who are called upon to risk their lives. It is important that pilots have total confidence in each other. They need to know that their wingmen are proficient and reliable.

Questions for Consideration

What effect do you think passing the struggling student had on other student aviators, both on those who stay in the Navy and those who attrite and go on to other careers in the military?

Is this CO's decision fair to other students who washed out after three failures, but who may have passed if given enough extra chances?

When the officer was trying to decide whether or not to say anything about his concerns, would it have mattered if no one would ever find out about the struggling student's extra chances?

Case 78: Cowardice

(From page 116)

What Happened

The officers in the squadron despised the XO for his bad behavior, but they also began to despise themselves because they felt they lacked the courage to address his actions. The squadron's morale suffered terribly. They had once won two Battle E awards in a row, but now performance and efficiency were poor.

Discussion

Lieutenant Ebbitt and the other junior officers were in an uncomfortable situation. The chain of command is vital to order in the military and it can be difficult for juniors to question the behavior of a senior officer. However, when a senior officer is violating the UCMJ, it is appropriate for a JO to speak directly to the CO. The CO needs to be given the first opportunity to address something that has an effect on the entire team.

It is also important for officers to speak out because failure to do so often compromises their self-respect. And officers without self-respect don't usually perform to the best of their abilities.

Questions for Consideration

Why did Lieutenant Ebbitt put concerns for his career over his sense of duty?

Why would the XO's behavior have such a detrimental effect on squadron morale?

When is it inappropriate to confront a senior officer about his or her behavior?

Case 79: The Accomplice

(From page 117)

What Happened

The board recommended removal. That, along with the other stresses in his life, persuaded the junior pilot to look for a way out. The CO offered him the opportunity to voluntarily withdraw from aviation and the junior pilot jumped at the chance. The CO achieved his goal of removing the junior pilot from flight status.

Discussion

What is the ethical issue here? The O-3 calls his own ethics into question because he participated in the entire process without once voicing his true opinion—that the junior pilot could be saved. The O-3 knew that the CO respected his opinion enough that had he made it clear he would not go along with the CO's intended course of action, the course may have been changed. Further, his evaluation as senior LSO was necessary for documentation of performance, and his role as PTO ensured that no other course of action other than FNAEB was pursued.

The O-3 who reported this case noted with regret that he believed he had failed ethically because he was "an accomplice to the whole process. I make no excuse for my actions, but I will say that when you see a young officer who is trying very hard to serve the CO, it is very easy not to see the forest for the trees."

The O-3 did not see clearly that the goals and desires of the CO may have been more personality-oriented rather than professionally motivated. What, at the time, seemed to be in the Navy's best interest, may not have been. Mismanagement of personnel issues never benefits anyone.

The CO, however, was obligated to remove an ineffective pilot from flight status. Though it isn't pleasant to document failure, the effectiveness of the service requires that those who may hurt or kill themselves or others, or compromise the mission be removed. The CO did what he thought was best and it may very well be that he did save the life of the junior pilot and prevent an aviation mishap by removing him from flight status.

The ethical failure in this case lies with the O-3 who failed himself and his commanding officer because he didn't have the courage to tell the CO his real opinion. Instead, he went along with the board without comment because he wanted to please his CO. If the O-3 thought the junior pilot could be saved, he should have made his case. While wanting to please seniors is a strong motivator, it must never be used as an excuse to shirk a duty, even if it is difficult.

Questions for Consideration

If the O-3 disagreed with the CO, how should he have made his case?
Was it fair that the board's decision seemed to be a foregone conclusion?
What happens when a junior officer's desire to please a senior gets in the
    way of his better judgment?

Case 80: The Investigation

(From page 119)

What Happened

The investigating officer acquiesced to the senior officer's suggestions for handling the case and the senior officer elected to cover up the whole issue. The offending JO was immediately transferred and a carefully worded report stated that all allegations were found to be without merit.

The entire command knew about this whitewash, and morale plummeted because the JO and other involved personnel were not held accountable for their actions. The investigating officer's senior lost credibility and was ineffective for the remainder of the tour. The JO had to be transferred from his follow-on duty station because that officer again engaged in fraternization with enlisted personnel.

Discussion

The course of action suggested by the senior officer was not only unethical, but also illegal. And the investigating officer's cowardly action in agreeing to the cover-up sent a strong message to the other officers that there is a limit to the risks an officer should take when a career is threatened.

If we are to strengthen our ethical climate, we must recognize there is room for improvement. A far stronger message would have been sent to the command had the JO and the other personnel involved been dealt with by the prescribed standards of investigating allegations. A proper investigation would, if the facts warrant it, be followed with administrative disciplinary action.

The officer corps has the deserved reputation of being a highly moral and ethical group, and our future growth in this area depends on the education of our junior officers, who will be the leaders of tomorrow. History has shown that a military that stops believing in itself, no longer respects its leaders, and doubts its mission is doomed to defeat when it comes up against an enemy who believes itself to be morally correct and who believes in what it's fighting for.

[*Editor's note:* The gender of the officer discussed in this case is not indicated because we want to make the point that the handling of unethical conduct by an officer should not be influenced by the gender of the defendant.]

Questions for Consideration

Why did the senior officer feel it was necessary to cover up the findings of the investigation?

Why is it so difficult to follow a leader you can no longer respect?

What happens to the rest of the service when a serious problem is overlooked and the participants go unpunished? What do you think happened in the fraternizing JO's follow-on command?

Case 81: Speaking Up

(From page 120)

What Happened

Lieutenant (jg) Carlton decided not to raise his concerns with Commander Buchanan.

Discussion

Carlton failed both himself and Commander Buchanan by not speaking up about his concerns. If a junior officer is not allowed to confront (or doesn't feel comfortable confronting) a senior officer in the cockpit, crew coordination breaks down and that breakdown could lead directly to a mishap and the possible loss of aircraft and crew.

Carlton wasn't concerned because he was timid. He had already survived one harrowing mishap and still continued to fly, so his courage was not in question. This was simply a matter of one pilot knowingly exceeding NATOPS regulations and another pilot keeping quiet about it.

Flying aircraft is inherently dangerous. In the past, some pilots have made it more dangerous by attempting to show off their skill with antics such as "flat hatting," maneuvering as close to the ground as possible, hopefully without crashing. Unfortunately, if a pilot fails in this situation, he doesn't just "look bad," he often dies. Many pilots have lost their aircraft and been killed performing these kinds of stunts.

Aviation's safety record is improving as these types of barnstorming antics are eliminated and as outstanding pilots speak up and make safe flying an issue. NATOPS regulations, designed to protect pilots and aircrew, are often a reflection of lessons learned at the high cost of crew and aircraft losses. It is often said, "NATOPS is written in blood" because all too often it is.

Training a military pilot is particularly expensive, and the result of that training should be junior officers who are committed to doing what is right. Most important, junior officers should be willing not only to set the example but also require that others follow set procedures.

Though it is heroic to have the courage to die for one's country, failing to preserve and live up to its rules represents an insidious kind of cowardice. It implies that an officer might fail to speak out because he fears losing his career. By not speaking out about his concerns, Carlton failed Commander Buchanan, the military, and aviation in general. One day, the CO might have a mishap because he ignored NATOPS regulations. Carlton will never know if he could have prevented it if only he had had the courage to speak up.

Questions for Consideration

How could Carlton have raised his concerns with Commander Buchanan? Would Carlton have had more credibility or less because of his involvement in a serious mishap?

What if Carlton raised his concerns and Commander Buchanan ignored him? What should Carlton do next?

Case 82: The Classified Inventory

(From page 121)

What Happened

No one knows what happened because Major Kovarik failed to carry out her simple assignment in a professional manner.

Discussion

Major Kovarik was responsible to see that all inventories were performed correctly. She was supposed to set an example for juniors by ensuring a complete and accurate inventory. The handling of classified material is a very sensitive issue and a proper monitor—and thus a proper inventory—usually takes only minutes. In addition to monitoring the inventory, she also had to initial the monitor check list to verify that all inventory requirements were met.

No one but Kovarik and the persons doing the inventory were ever likely to know if the inventory was done improperly. An officer is trusted to do the job correctly. There isn't enough money to have a team watch every officer to ensure the job is done right.

Kovarik's lax attitude set a bad example for all subordinates and was the weak link in a chain designed to make the unit operate successfully. Improper monitoring operations are counterproductive to the conduct of business, since the monitor is meant to find problems, identify causes, and correct the problems in order to make the system run smoothly.

Honor and integrity are the hallmarks of our profession. An officer must do the job right, every time, not just when others are looking. The officer corps of America's armed forces is one of the great strengths of the nation, but if its most trusted personnel fail to meet their obligations, eventually only a paper tiger will defend our nation because our leaders will rely on false reports. It hurts everyone when individual members of the team decide for themselves whether and to what extent they are going to obey the rules. Failure to act ethically is not a victimless crime. An officer's oath requires more than just a perfunctory meeting of standards.

Questions for Consideration

Why would Kovarik have been lax in her duties as inventory monitor? What kind of example did this set for her junior officers and her troops?

Case 83: The Air Show

(From page 122)

What Happened

The aircraft was destroyed, though no one was hurt.

Discussion

The after-accident investigation determined that the pilot had been experiencing burn out and was not current in annual flight time, number of approaches, landings, and aircraft qualification requirements. As to how the NATOPS evaluator could have retained his qualifications without being current, the answer goes to the heart of the need for and trust in the military service. The selection of an evaluator is based on the individual's past performance and his or her demonstration of integrity and the acceptance of responsibility, including maintaining proficiency.

In this case, the evaluator took advantage of the system. While the CO of a squadron is provided on a monthly basis with the state of each individual's meeting NATOPS requirements, the senior evaluator is expected to make sure that no one flies who is deficient. In addition, this case also highlights the failure of both the operations and training officers to check their records and ensure that only pilots who are "current" are allowed to fly. From their earliest crew coordination classes, pilots know that flying when NATOPS requirements have not been met will surely lead to the end of one's flying days, and in some cases, dismissal from the service.

There is also another issue here. The mishap may have been avoided if the copilot had spoken to the pilot about his concerns over the steepness of the approach. Officers have an ethical duty to tell their seniors when they think a mistake is going to be made. Being ethical means more than just that one doesn't lie, cheat, or steal. While writing or saying something false is wrong, withholding comment about the approach to be used on a mission—fearing perhaps that another might be hurt or offended—is also wrong and implies a lack of moral courage.

It is not easy to speak up to a senior, but loyalty demands that kind of service. Ethics are not just philosophical concepts that barely enter our lives; our ethics reflect our daily willingness to seek truth and justice. In the armed forces, our ethics also save lives and equipment.

Questions for Consideration

How did the pilot probably rationalize his violation of NATOPS standards? Why would the copilot keep quiet about his concerns?

Can you think of some other instances in which speaking out has saved lives and equipment?

Case 84: NATOPS Check Flight

(From page 123)

What Happened

In addition to permitting undue familiarity, the senior evaluating pilot allowed the junior pilot to exceed his level of skill and comfort in flying the aircraft. The aircraft was destroyed, and one life was lost.

Discussion

The "pilot appreciation" mind-set hindered flight preparation and aircrew coordination, which led to several errors in judgment that would later turn out to be fatal. The pilots apparently forgot that NATOPS requirements have been developed over a long period of time and are rooted in lessons learned the hard way.

When someone earns their wings as an aviator, they take on many responsibilities, including that of acting professionally. The barnstorming years of military aviation are over and have been replaced with precision flying. The Thunderbirds and the Blue Angels are disciplined aviators, not stunt flyers, and they are recognized for their ability to do precisely what the flight plan dictates.

The pilots in this case violated the ethics of their profession by failing to abide by the rules, failing to be professional at all times, failing to regard the trust placed in an officer as sacred, and failing to remember that everything an officer does affects others in the military and also affects civilian attitudes about the military. They paid a heavy price for their failure.

Questions for Consideration

How do you think the surviving pilot felt about the mishap?

How did the "social" atmosphere of the flight contribute to the mishap?

Case 85: Lack of Courage

(From page 124)

What Happened

As a direct result of the CO's behavior, respect for him waned and discontent was rampant throughout the command. In time, it was his total disregard and lack of respect for the full weight of his position that led to the demise of command unity. The command's operational efficiency suffered terribly.

The O-3 transferred during middeployment with an intact service record, though he felt great sadness that he and his fellow officers had lost sight of what it meant to be a leader. Several of the officers involved expressed deep regret that they "did not have enough moral courage to speak out against the prevailing lack of professionalism that existed in the unit."

Discussion

Everyone in the Navy is a sailor regardless of rank or time in service and accordingly, they are obliged to meet high standards of performance and discipline in both their personal and professional lives. Senior enlisted expect their officers to set an example for the troops. Failing to do so further complicates the job of maintaining discipline and ensuring that all activities are carried out in a timely and efficient manner.

In this case, highly trained, competent officers—trained and educated to put their country, mission, and comrades before themselves—failed to take responsible action and be accountable to their oath of office. They recognized how wrong things were, but they still did nothing. Though they were apparently prepared to sacrifice their lives for their country, they were not prepared to sacrifice their careers for the good of the service and the nation.

After their training, commissioned officers should be equipped with the basic tact and skill necessary to resolve serious unprofessional behavior such as that reported in this case. Commissioned officers should be above reproach. Junior officers must understand the negative effect such conduct has on an officer's respect and esteem. Avenues do exist to make sure this rampant lack of professionalism—even by a CO—does not go unnoticed. The legal officer or chaplain is always available for consultation.

Additionally, while the armed forces do not prohibit drinking, they do expect responsible behavior by their members.

Questions for Consideration

Why is it sometimes easier to risk our lives in service to our country than to risk our careers?

What could the concerned officers have done to confront the CO?

Do you think the officers involved are still bothered by their lack of action? Why?

Case 86: Ecstasy

(From page 126)

What Happened

The careers of all three Ecstasy-using JOs were over. They received OTH discharges.

For months afterward, the wardroom was in an uproar. Some officers felt that Pacy had betrayed his friends' trust. Others were outraged that officers were using illegal drugs. Though Pacy faced no legal ramifications for the incident, he was saddened by the loss of his friends. He also lost some of the pride he had in his unit because, by their actions, some of the other officers showed they did not approve of what he had done.

Discussion

Doing the right thing is not always easy or pleasant, but our country expects its officer corps to always do the right thing. Reasonable officers may disagree over an appropriate course of action, but all officers, in swearing allegiance to the Constitution, agree to uphold the laws of our nation.

Drug use has caused deaths in our military, and a true friend will not break the law and then expect their companions to overlook their actions. If the JOs had been Pacy's friends, they would never have put him in a position where the only thing he could do involved legal action. These three JOs tried to take advantage of Ensign Pacy because they thought he would either join in or say nothing. By their actions, they showed they didn't really think he was a professional officer.

As officers, it is our professionalism that binds us together; without that, we merely have a job. Junior officers who want to continue in their careers should conduct themselves as they would expect a senior officer to act and show by their actions that they are ready for advancement.

Illegal actions by a commissioned officer at any level are intolerable. Citizens trust in the efficiency of the military and in its obedience to existing laws and regulations. Violation of that trust is hypocritical and exceedingly unprofessional.

For further discussion of this point, see Plato's essay "Guardians of the Republic."

Questions for Consideration

Should a JO always turn in fellow officers who commit illegal acts? Or does friendship dictate that what you learn about your friends' off-duty activities remain private?

Are there any circumstances when it is okay to end another officer's career? Are there any circumstances when it is better to keep quiet?

What is the effect on the wardroom if one officer turns in his friends for illegal activities?

Case 87: The Munitions Case

(From page 127)

What Happened

The Office of the Secretary of Defense reviewed the boss's recommendation and sent back a letter of disapproval, stating that the munitions package should not be delivered to Iraq. The office's reasoning was essentially the same as Conrad's. Accordingly, the sale of classified technology to Iraq was prevented. In the Gulf War, Desert Storm forces did not have to face an enemy that would be fighting them with their own technology.

Discussion

This is a complex situation for many reasons. On the one hand, officers will often find that they are directed to carry out orders they may not fully understand. On the other hand, because they are so highly trained, educated, and trusted, officers are expected to have the common sense, intuition, and knowledge to recognize an illegal or unethical order. Unfortunately, the difference between the two situations is not always immediately apparent.

When an officer is in doubt, he or she should first ask for clarification. If the officer's first reaction is disagreement with a superior or a feeling that the superior is proposing something improper, the officer should attempt to prove the superior's actions are correct. An officer should always seek the truth of the matter and not just something that supports his or her individual concept of military propriety.

If, after trying to prove the superior right, the officer discovers the superior is indeed wrong, the officer should discuss his concerns with that senior and seek a resolution.

At times, officers will face decisions that may require more knowledge and experience than they have. When this happens, in addition to discussion with their senior, they may choose to consult the base judge advocate, the chaplain, and possibly their peers. Difficult decisions should always be discussed with others to increase the breadth and scope of perspective and thought.

It is important to note that Major Conrad's boss did not punish him. In delaying approval, Conrad had helped to save his superior from a lot of trouble, trouble the pressuring agency could not have saved him from, the same way the agency could not have saved the pilots who flew against Iraq in Operation Desert Storm.

Questions for Consideration

How did Major Conrad know his boss was asking him to do something improper?

Could Conrad have done anything to persuade his boss that his opinion was correct and the governmental agency was wrong?

What might have happened if Conrad hadn't stood up for his beliefs? Was he insubordinate for refusing to change his recommendation? Why or why not?

Case 88: The Friend

(From page 128)

What Happened

After much discussion and soul searching, the spouse and the unmarried officer decided that a one night stand would do nothing to help either the couple's marital problems or the officer's loneliness. The unmarried officer helped the couple begin formal counseling with the command chaplain. They eventually moved closer to town and the spouse resumed her career.

The unmarried officer felt his friendship with the JO was important, and he wanted to continue the tradition of protecting a military family.

Discussion

This was not necessarily an easy choice for the unmarried officer, but it did establish that he was a true friend to the JO. The hard right is usually not as initially satisfying as the easy wrong. But the unmarried officer knew he made the right choice on both a personal and professional level. In this case, the rights and wrongs were fairly obvious, which helped make the hard choice easier.

Questions for Consideration

Why is the preservation of the military family important to the service?

What would have happened if the unmarried officer and the spouse had been caught in an improper affair? Professionally and personally?

If the unmarried officer had begun an affair with the spouse, could they have ever really trusted each other?

Case 89: Tailhook '91

(From page 129)

What Happened

The lieutenants decided to do nothing to stop the gauntlet, though they made their room a haven for anyone trying to escape the fracas. They also warned several women what might happen if they tried to run the gauntlet. Their decision to do almost nothing, to try neither to stop the gauntlet nor to make a serious effort to find a flag officer, had extremely long range implications that they did not foresee.

Tailhook '91 is still infamous. It badly hurt the Navy in general and seriously damaged the reputation of naval aviation in particular. Many careers were ruined as a result of the scandal.

Discussion

Military history is full of examples of people who risked their lives and faced tremendous odds to save members of their unit. When Marine Corps captain John Ripley (winner of the Navy Cross) worked for two hours under constant enemy fire to mine and destroy the bridge at Dong Ha, he knew that if he succeeded forty-five thousand troops could be saved. When LT Audie Murphy, U.S. Army (winner of the Medal of Honor), ordered artillery fire on his own position in order to kill the surrounding enemy, he knew he was risking his own life for the good of others. When LCDR Eugene Fluckey (winner of the Medal of Honor) guided his submarine thirteen miles up a river to destroy the enemy fleet, he knew he would be under fire because the river was too shallow for the submarine to submerge. When physician Mary Walker (winner of the Medal of Honor) treated the wounded during the Civil War battles of Bull Run, Atlanta, and Chickamauga, she risked her life. And she continued to treat the wounded even after she was detained as a prisoner of war. Air Force major Richard Bong (winner of the Medal of Honor), a gunnery instructor who was neither required nor expected to serve in combat, risked his life in numerous missions. Signalman 1st Class Douglas Munro, U.S. Coast Guard (Medal of Honor winner), deliberately sacrificed his life by drawing enemy fire, thus saving others' lives. All of these individuals were trusted to do what was right, and their superiors had confidence that they would live up to that trust.

Tailhook '91 was hardly combat, but the few lieutenants who realized something was wrong had an opportunity to step forward. If they had stopped the gauntlet, they could have protected the military's reputation from the antics of a few selfish, drunken individuals who were unconcerned about the reputation of their community and their military service.

There are many messages to remember from this incident, but possibly the biggest is that when one fails to act ethically in any given situation, it is almost impossible to know how that failure will ultimately play out. Though they didn't know it at the time, those lieutenants had the chance to save many careers and millions of dollars, and there was no chance that they would lose their lives in the process. They probably were ready to risk death flying into combat, but they were not willing to risk their careers and the reputation of their aviation community to stop the gauntlet. To be sure, if they had intervened, there may have been a fight, but it would likely have been over very quickly—a small, local incident, probably quickly forgotten. Instead, because no one stepped forward to stop it, the Navy has suffered years of struggle to rise above the shadow of Tailhook '91.

The incident and its disastrous aftermath allow the military an opportunity to view the terrible results of unethical action, inaction, and tacit approval of unprofessional conduct. In this case, even one lieutenant could have made a difference. As the wife of Command Pilot Michael Smith (USNA '67) said when she presented materials recovered from the *Challenger* disaster to the Naval Academy Brigade of Midshipmen, "One person can make a difference. My husband, Michael Smith, did and so can you."

Questions for Consideration

Why is it sometimes so much easier to contemplate risking our lives than to risk ridicule by stepping forward to stop something that is obviously inappropriate?

What else could the lieutenants have done to stop the gauntlet?

What could group and squadron commanders have done prior to Tailhook '91 to prevent such an occurrence?

Should senior officers have been concerned that the Tailhook Association president had sent letters to the squadron commanders prior to Tailhook '91 warning about underage drinking and "late-night gang mentality" at past conventions?

Case 90: The Prank

(From page 130)

What Happened

Bender and Armstrong decided to participate for several reasons: (1) to gain the acceptance from their peers, the O-3 instructor pilots; (2) to poke fun at the unpopular chief of staff; (3) to indirectly show support to the CO, whom they considered an outstanding, well-respected, and well-liked officer; and (4) to get out of standing at attention for an entire hour during the ceremony, and to be first in line for beer at the reception. They considered the prank harmless and were unconcerned about the impropriety of its illegal and unethical nature.

Though they gained acceptance among their peers and immediate seniors, they lost face with higher ranking officers. But unlike Tailhook '91, this matter was resolved in-house, and the behavior of the officers involved was never made public.

Discussion

While some might classify this prank as harmless fun, the facts are that Bender and Armstrong had possession of stolen property, were UA from a mandatory command function, were at the Officer's Club when they shouldn't have been, and were disparaging of the chief of staff, who was both senior to them and in their chain of command.

In a small way, they were trying to honor their CO, but they also may have been interested in making a statement of their own. Whatever their intent, they certainly didn't honor their CO by calling attention to any personality differences he might have had with the chief of staff. Officers who want to honor seniors don't do it by actions that indicate the senior has failed to teach the junior officers what it really means to be an officer. This was not the first time the unit's officers had embarrassed the CO with their lack of professionalism and selfishness. This prank showed that the training squadron harbored a bunch of clowns and suggested that the CO tolerated their antics.

By their actions, the architects of the prank and the participants showed that they lacked an understanding of loyalty, responsibility, integrity, accountability, and any realization that the chief of staff has a difficult job. All of these junior officers were being paid to be officers first and aviators second. The prank also sets a bad example for others who hear about it. It suggests that any officer can express an opinion about a senior in inappropriate ways, as opposed to addressing personality conflicts and disputes in a more professional manner.

As for the officers who knew about the prank but did not participate, their failure to step in and stop it is a complete dishonor to the corps of American military officers.

Questions for Consideration

Why didn't the O-3s hang the picture in the bathroom themselves? Why would they involve Bender and Armstrong?

How might the CO have felt when he learned of the prank?

What do you think the other senior officers at the ceremony thought of the CO? What do you think they thought of the JOs involved?

Case 91: The Stories

(From page 132)

What Happened

Lieutenant (jg) Hannifin advised all personnel that the inappropriate storytelling had to stop. He also talked to the troops about the importance of providing work areas free of the threat of harassment or degradation. He explained the reasons for his action and noted that the social mores of the armed forces were changing for the better and it was up to all hands to support the new policies and strive to achieve harmonious working relationships. The troops agreed with his decision unanimously and the storytelling ended without comment. The crew's quality performance continued, and their productivity increased.

Discussion

When something is wrong, the time to stop it is when you first discover it. Not to take action immediately usually means you become part of the problem rather than a means to a solution. If Hannifin had overlooked the matter and another individual who joined the group later had openly objected to the storytelling, Hannifin would have had a difficult time stopping a practice that he had allowed to continue.

Lieutenant (jg) Hannifin considered his actions carefully because the team seemed to be working very productively in spite of the storytelling. As the saying goes, "If it ain't broke, don't fix it." But this catchy slogan fails to take into consideration the fact that almost any system can be improved and ultimately produce better results.

The armed forces have a long history of working ahead of the nation to bring positive social changes and improve the operation of the military. The U.S. Navy outlawed flogging at the beginning of the twentieth century, and many old-timers wondered how discipline would be maintained without the threat of beatings to remind the men who was boss. Drinking was common on ships during the nineteenth century. As late as the 1960s and 1970s, drugs were beginning to take hold in the military, until ADM Tom Hayward (former CNO) uttered his famous statement, "Not on my ship, not on my watch, not in my Navy" and made it stick.

The integration of women into the armed forces is not new. Females served well in both world wars and have, since then, continued to make positive contributions to military effectiveness. In the civilian sector, women have advanced from the years when they couldn't even vote to holding senior positions in industry and government. The treatment of women is slowly changing to one of total equality without regard to gender.

It is no more appropriate to tell jokes that are offensive to women than it is to tell ethnic or religious jokes or to malign any segment of society.

Questions for Consideration

To what extent is the storytelling wrong, especially if it is done on work breaks? Are all personal stories inappropriate?

How could stopping the stories damage morale? Why would that hurt productivity?

How do you think the women really felt about the graphic stories? If it bothered them, why didn't they say anything?

Case 92: Rescue Mission

(From page 133)

What Happened

The rescue mission failed. Many years later, Commander McPherson still regretted his decision to take the easy way out and let the falsified report go without protest.

Discussion

Though doing the right thing might have cost Commander McPherson his career, not doing the right thing cost him something far more precious—his peace of mind. Though his record showed he had risked his life many times in service to his country, in the end, he was not willing to risk his career.

McPherson made a mistake by confusing loyalty to a person with loyalty to both the truth and the military. It was even more troublesome because in the fast-paced world of the modern Navy, officers must be able to rely on one another's word if they are to accomplish their dangerous and challenging missions.

Even if the task force commander sent the false report to throw off a listening enemy, at a minimum, McPherson should have written a "memo to record" stating that the report was filed over his objections. He should also have sent a copy to the task force commander noting that, though there may have been good reasons for it, the report that had ultimately been sent to headquarters was not the report that McPherson had filed.

Commander McPherson could and probably did rationalize that he didn't know all the facts, that others had the big picture, and that the chain of command was in control. All of these things are generally true, but the falsification of an officer's report is patently illegal. So his rationalization was weak because no officer is ever obliged to obey an illegal order under any circumstances.

If you are amoral or without conscience, doing wrong will never cause you ulcers or worry. But if you do know right from wrong, failing to act on what you know is right will haunt you for the rest of your life.

Questions for Consideration

Why would false reports be damaging to the effectiveness of the military?

Why would the task force commander ask his junior to falsify a report in this manner?

How do you think McPherson and the task force commander felt after the mission failed? Did they wonder if it was because McPherson's aircraft were not up to full readiness?

Case 93: Training Supervision

(From page 134)

What Happened

While performing vertical maneuvers, Lieutenant Erickson stalled the aircraft (experiencing negative and near zero G flight conditions) and failed to use proper recovery techniques. Erickson was seriously injured, and the aircraft was lost.

During the mishap investigation, it was determined that despite what he had said, Erickson had not had enough flight or practice hours in that particular aircraft, nor had he had *any* stall training in it. The squadron had failed to monitor Erickson's proficiency training, and they had not received an indication from his previous command that he had completed the requisite stall training.

By the time the investigation was complete, it was clear that Erickson should not have been allowed to fly this particular mission and that complete training records should have been obtained before he was ever assigned any mission.

Discussion

Every risk that can be imagined and subsequently trained for should be included in a pilot's training program to ensure the greatest chance of successful missions. This mishap could have been avoided if the CO had been more willing to risk hurting Erickson's feelings and pride by not allowing him to fly until his training record was fully known.

Enthusiasm is never a substitute for knowledge, and a CO must make decisions based on facts rather than feelings. This is an ethical matter because the CO has to consider what is best for the squadron. There is an inherent risk in flying, and it's every senior's responsibility to provide subordinates with opportunities that are as safe as possible to show what they can do and thus further their career opportunities in the military.

Courage on the part of a CO means not only the courage to fly dangerous missions, but also the courage to make sure personnel are not taking on more than they are ready for (especially in peacetime). In a high-tempo operation, it is especially tempting to assume that everyone knows what they are supposed to know. Unfortunately, that isn't always the case. Being courageous is not always synonymous with being ethical, but having the courage to do the right thing and make the hard decision is always ethical.

Questions for Consideration

How much can commanding officers realistically be expected to know about the capabilities of their subordinates?

Was Lieutenant Erickson lying when he told the training officer he was qualified for the mission? Or was he just being an aggressive team player, wanting to do his part?

Must a commanding officer always know how every single one of his subordinates will act in a given situation?

Who should bear the final blame for the mishap?

Case 94: The Submarine Inventory

(From page 135)

What Happened

The lieutenant received a lengthy lecture on the chain of command from his CO and an already strained professional relationship was virtually destroyed. Additionally, his detaching fitness report reflected the CO's displeasure.

Discussion

Although it was the most difficult decision the lieutenant had made so far in his career, he still felt certain it was the proper one. He felt he had been forced into the uncomfortable position of having to put his CO on report with his CO's boss. And even though it affected his fitness report, the lieutenant was proud of the way he had handled a situation that challenged both his personal and professional ethics.

The lieutenant did have another alternative. He could have asked his CO to go with him when he went up the chain of command. Although this wouldn't have made the CO very happy, he probably would have allowed the inventory to go ahead and might not have felt that the lieutenant had jumped the chain of command behind his back.

[*Editor's note:* With the help of the commodore, the lieutenant's negative fitness report can be thrown out—expunged from his record by an appeal to the Board of Correction of Naval Records.]

Questions for Consideration

Were the CO's reasons for wanting to skip the inventory valid? Why or why not?

Why was the lieutenant so concerned about ensuring the inventory was performed correctly?

How do you think the relieving officer felt about all of this? Do you think it affected his relationship with the CO? What would you have done if you were the relieving officer?

Case 95: Billet Assignments
(From page 137)

What Happened

Commander Jacobs recognized the imbalance of previous crew assignments. He determined that both seamen were trainable and equally capable and assigned the minority to operations and the nonminority to supply. He also met with the operations officer and all division officers to say he expected the integration of the two seamen into their respective sections to be harmonious and fair.

Discussion

If Commander Jacobs had assigned the new seamen according to prior practice on the ship, it would have perpetuated the ship's past discriminatory practices and further eroded the morale of the minority members of the crew, who might see themselves as trapped in jobs less glamorous than operations. By continuing the practice of assigning duties based on minority or nonminority status, Jacobs would have sent a message to the rest of the officers and the crew that race, not merit or potential, was the determining factor in job assignment.

By assigning the new seamen differently, Jacobs sent a clear message that segregation was over and all assignments would be made on the basis of merit in the case of equally qualified personnel and that every effort would be made to ensure a homogeneous crew.

Questions for Consideration

Do you think Commander Jacobs's initial impulse to follow the past trends of the ship and assign the new seamen each according to their race was well intentioned?

Was the past assignment of crew members intentionally discriminatory or was it a case of following past practices without consideration?

If you noticed such a trend in your command, would you bring it to the attention of a senior officer? Why or why not? How would you do it?

Case 96: Systems Acceptance

(From page 138)

What Happened

Instead of signing the acceptance document as he had been directed, Captain Nathan mailed the unsigned acceptance document and his report, along with a letter of recommendation, to the O-6 for his review and signature. Nathan's career was not hurt by his actions, and his boss directed the contractor to fix all discrepancies before he accepted the system.

Discussion

It is true that bosses don't always have the time or the inclination to explain their actions to subordinates. The military runs on trust and chains of command. To do other than what he was directed made Nathan uncomfortable because it might be seen as an attempt to impugn the integrity of his senior officer.

But against the background of military expectations between seniors and subordinates, it is important to remember that officers swear allegiance to the Constitution and not to a particular boss. When officers sign something, they are attesting that to the best of their ability, they know that what is on the document they signed is correct and complete.

Questions for Consideration

Was Captain Nathan right to view his situation as a dilemma?

What if the O-6 had been angry with Nathan's actions? What could have happened?

What might have happened if Nathan had accepted the system against his own better judgment? How could accepting a flawed system ultimately effect troops in the field? Could Nathan's actions ultimately have terrible consequences for others besides himself? How?

Case 97: Communication

(From page 139)

What Happened

Neither the CMC, the XO, nor the CO took action to resolve the situation. The CO believed it was up to Lieutenant Johnson and ADCS Whitman to work out a method to improve their relationship.

In the end, the officer candidates training with the unit were most hurt by the situation. Their understanding and interpretation of the standards for proper communication and conduct within the chain of command were skewed and confused.

Discussion

Communication between individuals who work closely together is necessary and should be automatic. The need for the services to work with the minimum number of personnel needed to do the job is important because national defense resources are limited, and there is a general need to maximize both the use of available funds and the accomplishment of personnel.

In the military, teamwork is the key to everything. Each member is expected not only to know their own job but also to keep an eye out for their teammates so that they can offer help if the need arises.

By failing to take the first step, Lieutenant Johnson showed that he had neither the knowledge nor the desire to resolve the communication problem he had with Whitman. No matter what grade you are, there is more to being an officer than doing your own job and ensuring that your immediate subordinates also do theirs. The position of commanding officer—whether you are an O-7, O-5, or O-3—includes responsibility for everything that happens in the unit from your level down to the lowest rated enlisted in the ranks.

In the final analysis, the ultimate responsibility for activity or inactivity, as the case may be, rests with the commanding officer. If there is trouble in any organization, it is usually considered to come from the top down rather than from the bottom up. At every level of command, it is the responsibility of those who are senior in the chain of command to know what is going on below them and to take steps for improvement when necessary.

The ethical failure in this case is partly the responsibility of both Johnson and Whitman for failing to resolve their differences themselves. But their CO also failed by not intervening and resolving the communication problems that existed in his command. The organizational benefit derived from an involved commander is often underestimated. Their CO should have spent time with them to show them how and why they should resolve their problems for the benefit of the entire unit. If the CO had taken the proper action, the officer candidates who were training with the unit might have benefited from his involvement as well.

Questions for Consideration

Can a CO order people who dislike one another to get along?

Why was it Lieutenant Johnson's responsibility to take the first step to resolve the situation?

How do you think this difficult situation affected the officer candidates' understanding of the chain of command?

Case 98: The Competition

(From page 140)

What Happened

When the actions of the CO and the OpsO were discovered, the rest of the aviation community was outraged by their conduct, and they decided to withdraw from the competition. The CO's and OpsO's service reputations and futures were damaged beyond repair.

Discussion

While the idea of cheating is abhorrent in the military, the drive to win constantly requires officers to perform reality checks on their ethical approach to achieving victory. For the CO and OpsO, winning the competition had become their primary goal, and they were apparently prepared to win at all costs. Even though it was only a training exercise and not real combat, the idea of winning consumed them both. And the consequences of their unethical actions had long-term consequences for both of them.

This ethical issue could be seen as a bit gray. It is too easy to say that a win-at-all-costs attitude will cause a squadron to act unethically. In combat, an aircrew is expected to do everything possible to get to the target and return. Anything less than that is obviously a foolish and unacceptable goal.

In tactical training and competition, it is up to each individual to decide how far he or she is willing to go to win. The question is really: Is everything that might be justified in combat also justified in training? It helps to remember that we don't try to kill our teammates during training, and neither are we quite as prepared to die during training as we are during combat. The point is that in training, winning is important, but it isn't everything.

We must do things right; not because we are afraid of being caught, but because we can feel a greater sense of satisfaction knowing we have bested the competition in a fair fight. We should have enough regard for other members of our military that we consider them a team rather persons we are trying to take advantage of and defeat.

Remember the test of whether your actions may or may not be ethical: Are you willing to discuss them with others whose opinion you respect? If you are not prepared to do so, your actions may very well be unethical.

Questions for Consideration

Why do you think the CO and the OpsO felt such pressure to win the competition?

How do you think the other aviators in their squadron felt when they learned of the attempt to cheat?

Is a win-at-all-costs attitude ever acceptable?

Case 99: Fraternization

(From page 141)

What Happened

The fraternization ended the JO's career and prevented the enlisted person from reenlisting. Additionally, the enlisted never received any professional military counseling.

Discussion

While helping another service member is to be accomplished whenever and wherever possible, the conscientious officer must always keep in mind military fraternization policies. All personnel in the chain of command are concerned with what happens to their people. In this case, the JO should have offered assistance on the spot but then sought assistance for the enlisted through the proper channels. It would have been appropriate to advise the enlisted to contact his or her supervisor, the home command master chief, or the home Family Service Center about the problems. The JO should not have become emotionally involved with an enlisted married person.

Officers are granted special trust and confidence and a great deal of latitude may be taken without necessary approval by seniors. It is the trust placed in officers that makes it imperative that they carefully think through all of their actions in advance.

The JO forgot that all officers are sometimes judged by the actions of a few. By failing to seek counsel from the local military chaplain and a judge advocate, a situation developed that was almost predictable, but nevertheless ended two careers.

As a leader, an officer should also be aware of all services available for subordinates. If this JO had been more aware of the assistance available for the enlisted, it might have helped the officer make a better decision about the appropriate senior–subordinate relationship.

It's important to remember that fraternization can occur on or off base. The commissioned officer must always remain above reproach—even when away from home port or the home command. The location where a violation occurs is never an excuse. You are an officer of the armed forces of the United States twenty four hours a day, seven days a week. You can never escape the responsibility.

Questions for Consideration

Do you think the JO realized the situation would ultimately result in a violation of the policy against fraternization?

How do you think this affected morale in the home command?

Case 100: Video Harassment

(From page 142)

What Happened

The video was destroyed, the individuals who made up the skit were censured, and the XO was given a letter of reprimand.

Discussion

If we, as American military officers, do not embrace the responsibilities and accept the challenges of ending discrimination within our work place, decreased morale and animosity between the races will continue.

High morale and effective mission accomplishment can only be achieved in an environment of equality and fairness. Established policies and procedures dealing with equal opportunity must be enforced and adhered to in order to obtain equal treatment within the armed forces.

You must always do the right thing, even if it brings you under fire from those senior to you in the chain of command. Each of us is prepared to die for our country. Let's make sure we are also prepared to live for it, even if it means sacrificing our career to encourage growth within the military.

Questions for Consideration

If Lieutenant Kerry had not pursued the matter further, could he have claimed that he had fulfilled his responsibility by informing the XO? Why or why not?

Was it Kerry's responsibility as a junior officer to ensure that equal opportunity issues were brought to the attention of the CO after the XO had declared the matter closed? Why or why not?

What should Kerry have done if the CO had also dismissed the video harassment?

Case 101: Designation

(From page 143)

What Happened

Lieutenant Lupo did nothing.

While some of the unqualified officers benefited from the lax standards, the remainder of the squadron felt that morale, training, and readiness were compromised. The majority of personnel in the squadron lacked the confidence that the "special" individuals were fully qualified to assume their designated duties. As a result, many of the aircrews requested not to fly with the "special" people during both training and operational tasks. This, of course, had an adverse effect on flight/crew scheduling, as well as operational performance and further affected the squadron's operational readiness.

Discussion

Confidence in command is important and is enhanced when a high number of personnel pass their qualification exams. (This in turn helps these individuals pursue their military careers.) However, the validity and prestige of the important designations is lost if the exams are compromised when a command passes unqualified individuals. Safety may also be compromised, and there is an overall negative effect on morale.

Lupo's squadron was obviously concerned about looking good by having a high number of personnel pass the qualification exams, but the commanding officers failed to realize they would still look good for refusing to relax the standards rather than being concerned primarily with numbers.

The message is clear: Do not qualify any individual who does not fully meet the standards and expectations of the position. Individuals who cannot legitimately qualify will be directed into a military occupational specialty more suited to their abilities.

It's not easy to take a stand on an issue when you first join a unit. However, if you don't take a stand when you view or hear of unprofessional conduct or possible unethical behavior, you quickly become part of the problem rather than a mere onlooker.

Questions for Consideration

Why would the commanding officers designate unqualified individuals? How would this undermine morale?

How do you think the fully qualified officers felt when they had to fly with those whose performance they knew was substandard? How do you think the enlisted aircrews felt?

Case 102: The Complaint

(From page 144)

What Happened

The officer receiving the complaint decided that though the enlisted was not an immediate subordinate, there was a call for help. The officer reported the incident up the chain of command, and an investigation began. The enlisted, as well as others who knew about the incident, felt the command was concerned about its people. (As General Order 21 of the Navy states, "When the Navy shows an interest in its people, its people will show an interest in the Navy.")

The accused officer was found to have taken some ill-considered actions, and the CO determined that a warning was in order. This action stopped harassment across the board and may have (assuming that no other instances of harassment take place) saved the accused officer from committing an act that would result in a more intensive investigation in the future.

Discussion

An officer's overall responsibility is not limited to those areas for which he or she is held directly accountable. By their oath, officers swear allegiance to the Constitution and to uphold the laws of the land. Harassment is not only illegal, it is also wrong. If the officer receiving the complaint had done nothing, that lack of action would have spoken volumes to the enlisted. The officer would be saying to the enlisted that the complaint was wrong and not important enough to act upon.

The officer receiving the complaint knew that doing nothing would not make the problem go away. The officer also knew the enlisted's complaint could ultimately reappear in ways that would be far more embarrassing to the command. Although talking to the accused officer might either stop the action or determine that nothing had happened, that course of action would not stop the complaining enlisted from complaining to others, including the inspector general.

Officers are human beings. They can make mistakes. It is up to their peers to care enough about fellow officers to take action because doing so may actually save a career rather than end one. It might have turned out that the complaint had no merit, but the officer who received the complaint did the right thing by allowing the chain to investigate. Being an officer sometimes requires us to take actions and make choices that might not be universally accepted, but we get paid to make hard decisions.

Questions for Consideration

Why would an enlisted member choose to complain to an officer outside the enlisted's chain of command?

Why was the officer concerned about alienating the other officers by forwarding the complaint up the chain of command?

Would not reporting the complaint to the proper authorities hurt morale? Why or why not?

Case 103: The Haircut

(From page 145)

What Happened

To avoid undercutting the chief's authority with the crew, Ensign Fiske discreetly advised him to get a haircut.

Discussion

This was one of the many times an officer is faced with making the easy wrong decision over the more difficult right one. It would certainly have been easier for Fiske to defer to the senior status of the chief and not embarrass the senior enlisted before juniors. It's important to remember, however, that the chief knew the rules and still made the decision to appear as he did before the OOD and the other enlisted.

All of us in the armed forces want to trust and have confidence in our seniors, yet that loyalty can be broken if juniors see seniors obeying a standard different from that in place for everyone else.

The chief does, in fact, have certain privileges not enjoyed by those more junior, but those privileges do not include failing to meet the ship's appearance standards. If the chief is a professional, he will carry out the ensign's order to get a haircut without comment. If he is not a professional, the officer will have to insist. The OOD is the direct representative for the commanding officer and must ensure that all orders are obeyed and enforced as if issued directly by the commanding officer.

In the final analysis, by upholding the ship's policy for all hands, Ensign Fiske prevented the establishment and the appearance of a double standard aboard the ship. He made a difficult decision and met the test of ethical conduct.

Questions for Consideration

Why would it have been easy for Ensign Fiske to let the chief go with just a warning?

How do you think the junior enlisted working on deck would have felt if they saw the chief leave the ship without meeting the appearance standards?

How do double standards undercut morale?

Case 104: Discipline

(From page 146)

What Happened

Lieutenant Wilkins met with the junior petty officer and was careful to make it clear that while he disapproved of the junior's actions, he did not disapprove of the junior petty officer in general. Wilkins then explained that he was entering a drop in marks for military bearing and personal behavior in the junior petty officer's service record.

Discussion

What makes this an ethical dilemma for Lieutenant Wilkins is the conflict he feels between sympathy for the junior enlisted's family and his responsibility to maintain good discipline and order.

When he talked with the junior petty officer about his behavior, Wilkins encouraged him to apologize to the chief and try to work even harder in the future so that his lowered mark wouldn't end his career. Wilkins also explained how the junior petty officer should have handled his annoyance with the chief. He told him he should have met with the chief to politely try to resolve the situation. If that approach had failed, the junior should have taken his concerns up the chain of command. Wilkins emphasized that the chain of command and proper respect toward seniors is essential for the military to meet its mission requirements.

Wilkins also explained to the junior petty officer why it was important that the junior's actions not go unpunished. A lack of action would have sent a strong message to others in the unit that the chief really wasn't that important to the organization, the kind of message that would have thoroughly undermined the chief's authority within the unit. The chain of command and the need for respect between juniors and seniors applies equally in the enlisted ranks and officer corps and should be followed—both on and off duty.

Questions for Consideration

Did Lieutenant Wilkins handle the situation correctly? Why or why not? Was there another way to handle this that might not have harmed the junior petty officer's record?

Should Wilkins have allowed his concern for the junior's career and family to effect his disciplinary decision?

Appendix A
Integrity

ADM Arleigh Burke, USN

[*Editor's note:* The classic treatise on the subject of integrity was written by ADM Arleigh Burke in a letter to Prof. Karel Montor. This treatise was published in the October 1985 issue of *Proceedings* and is produced here in its entirety. Brief definitions cannot do justice to this most important topic. This article, while it does not cover all aspects of integrity, will provide the reader with a good frame of reference for further thought.]

Integrity

> First you find yourself overlooking small infractions that you would have corrected on the spot in the past.
>
> Soon, you are a participant in these infractions. "After all," you say, "everybody's doing it."
>
> All too soon you find yourself trapped: You no longer can stand on a favorite principle because you have strayed from it.
>
> Finding no way out, you begin to rationalize, and then you are hooked.
>
> The important fact is, the men who travel the path outlined above have misused the very basic quality and characteristic expected of a professional military man, or any other professional man for that matter:
>
> They have compromised their integrity.

This quotation, from a plaque hanging in the office of the chief of staff, Marine Corps Development and Education Command, Quantico, Virginia, is remarkable in its simplicity and truthfulness. My old college dictionary defines *integrity* as (1) an unimpaired condition; soundness; (2) adherence to a code of moral, artistic, or other values; (3) the quality or state of being complete or undivided; completeness. As synonyms, it lists *honesty* and *unity.*

These are good definitions, but they are not precise. They allow a great deal of leeway because the descriptive words may mean different things to different societies, different cultures, and different people. What is integrity for a German may not be so for an Iranian. What is integrity for a cowboy may not be considered integrity by a minister (the disposition of horse thieves, for example). Integrity also varies widely among individuals in the same group. Probably no two individuals have the same ideas about all aspects of integrity. The point is, there exists no absolute definition of integrity.

Since no two people have the same values, how does a person acquire integrity, a code of conduct, a set of standards by which to live? How does a person develop a sense of obligation toward others, whether they make up a civic group, a military service, or a country? Most individuals' standards are learned when they are very young, from family, associates, and other contacts, from reading, and from watching television. It is well to remember, though, that families with high standards have had children who rejected the beliefs of the families and turned out to be first-class scoundrels. The reverse is also true. People with integrity have come from families that have lacked it. Perhaps this does not happen often, but it does happen. The point is that it is impossible to guarantee that any one person will acquire integrity. Development of integrity depends primarily on the individual.

There will be wayward priests, crooked politicians, and wicked naval officers. In a highly moral organization, people who fall below the standard will eventually be recognized and removed from the organization. In an organization of lower standards, they may be punished but still tolerated. In an immoral organization, such as in a criminal family, they will be measured by their contribution to their organization.

Individuals are responsible for their own integrity. They will be influenced by many people and events, but, in the end, their integrity quotient is of their own making. People are responsible for establishing their own standards, and their choices determine the kind of person they will be.

The integrity an individual should look after is his own—not his neighbor's, his subordinate's, his senior's, or his associate's, but his own. You can try to influence people to accept your views, but whether they do or not is up to them. A society or an individual may force rules on others, but no one can ensure that integrity will be inculcated. Only the individual concerned can accomplish that.

The integrity of a society or a group is approximately equal to the lowest common denominator of its people. When the standards are lowered for an individual, the standards of the group or society to which the individual belongs are lowered. Sometimes standards are raised in groups, but more frequently there is a gradual disintegration of standards.

Since the integrity of individuals varies, an organization cannot maintain an absolutely uniform integrity; not even sequestered groups can accomplish this. A general level of integrity can be approximated, but individuals may deviate greatly from the norm, even in organizations that try to keep standards high.

In these days of high-speed teaching methods, young people receive guidance from their families and literally dozens of other groups. They are even given computerized, capsulized advice. Developing individuals observe the people who dole out the plentiful and diverse guidance, and the observations they make influence their acceptance of what is right or wrong, good or bad. The following example is frequently mentioned in regard to education: If merit and capability are not requirements for success in the teaching profession, then young people are likely to judge that merit and capability are not important. Likewise, if developing individuals observe that people with known moral defects, or people who are known to be crooked or liars, are accepted in society without penalty, they might well conclude that integrity is not worth their effort, either.

Still, individuals determine what convictions they want to have and what they want to do about them. They continually adjust what they think is correct, what they want to learn, and how much effort they are willing to devote to each subject. Individuals determine whom to like and whom to avoid, whom to admire and whom to emulate, and they make decisions about what is important and how to go about self-improvement. Individuals also determine what obligations they are willing to undertake on their own volition.

Since individuals create their own integrity, it follows that integrity is not fixed permanently. Integrity is a variable in one individual, among individuals of the same family and society, and among different societies and cultures. Integrity may be changed throughout life as individuals determine what actions they are willing to take to improve themselves and their integrity. Deciding how much integrity individuals want to develop is one of the most important decisions they make, whether they are conscious of the process or not. The basis of all education is learning to make judgments. This holds true for developing character as well as for becoming expert in any particular field. Individuals' judgments on material matters can be based on what other people have developed, and so can their judgments pertaining to integrity, but the final choices in both areas are made by the individual concerned.

Olympic athletes have devoted nearly all their efforts and time—often their whole lives—to becoming expert in their chosen field. If a person wants to become one of the best gymnasts in the world, that person ought to start training by the age of three. Since many people find that their dreams exceed their natural capabilities, they will make the sound judgment not to continue to try to accomplish the impossible, but to restrict themselves to what they can do well. The lesson must be learned early in life that very few people can ever be number one. This insight is part of learning to make sound judgments.

Individuals who get away with schemes not to mow the lawn do not increase their sense of obligation very much. When individuals decide not to make the efforts necessary to learn arithmetic or calculus, it is not likely that they will be very good in any profession requiring a knowledge of math. The young person who fools around at the piano, not really trying to learn, is making the choice not to be a piano player. If people worked as hard at learning academics and professional knowledge as they do at performing in athletic contests, it is probable that the world would be a better place to live.

It must be understood that a judgment on anything is not irrevocable, although action taken as a result of a judgment, such as hanging the wrong man as a horse thief, frequently has irrevocable consequences. A person with low grades can see the light, for example, and decide to become more proficient in math. If desire is there, most things can be accomplished. It takes more effort, more time, more determination to correct an original wrong judgment—but it can be done. Grandma Moses became a great artist after she decided to try painting later in her life.

Of course, individuals can alter their integrity. Too frequently the alterations are on the side of lowered standards, as has been demonstrated in a number of professions and in government. The crux of this is that individuals make their own integrity by reason of their own decisions, choices, and judgments, and they change their integrity by the same means. At the same time, people should make judgments on other people's integrity gingerly. The many different concepts of integrity held by different individuals, groups, and cultures should be treated with all due respect.

Some of the most vicious wars in history have been fought in the name of religion by societies that had very strong—and very different—convictions concerning integrity. They disagreed on what was right, on the means of implementing what was right, and on their sacred writings, and thus, each side resolved to force its views on the other side. Both sides were absolutely certain they had the monopoly on integrity, and that the other side had no integrity at all.

The extended upheaval in the Middle East is primarily based on different views of religion: what is right, what is good, and what is the word of God. These differences have been exacerbated by greed, desire for power, and self-interest. The Middle East (like a number of American cities) is full of strong and conflicting views on integrity and full of people who do not seem to have much integrity. Some leaders in the Mideast appear to be scoundrels, liars, selfish in the extreme, and generally without socially redeeming features. It is likely that few people in this country agree with, or understand, their philosophy, and that fewer still would stand for any attempt to force that philosophy on them.

Keeping our own integrity up to par is problem enough. We are responsible for our own conduct; we are not responsible for another's integrity. If we have made the normal number of correct judgments during our lives, we have probably concluded that we should not try to interfere with the religion of others or to determine what is right or wrong for them. We should not interfere unless another group tries to force its views of integrity on us or our organization. Then we must resist, or the other group's efforts will appreciably lower the standards of our organization. In relation to the naval profession, in particular, the following observations are applicable:

1. Integrity and motivation are necessary in naval officers, but competence in the profession is also essential.

2. Good intentions are most desirable, but nothing can be built or done by good intentions alone—except maybe paving the road to hell. Performance is required. Good intentions may help get performance, but the required end product is performance, not "I meant well."

3. Integrity, or lack thereof, is not always discernible. Many people practice successfully to appear to have great integrity, or more than they do have. They can fool many some of the time. But always guard against making a final judgment on another's integrity based only on his own statements or on what appears to be.

4. Be wary of self-proclaimed virtue. Do not rely on other people's evaluation of their personal integrity. If they had integrity, perhaps they would not need to be their own press agents.

5. The marketing of reputations for integrity is a good business. Many leaders have made good livings allowing their reputations to be used to represent organizations with no or poor reputations of their own.

Despite the cynical tone of these observations, most people and a large percentage of naval officers are people of integrity. They are honest, they are reliable, they are professional, and they do have good professional ethics. Have faith in your fellow officers, but be ready if one of them is less valiant, less competent, or less honest than you thought.

All of us can learn from the past. As wise as Moses was, he had difficulty hearing the disagreements of all the people who came before him. The people wanted Moses to settle matters between them and make known to them God's decisions and regulations. His father-in-law, Jethro, observing that Moses was having great difficulty handling the work, suggested:

> Be thou for the people to Godward, that thou mayest bring the
> causes unto God. And thou shalt teach them ordinances and
> laws, and shalt show them the way wherein they must walk,
> and the work that they must do. Moreover thou shalt provide
> out of all the people able men, such as fear God, men of truth,
> hating covetousness; and place such over them to be rulers of
> thousands, and rulers of hundreds, rulers of fifties, and rulers
> of tens. And let them judge the people at all seasons; and it
> shall be, that every great matter they shall bring unto thee, but
> every small matter they shall judge; so shall it be easier for

thyself, and they shall bear the burden with thee. If thou shalt do this thing, and God command thee so, then thou shalt be able to endure, and all this people shall also go to their place in peace. (Exo. 18:19–23)

The point is that, when considering weighty matters, an individual can be helped greatly by turning to and relying on others for support, for no one individual has all of the knowledge necessary to be 100 percent correct all of the time.

One question to be considered is, What should an officer do when he thinks that a senior is lying to the next senior officer in the chain-of-command? Certainly a junior officer who believes a senior is making a mistake—any serious mistake, not just a mistake with regard to integrity—should inform that senior officer. For example, suppose that the officer of the deck has the conn, and he orders, "Come to 080." The junior officer of the deck believes that it is an incorrect order, and he tells the OD right away. The OD rechecks and either corrects the order or tells the junior officer that the order will not be changed and why. This sort of exchange is common in the Navy. Usually the senior will ask for the junior's opinion as a matter of training if for no other reason. Seniors do not want to make mistakes, and they appreciate being informed of an error before any damage is done.

Thus, it is a good habit to question suspected errors in normal operations. An officer, however, does not often deliberately lie to a senior.

This example illustrates how important it is for a naval officer to have experience in making judgments. There are, unfortunately, no general guidelines that can be laid down for the contingency of lying. The appropriate reaction to lying depends on circumstances, which are unpredictable. If a junior officer believes that a senior is lying, the junior officer must ask himself questions. Is the junior officer sure that the senior is lying, or is it possible that he is only guessing that the senior is lying? Is it possible that the issue involves a difference of opinion? Could it be a question of interpretation? Finally, does the matter have significance?

The junior must judge whether the lie will have an effect on the organization. If the junior concludes that the senior is lying on a significant matter, and that the senior's integrity is involved, then it is the duty of the junior to tell that senior that the matter will be reported to the next senior in the chain of command as well as the reasons why the junior believes the report is necessary. It is particularly important for an officer to confront a senior accused of dishonesty or another breach of integrity, and to advise that officer on the intended course of actions before he besmirches the reputation of that officer.

The decision to accuse is never to be taken lightly. An officer who accuses peers or associates of any kind of wrongdoing knows well, before he utters the first words of accusation, to expect judgments from shipmates and perhaps from larger groups on the appropriateness of the charges made. This is in accordance with "Judge not, lest ye be judged" (Matt. 7:1).

Therefore, when the junior starts wrestling with his conscience to make the judgment on where his duty lies, he should resist impulsive actions and even consider searching out a second opinion. Friends in the unit will likely take the issue seriously, or at least the more conservative ones will. There may be one or two who have noted the alleged misconduct themselves. I suppose that this sort of a drum-head court martial without the presence of the accused would come to a general conclusion, one way or another. Still, the final decision is in the hands of the originator of the charge, and that individual must make the final judgment on what should be done, no matter how much advice was sought and received from others. The decision belongs to the officer—and no one else.

Matters such as these are difficult for a junior officer, a chief of naval operations, or a president. At the Naval Academy, in the year just before they graduate, midshipmen are taught the relationship between duty and honor: "We serve the country first, our seniors second, and ourselves, last." The future officers are counseled on honor versus loyalty in the naval service, and specific attention is given to the difference between a professional and a careerist. These definitions are given: "A military professional is someone who upholds the highest standards and serves the country with unquestioning loyalty; the professional is not motivated by personal gain. . . . A careerist is someone who serves the country in the best way fit to further his own career." It is noted in this lesson given to our future officers that the careerist is more likely to fall into the zero-mentality syndrome, to be someone who would choose to cover up those things that might draw discredit to his own unit. The professional takes on the issues directly and does not swerve to avoid criticism. These matters are never easy for the officer, but he must take on the issues to fulfill the obligations he holds to country, service, unit, personnel therein, and self.

As a junior officer on a battleship, I was once involved in a delicate situation that I did not handle properly. I recount it here so that others may not need as much time to learn when the proper action should be taken in such a situation. On a Labor Day weekend I had duty as one of three officers of the deck. My relief did not return to the ship on Monday morning to relieve me, so I stood his watches on Monday without reporting anything amiss. When the derelict officer showed up on Tuesday, he told the senior watch officer that he had made arrangements with me to stand his watches before he left for the weekend. That was not true. He simply took the chance that some dope would fill in for him. I did not do anything about that misstatement, either. Within two years that officer was dropped from the rolls of the Navy for a similar offense. Had I reported him the first time, he might have been jolted out of his expectation that there would always be some volunteer who would step in to carry his part of the load.

There is also the question of what to do about a "whistle blower." The answer involves knowing whether the individual has made an honest effort to correct the wrong by using the chain-of-command channels that are available. A clever whistle blower can parlay an error into something that produces publicity and promotion that is not deserved. Recognizing the media's hunger for material to present to the public should cause any person to ask, before he blows the whistle, whether all possible steps have been taken to correct the situation. The naval service is an organization made up of people, and people are subject to making mistakes, but it is important for the public to know that efforts are being made to find mistakes and to correct them. It is wise to wait before making a judgment until you know why the usual steps were not taken or why those steps were not successful. It is also wise to listen and not make a premature judgment. Every organization needs good internal checking, internal policing, and internal corrective apparatus, just as every organization needs an external inspector, an external check, and means for external correction.

It is suggested that codes of honor and integrity must not be so rigid that they are beyond the capability of human beings to follow. I believe it should be the personal responsibility of individuals to decide whether to report lying, cheating, and stealing, and that they should do so only after completely scrutinizing their own conscience regarding integrity. When a person steals a pencil, perhaps absentmindedly picking it up from someone's desk, the observer should have the discretion to judge whether the theft should be reported. A person can dream up many examples and possibilities, most of them minor, when there is no doubt that a theft, a lie, or a cheating incident has occurred. But the incident may have been so inconsequential that an individual of good conscience could interpret it as not significant enough to be reportable.

In summary, we must instill in individuals a sense of personal honor, an obligation to their organization and other groups, a desire to keep their own standards high and to keep the standards of their organization high. This sense of honor gives real meaning to the feeling engendered from belonging to a "Band of Brothers" and to other nostalgic emotions that are essential to a taut, high-standards organization. However, an honorable person should have the option of determining whether to believe that others are honorable and whether to take appropriate action in each case. The appropriate action is not usually reporting the offender to the senior, but confronting the suspected culprit with the charge first. What should be done must be individually decided at every step. A fixed rule that insists that a person never squeals on a classmate, a shipmate, or a buddy is just as wrong as a rule that says that everything that could be construed as lying, stealing, or cheating should he reported to a senior.

Likewise, it is also important to comment on the issue of "pleasing the boss." "Greasers"—those who play up to their bosses strictly for personal gain—do not last very long in the service, because their method of operating is discovered and disliked, and they are discharged. But also keep in mind that bosses are pleased to have confidence in the competence of their subordinates, and that there are few subordinates in any profession who do not want to please their bosses. Bosses have been put in positions of responsibility and authority because their bosses think the individuals know what they are doing—and what their subordinates, in turn, should do. What pleases the boss is usually getting done what should be done. It is proper that all officers of the naval service should want a reputation for contributing to the improvement of their service. There is nothing wrong with that. Every unit's effectiveness is determined by the way the bosses, and everyone else in the unit, do their respective jobs. The reputation of the naval service, the unit, and the individuals in the unit depends on overall unit effectiveness.

Since the boss usually desires a reputation for being a capable officer, including being a capable leader, it is laudable in a subordinate to want to please the boss. There is certainly nothing wrong in pursuing that trait, unless pleasing the boss results in turning in a poor performance. It is usually not too difficult for the boss to recognize insincere support. Greasing seldom works in a classroom, and it succeeds almost as often in the fleet.

Each of us must make his own decisions about the meaning of integrity. I suggest that officers who want to be ready for the difficult decisions of life study the great military leaders of the world, their similarities and differences. Frankly, there is no shortcut to wisdom. Rules to cover all situations do not exist. All of us must find our own way. Our ability to make the best decisions at the time will certainly be influenced by our knowledge of the past, our consultation with others, and our ability to "see" the future. At the moment of decision, we will have to use our best judgment on what we in turn will do about it. Good luck!

Appendix B
Courage

Gen. Charles C. Krulak, USMC

Let me tell you a story about personal courage. In April of 1966, a young Marine, Capt. Thomas V. Draude, Naval Academy class of 1962, was the company commander of Mike Company, 3rd Battalion, 7th Marine Regiment. Mike company was conducting a search and destroy mission in the Quang Ngai Province of Vietnam. One morning they came under intense small arms, automatic weapons, and mortar fire from a concealed and entrenched enemy company inside a hamlet. Captain Draude directed his unit to attack this hamlet, which was later determined to be the base for Viet Cong operations. The attack encountered heavy and determined resistance. Repeated artillery and air strikes failed to reduce the defensive positions of the enemy. The fight raged on.

Determined to seize the objective, Captain Draude said that for the first time in his career he gave the order to his unit to "fix bayonets." It is a solemn moment when combat Marines fix bayonets on their weapons. Individuals look at that rifle with renewed respect because they know that in a few minutes someone is about to die–on one end or the other.

Late in the day, they attacked and seized the hamlet. Thirty-one Viet Cong had been killed. But as night approached Captain Draude decided to have the company, still in contact with the enemy, fall back to a more defensible position. After they had fallen back Captain Draude was informed that one of his Marines, Cpl. Fredrick Miller of Berlin, Ohio, had been hit and lay dead in the hamlet. Although physically exhausted from the nonstop all-day fighting, Captain Draude and two other Marines immediately ran back into the hamlet, still receiving small arms fire, and, by the light of burning huts, searched for Corporal Miller. When Captain Draude finally found where the Marine had fallen, he picked up Corporal Miller's body, and, while dodging bullets, carried him back four hundred meters to friendly cover.

Now that is physical courage, the ability to overcome the fear of bodily injury and death. That fear is real. I'm not talking about being scared on the first time out; even seasoned combat veterans must overcome fear. When you see bodies torn apart by the horrors of combat, when you hold someone you know as they bleed to death in your arms, when you write a letter to a friend's family explaining that a loved one is not coming home—you understand the reality of our business. In the naval services you cannot escape fear; you must deal with it. How did Captain Draude overcome this fear; Where did his physical courage come from? First, he was well trained; second, he had convictions; and third, he understood the real reason we fight. We fight for one another. Now, I'll come back to this, but let me tell you what else happened.

The day after the battle the battalion commander came to Mike company's position and noticed that the company commander's flack jacket was covered with blood. When the battalion commander heard that during the battle Captain Draude had gone back into the hamlet to recover the body of a dead Marine, he flew into a rage, yanked Captain Draude aside and fiercely reprimanded him. The battalion CO told Draude his actions were stupid, foolish, and had endangered himself and his Marines needlessly. After five minutes of admonishment, the battalion commander demanded that Draude never do anything like that again and threatened to relieve him if he did. Then the battalion CO finally fell silent. Captain Draude said that moment of silence seemed like an eternity and became a defining moment in his life. He had a golden opportunity to keep his mouth shut and walk away. But that would have been lying by omission and misleading his senior. Instead, he looked up at his battalion commander and said, "I understand what you are saying, sir; however, given the same situation with a dead or wounded Marine left behind, I'm afraid I would have to do the same thing."

This time the battalion commander went ballistic. He told Captain Draude he was fired and relieved him of his company command. To make matters worse, a helicopter flew over and then proceeded to land. Out jumped the assistant division commander, Brigadier General Stiles, who was shouting at the top of his lungs, "Where is the CO of Mike company?" Captain Draude said he felt like it was the worst day of his life. He had just been chewed out, was now in the process of being relieved by his battalion commander, and in a few minutes he was probably going to be placed under arrest and court-martialed by a Marine general. Captain Draude remembers thinking how here he was, a young Marine, just four years out of the Naval Academy, and now his military career was over.

Now that is moral courage, the ability to overcome the fear of hurting someone or something you love in order to stand up for what is right. Once again, that fear is very real. You may think it is always easy to stand up, speak out, or take action in order to do what is right, and that by doing so you could never hurt something you love. It is not always so easy.

Captain Draude loved the Marine Corps. If he was relieved, he would probably not be promoted and forced to leave. Captain Draude loved his Marines. If his Marines ever learned the details of why he was fired or maybe even punished by a court martial, he would lose their respect. Captain Draude loved his family. If he was disgraced, he would hurt and shame them. How did Captain Draude overcome this fear? Where did his moral courage come from? First, he was well trained; second, he had convictions—the same sources of strength for physical courage—and third, he understood the real reason we do the right thing. We do the right thing because our ideals are more important than ourselves. I'll get back to this, but let me tell you what happened to Captain Draude.

When the Marines pointed out Captain Draude, General Stiles rushed over to where Draude and his battalion commander were standing. The general grabbed Draude's hand and shook it, and slapped him on the back. General Stiles told Draude what a great job he had done and went on and on about how proud the general was to have Draude in the division. Finally, the general looked at the battalion commander and said, "How can you go wrong with such fine young men as this?"

Well, needless to say, instead of being relieved of his command and ending his career, Captain Draude went on to much more. For his actions that day, he received the Silver Star, one of two he was awarded for heroism in Vietnam. He went on to become a brigadier general and was himself an assistant division commander in combat, serving with the 1st Marine Division during Desert Storm.

General Draude is a courageous man. Not only did he receive two Silver Stars for heroism, he was awarded the Purple Heart, the Legion of Merit, the Bronze Star Medal, and the Navy Commendation Medal. The last three with the combat "V" for valor. But he would tell you that it was much harder for him, when he could have remained silent, to speak up and tell his battalion commander something that he knew would get him relieved than it was to risk death and go back into the hamlet to recover Corporal Miller's body. And that leads us to two important points that I want to make about courage. First, moral courage is tougher than physical courage. And second, you will be required to display moral courage far more often than you will be required to show physical courage.

Appendix C
Bedrock Standards of Conduct

To maintain the public's confidence in our institutional and individual integrity, personnel of the armed forces *shall:*

1. Avoid any action, whether or not specifically prohibited by the rules of conduct, which might result in or reasonably be expected to create an appearance of

a. using public office for private gain;

b. giving preferential treatment to any person or entity;

c. impeding government efficiency or economy:

d. losing complete independence or impartiality;

e. making a government decision outside official channels; or

f. adversely affecting the confidence of the public in the integrity of the government.

2. Not engage in any activity or acquire or retain any financial or associational interest that conflicts or appears to conflict with the public interests of the United States related to their duties.

3. Not accept gratuities from Department of Defense contractors unless specifically authorized by law or regulation.

4. Not use their official positions to improperly influence any person to provide any private benefit.

5. Not use inside information to further a private gain.

6. Not wrongfully use rank, title, or position for commercial purposes.

7. Avoid outside employment or activities incompatible with their duties or which may discredit the armed forces.

8. Never take or use government property or services for other than officially approved purposes.

9. Not give gifts to their seniors or accept them from their subordinates when it is not appropriate to do so.

10. Not conduct official business with persons whose participation in the transaction would violate laws or regulations.

11. Seek ways to promote efficiency and economy in government operations.

12. Preserve the public's confidence in the Armed Forces and its personnel by exercising public office as a public trust.

13. Put loyalty to the highest moral principles and to country above loyalty to persons, party, or government department.

14. Uphold the Constitution, laws, and regulations of the United States and never be a party to their evasion.

15. Give a full day's labor for a full day's pay, applying earnest effort to the performance of duties.

16. Never discriminate unfairly by the dispensing of special favors or privileges to anyone, whether for remuneration or not, and never accept for himself or herself or for family members, favors or benefits under circumstances which might be construed by reasonable persons as influencing the performance of governmental duties.

17. Make no private promises of any kind binding upon the duties of office.

18. Not engage in business with the government, either directly or indirectly, inconsistent with the conscientious performance of governmental duties.

19. Expose corruption wherever discovered.

(Derived from U.S.C. 2635.10, published in the Federal Register, vol. 57, no. 153, August 7, 1992 [Rules and Regulations].)

APPENDIX C

Bibliography

Books, Articles, and Speeches

Bach, Brian J. "Soldierly Ethics." *Marine Corps Gazette,* Sept. 1984, 56–59.

Beran, Walter F. "How to Be Ethical in an Unethical World." *Vital Speeches,* June 1976, 602–8.

Bloom, Allan. "Liberal Education and Its Enemies." Colorado Springs, Colo.: U.S. Air Force Academy, 14 Nov. 1991.

Bok, Sissela. *Lying: Moral Choice in Public and Private Life.* New York: Pantheon Books, 1978.

Brennan, J. G. *Foundations of Moral Obligation: The Stockdale Course.* Newport, R.I.: Naval War College, 1992.

Brown, J., and M. J. Collins. *Military Ethics and Professionalism.* Washington, D.C.: National Defense University Press, 1981.

Buckingham, C. T. "Ethics and the Senior Officer: Institutional Tensions." *Parameters: Journal of the Army War College* 15, no. 3.

Carroll, Robert C. "Ethics of the Military Profession." *Air University Review* (Nov.–Dec. 1974): 39–43.

Carson, Frank L. "Teaching Military Ethics as a Science II." In *Research Report.* Maxwell Air Force Base: U.S. Air University, Air War College, Mar. 1989.

Chalker, Edsel O. *Ethics for the Air Force Officer.* Maxwell Air Force Base: U.S. Air University, Air War College, Air Force ROTC, 1973.

Corey, G., M. Corey, and P. Callanan. *Issues and Ethics in the Helping Professions.* Monterey, Calif.: Brooks/Cole, 1984.

Coutu, D. L., and F. Ungerheuer. "The Money Chase." *Time,* 4 May 1981, 58.

Creating a Workable Company of Ethics. Washington, D.C.: Ethics Resource Center, 1990.

DeGeorge, Richard T. "When Integrity Is Not Enough: Responding to Unethical Adversaries in Business and the Military." Colorado Springs, Colo.: U.S. Air Force Academy, 10 Nov. 1991.

Denise, Theodore C., and Sheldon P. Peterfreund. *Great Traditions in Ethics.* 7th ed. Belmont, Calif.: Wadsworth Publishing, 1992.

Diamond, D. B. "Private Agony—Public Cause." *Ladies Home Journal,* June 1990, 125.

Diehl, William F. "Ethics and Leadership." *Military Review* 65, no. 4 (1985): 35–43.

Ethics: A Selected Bibliography. 3d rev. ed. Carlisle Barracks, PA: U.S. Army War College Library, Jan. 1993.

Ethics in America. Pt. 1, Military Combat; Pt. 2, Under Arms, Under Fire. Maryland Public Television, 31 Oct. 1987.

Ethics Journal. Washington, D.C.: Ethics Resource Center.

Futernick, Allan J. "Avoiding an Ethical Armageddon." *Military Review* (Feb. 1979): 17–23.

Fotion, N. *Military Ethics: Looking toward the Future.* Stanford, Calif.: Hoover Institution Press, 1990.

Fotion, N., and G. Elfstrom. *Military Ethics: Guidelines for Peace and War.* Boston: Routledge & Kegan Paul, 1986.

Gabriel, R. A. *The Nature of Military Ethics.* Westport, Conn.: Greenwood Press, 1980.

———. *To Serve with Honor: A Treatise on Military Ethics and the Way of the Soldier.* Westport, Conn.: Greenwood Press, 1982.

Ginsburgh, Robert N. "Military Ethics in a Changing World." *Air University Review,* Jan.–Feb. 1976, 2–10.

Greene, W. M. "What Is Right." *Marine Corps Gazette,* June 1984, 44–46.

Halloran, Richard. "Washington Talk: Officers and Gentlemen and Situational Lying." *New York Times,* Aug. 6, 1987.

Hamel, Raymond F. "Are Professionalism and Integrity Only a Myth?" *Air University Review,* May–June 1978, 60–67.

Hauser, William L. "Careerism vs. Professionalism." *Armed Forces and Society* (Spring 1984): 449–83.

Hill, Ivan. *Common Sense and Everyday Ethics.* Washington, D.C.: American Viewpoint, 1980.

Huxley, T. *Evolution and Ethics and Other Essays.* New York: AMS Press, 1970.

Johnson, Kermit D. "Ethical Issues of Military Leadership." *Parameters: Journal of the Army War College* 2 (1974): 35–39.

Kilpatrick, William. *Why Johnny Can't Tell Right from Wrong: Moral Illiteracy and the Case for Character Education.* New York: Simon & Schuster, 1992.

Kreeft, Peter. *Back to Virtue: Traditional Moral Wisdom for Making Moral Confusion.* San Francisco: Ignatius Press, 1992.

Matthews, Lloyd J., and Dale E. Brown. *The Parameters of Military Ethics.* Washington, D.C.: Pergamon-Brassey's International Defense Publishers, 1989.

Military Ethics. Washington, D.C.: National Defense University Press, 1987.

Montor, K., and A. Ciotti. *Fundamentals of Naval Leadership.* Annapolis, Md.: Naval Institute Press, 1984.

Montor, K., T. McNicholas, A. Ciotti, T. Hutchinson, and J. Wehmueller. *Naval Leadership: Voices of Experience.* Annapolis, Md.: Naval Institute Press, 1987.

Moore, G. E. *Principia Ethica.* London: Cambridge University Press, 1951.

O'Hara, Michael J. "The Challenge of Moral Leadership." U.S. Naval Institute *Proceedings,* Aug. 1977, 58–62.

Piper, Thomas R., Kenneth E. Goodpaster, and Mary C. Gentile. *Managerial Decision Making and Ethical Values.* Boston: Harvard Business School, 1989.

Potter, J. V. "War Games." *Journal of Professional Military Ethics—U.S. Air Force Academy,* Dec. 1982.

Purtilo, Ruth. "Ethicist Helps to Resolve Dilemmas in Patient Care." *Boston Massachusetts General Hospital News* 47, no. 2 (Mar. 1988).

Raspberry, William. "Ethics Without Virtue." *Washington Post,* 16 Dec. 1991, A23.

Rescher, Nicholas. "In the Line of Duty: The Complexity of Military Obligation." Colorado Springs, Colo.: U.S. Air Force Academy, 15 Nov. 1990.

Shiner, John F. "The Need for Military Professionals." *Journal of Professional Military Ethics* 2, no. 1 (Sept. 1981).

Spinoza, B. *Ethics.* New York: E. P. Dutton, 1938.

Stockdale, James B. *A Vietnam Experience.* Stanford, Calif.: Hoover Institution Press, 1984.

— — —. "The World of Epictetus: Reflections on Survival and Leadership." *Atlantic Monthly,* Apr. 1978, 98–106.

Stratton, R A. "Where's Our Code of Ethics?" U.S. Naval Institute *Proceedings,* Dec. 1986, 83.

Stromberg, P. L., M. M. Waikin, and D. Callahan. *The Teaching of Ethics in the Military.* Hastings-on-Hudson, N.Y.: Institute of Society, Ethics, and the Life Sciences, Hastings Center, 1982.

Taylor, Maxwell D. "A Professional Ethic for the Military?" *Army* (May 1978): 18–21.

Toner, James. *The Cross and the Sword: Reflections on Conscience and Command.* New York: Praeger, 1992.

Turkelson, Donald R. "The Officer as a Model of Ethical Conduct." *Military Review,* July 1978, 56–65.

U.S. Air Force Academy Journal of Professional Military Ethics.

Wakin, Malham M. *War, Morality, and the Military Professions.* Boulder, Colo.: Westview Press, 1986.

Walton, C. *The Ethics of Corporate Conduct.* Englewood Cliffs, N.J.: Prentice-Hall, 1977.

Webb, Ernest L. "When Ethic Codes Clash: Absolute vs. Situational." *Army* (Mar. 1978): 31–33.

Wenker, Kenneth H. *Ethics in the U.S. Air Force*. Maxwell Air Force Base: Air University Press, 1988.

Wiener, Philip O. *Dictionary of the History of Ideas*. New York: Charles Scribner's Sons, 1973 ("Right and Good," 173–86; "Moral Sense," 230–34).

OPNAVINST and SECNAVINST Sources

Boats and Small Craft Inventory and Accounting. OPNAVINST 4780.6 series.

Contractor Support Services. SECNAVINST 4200.31 series.

Dependent Care Certification. OPNAVINST 1740.4 series.

Efficiency Review. SECNAVINST 5010.1 series.

Environmental Protection and Natural Resources Program Plan. OPNAVINST 5090.1 series.

Equal Opportunity. OPNAVINST 5354.1 series.

Follow-up on Reports of Audits. SECNAVINST 5200.34 series.

Fraud, Waste, and Abuse. SECNAVINST 5430.92 series.

Hazardous Material Control and Management. OPNAVINST 4110.2 series.

Information, Personnel, and ADP Security. OPNAVINST 5510.1 series.

Management Control Program. SECNAVINST 5200.35 series.

Navy Sponsor Program. OPNAVINST 1740.3 series.

Operations Security. OPNAVINST 3070.1 series.

Physical Readiness. OPNAVINST 6110.1 series.

Physical Security. OPNAVINST 5530.14 series.

Pre-Separation Counseling. OPNAVINST 1900.1 series.

Sexual Harassment. SECNAVINST 5300.26 series.

Standards of Conduct. SECNAVINST 5370.2 series.

Substance Abuse. OPNAVINST 5350.4 series.

Tobacco Prevention. SECNAVINST 5100.13 series.

Traffic Safety. OPNAVINST 5100.12 series.

Index

acceptance of gratuities, Cases 42, 46, 47, 48, 51, 57

Administrative Discharge Board, Case 40

alcohol abuse, Cases 28, 55

appearance(s):

    assignment of personnel, Cases 32, 95

    assumption of authority, improper, Cases 68, 71

    attention to detail, Case 29

    of inappropriate behavior, avoidance of, Cases 43, 47, 50, 51, 57

    perception of wrongdoing and, Cases 35, 51

    personal, maintaining proper standards of, Case 103

Bedrock Standards of Conduct. *See* Standards of Conduct

behavior:

    aberrant, inquiring into cause of, Case 34

    inappropriate, immediate action to correct, Cases 71, 91. *See also* appearance(s), of inappropriate behavior, avoidance of

bias. *See* gender bias; racial bias; sexual harassment

briefing, inattention to, Case 18

chain of command:

    inquiry via, *versus* hot-line report, Case 43

    use of: to rectify a grievance, Cases 73, 75, 76, 87, 94, 96, 100, 102, 104; to solve ethical dilemma, Cases 21, 52, 57, 58, 71, 78

chaplain:

    marital counseling by, Case 88

    seeking advice from, Cases 2, 12, 87, 99

cheating:

    by contractor, Case 58

    in training competition, Case 98

civilian attire, inappropriate, Case 38

claim, false, Cases 14, 48, 55

classified material, safeguarding of, Cases 11, 33, 82

combat readiness:

    pressure to "go along" *versus*, Case 101

    pressure to please senior *versus*, Cases 6, 9, 60, 72

    self-interest *versus*, Cases 6, 72

commanding officer. *See also* senior(s)

    approval of, required for off-duty work of subordinate, Case 28

    inappropriate behavior by, Cases 71, 85

    responsibility of, for harmony within command, Case 97

communication(s), adequate, need for, Cases 24, 97

community, relationship of military base with, Cases 35, 44

competition, unfair, Case 98

conduct unbecoming an officer, Cases 1, 8, 13, 21, 24, 27, 48, 49, 62, 63, 64, 67, 71, 78, 85, 86, 99

confidence, breach of, Case 21

conspiracy to falsify document, Case 7

Constitution, officer's duty to, Cases 3, 7, 21, 33, 61, 85, 96

contractor(s), relations with, Cases 7, 41, 46, 47, 48, 57, 58, 96

conversion of government property for personal use, Cases 55, 64

counseling of a subordinate, Cases 34, 99

courage, moral. *See* moral courage

criminal offenses, major, requirement to report, Case 24

cumshaw, Case 37

deception, straightforwardness *versus*, Case 1

detail, attention to, Case 29

disbursement, discrepancies in, Case 49

document(s). *See also* record(s); report(s)
  customs, falsification of, Cases 8, 65, 69, 96
  forgery of, Case 2
double standards, preventing establishment
    of, Case 103
drug abuse, Cases 40, 55, 86
  reporting of, self-interest *versus,* Case 12
  testing for, Case 27
duty:
  to Constitution. *See* Constitution, officer's
    duty to
  failure to report for, Case 67
  inattention to, Cases 18, 82
  unfitness for, failure to report, Cases 16,
    17, 18

enlisted:
  equal opportunity, Cases 66, 75, 95, 100
  family, sympathy for, Cases 40, 104
  officer's improper financial dealings with,
    Case 56
ethical climate, Cases 60, 52, 101; of "look
    the other way," Cases 53, 54
ethical loyalty, Case 83
extra-marital relationship, Case 48

false-claim, submission of, Cases 14, 48, 55
falsification:
  of official documents, Cases 15, 65, 69, 96
  of official records, Cases 8, 11
  of report, Cases 5, 7, 9, 11, 13, 17, 59, 60,
    72, 80, 92
  of travel orders, Case 2
fraternization, Cases 80, 99
fraud, Cases 2, 10, 14, 25, 30, 35, 43, 51, 52,
    54, 58, 65, 87
friend(s):
  counseling of, Case 10
  interest of, *versus* duty to unit, Case 20
  loyalty to: *versus* duty to unit, Case 86;
    versus safety, Case 61
fundraising, Case 44

gender bias, 32, 74, 75, 76, 85, 91
good order and discipline, prejudice to,
    Case 99
government facilities, unauthorized use of,
    Case 25
government property:
  conversion of, for personal use, Cases
    55, 64
  unauthorized disbursement of, Case 37
  use of: for personal business, Cases 30, 50,
    55; unauthorized, Cases 25, 30
gratuities, acceptance of, Cases 42, 46
gundecking, Cases 13, 59, 60, 69

harassment, Case 73. *See also* sexual
    harassment
hot-line(s):
  chain of command inquiry *versus,*
    Case 43
  use of, Cases 30, 31, 42, 44, 51, 57

IG. *See* Inspector General, investigations by
illegal order, obedience to, Cases 5, 92, 94
impropriety, appearance of. *See*
    appearance(s), of inappropriate
    behavior, avoidance of
inattention to duty, Cases 18, 82
injury, reporting of, *versus* self-interest,
    Case 16
inspection, borrowing material for, Case 1
Inspector General (IG), investigations by,
    Cases 22, 31, 47
integrity:
  components of, Case 92
  defined, Case 1
  personal, Cases 7, 52
investigation(s):
  of contractor, Case 58
  by Inspector General, Cases 22, 31, 47
  by subordinate, of senior's behavior,
    Case 76
JAG. *See* Judge Advocate General's Corps,
    seeking advice from

Judge Advocate General's Corps (JAG),
seeking advice from, Cases 2, 19, 25,
28, 30, 35, 39, 43, 44, 46, 56, 57, 85, 87
juniors. *See* subordinate(s)

legal officer. *See* Judge Advocate General's
Corps, seeking advice from
loyalty:
ethical, Case 83
misplaced, Cases 3, 62
to peer, *versus* safety, Case 61
to senior, *versus* following standard orders,
Cases 68, 69, 70
to subordinate, Case 68
lying:
versus admission of drug use during youth,
Case 12
on classified document destruction report,
Case 11
by subordinate, Cases 1, 19

marital problems, counseling peer and peer's
spouse with, Case 88
Medal of Honor, Cases 1, 44
merchants, town, relationship of military
base with, Case 35
misplaced loyalty, Cases 3, 62
misrepresentation of status, Case 2
mistake:
advise senior of, Case 83
owning up to, Cases 4, 17, 49, 75
moral courage, Cases 4, 12, 16, 18, 21, 36,
52, 53, 58, 62, 63, 73, 75, 76, 79, 81,
87, 89, 91, 94, 96, 100
morale, destruction of, Cases 21, 62, 74, 78

NATOPS, consequences of failure to follow,
Cases 18, 29, 36, 65, 72, 81, 83, 84. *See
also* regulation(s); standard operating
procedures, failure to follow
Naval Criminal Investigative Services,
Case 24
off-duty employment, Cases 19, 28; wearing

of uniform during, Case 35
official documents, forgery of, Cases 2, 10
operating procedures, standard. *See* standard
operating procedures, failure to follow
order(s):
forgery of, Case 2
illegal, obedience to, Cases 5, 65, 71, 92, 94
sealed, unauthorized reading of, Case 70

parking pass, forgery of, Case 10
pay, failure to correct in timely manner,
Case 45
peer(s):
acceptance of, *versus* ethically correct
action, Cases 38, 67, 89
counseling of, Case 10
failure of, to report unfit condition of crew
member, Case 18
illegal behavior by, Case 86
loyalty to, *versus* safety, Case 61
with marital problems, counseling of,
Case 88
pressure from, to act unethically, Case 53
request of, to sign false record, Case 11
responsibility of, to intervene on behalf of
officers being sexually harassed,
Case 89
suspicious regarding, Case 89
perception. *See* appearance(s)
personal business:
conduct of, while on duty, Cases 18, 55
use of government property for, Cases 19,
30, 50, 55
personal integrity, Cases 7, 52. *See also*
integrity
personnel, assignment of, Cases 32, 95
physical exam, Case 16
Pollard spy case, Case 33
prank(s):
participation in, to achieve peer
acceptance, Case 90
serious implications of, Case 10
as sexual harassment, Case 74

prejudice to good order and discipline, Case 99

private business. *See* personal business

procedures, standard operating. *See* standard operating procedures, failure to follow

procurement, Cases 42, 43

professional services, subordinate's need for, Case 99

property, government. *See* government property

psychological services, need for, Case 34

purchasing, Cases 42, 43

qualifications, falsification of, Case 69

racial bias, Cases 66, 75, 95, 100

random drug testing, Case 27

reading, while being briefed, Case 18

record(s). *See also* document(s); report(s)
need for completeness of, Case 93
official falsification of, Cases 8, 11

regulation(s). *See also* NATOPS, consequences of failure to follow; standard operating procedures, failure to follow.
consistency in enforcement of, Case 38, 103
failure to follow, Cases 6, 8, 15, 17, 18, 29, 33, 36, 49, 61, 67, 68, 71, 72, 82, 84

reimbursement for false claim, Cases 14, 48

report(s), Cases 5, 6, 7, 9, 11, 13, 17, 59, 80, 92. *See also* document(s); record(s)

rules. *See* regulation(s)

safety:
failure to follow procedures for, Cases 17, 39
loyalty to friend *versus*, Case 61
pressure to "go along" *versus,* Cases 17, 101
pressure to please senior *versus,* Case 72
self-interest *versus,* Cases 6, 16, 72

SECNAVINST:
5200.3 Series, Case 24
1700.11 Series, Case 28

security procedures, violation of, Cases 8, 10, 11, 22, 33, 70, 82

self-interest:
versus combat readiness and safety, Cases 6, 16, 72
versus reporting: of error, Cases 4, 49; of improperly operating equipment, Case 15; of injury, Case 16; of personal infraction, Case 23
violation of trust *versus*, Cases 37, 71

senior(s). *See also* commanding officer
breach of confidence by, Case 21
communication with, by subordinate, Case 24
fallibility of, Cases 26, 77
inappropriate behavior of, Cases 71, 78; possible, Cases 25, 75, 76, 89
intimidation of subordinate by, Cases 5, 30, 65, 71, 94
loyalty to, *versus* following standard orders, Cases 17, 68
pressure exerted upon subordinate by: to follow ethically inappropriate behavior, Cases 77, 87, 96; to follow illegal order, Cases 64, 65; to submit false report, Case 80
pressure to please: *versus* combat readiness and safety, Case 72; *versus* recommendation contrary to wishes of, Case 79
questionable order from, Cases 36, 77
responsibility of: to face possibility of own fallibility, Case 26; to inform subordinate of recommendations against subordinate, Case 73; to know capabilities of subordinates, Case 93; to observe performance of subordinates, Case 82; to seek advice from others, Case 26; for training of subordinates, Cases 9, 13, 42, 60, 83
testimony against, Case 63
willingness of, to hurt feelings of subordinates, Case 93

sexual harassment, Cases 74, 76, 91, 102; and failure of peers to take action to stop, Case 89. *See also* gender bias; racial bias.

sexually suggestive comments, Case 91

sexual relations, improper, avoidance of, Case 88

signature, meaning of, Case 96

sleeping on watch, Case 23

special treatment, improper acceptance of, Case 51

standard operating procedures, failure to follow, Cases 15, 17, 29, 33, 36, 61, 67, 68, 72, 82, 84. *See also* NATOPS, consequences of failure to follow; regulation(s)

Standards of Conduct, Cases 3, 8, 10, 13, 15, 17, 19, 20, 22, 23, 34, 35, 37, 38, 39, 40, 42, 44, 46, 47, 56, 57, 59, 67, 68, 69, 88, 90, 96, 97, 103; violation of, for personal gain, Case 54

standing orders, failure to follow, Cases 17, 68

status, misrepresentation of, Case 2

subordinate(s):

communication with senior by, Case 24

counseling of, Case 99

discipline of, Cases 40, 104

disrespect of seniors by, Case 90

failure of: to get CO's approval of off-duty work, Case 28; to deal with inappropriate actions of CO, Cases 71, 85; to follow standing orders, Cases 17, 68; to properly inform senior, Case 68; to report infraction to senior, Case 68, 23

intimidation of, by senior, Cases 5, 17, 30, 87, 94

loyalty to, Case 3

lying by, Case 1

off-duty employment of, Cases 19, 28, 35

poor performance of, Case 34

questionable order from senior and, Case 36

report of, falsified by senior, Case 92

responsibility of: to advise senior of investigation of senior's behavior, Cases 17, 76; to advise senior of pending mistake, Cases 77, 81, 83; to confront senior regarding inappropriate behavior of senior, Case 76; to properly inform senior, Case 6; to report possible inappropriate behavior of senior, Cases 17, 71, 78

training of, senior's responsibility for, Cases 9, 13, 60, 83

willingness of, to hurt feelings of seniors, Case 83

Tailhook 1991, Cases 24, 89

thefts within unit, appropriate course of action regarding, Case 20

town merchants, relationship of military base with, Case 35

training:

competition during, cheating in, Case 98

records of. *See* training records, falsification of

senior's responsibility for. *See* senior(s), responsibility of, for training of subordinates

training records, falsification of, Cases 9, 13, 59, 60, 101

travel claim. *See* claim, false

travel orders, forgery of, Case 2

unethical assistance, acceptance of, Case 77

unfair competition, Case 98

uniform, wearing of, during off-duty employment, Case 35

violation:

discovery of, *versus* violation itself, Case 2

of security procedures, Cases 8, 11, 22, 33, 82

of Standards of Conduct, for personal gain, Case 54

of trust, *versus* self-interest, Case 37

voluntary disclosure of wrongdoing, Case 27

Walker spy case, Case 33

waste, Cases 31, 41, 53, 58

watch:

failure to relieve on time, Case 67

sleeping on, Case 23

whitewash, Case 80

work, off-duty. *See* off-duty employment

wrongdoing:

perception of, Cases 35, 51

voluntary disclosure of, Case 27

zero tolerance policy, Cases 27, 40

The Naval Institute Press is the book-publishing arm of the U.S. Naval Institute, a private, nonprofit, membership society for sea service professionals and others who share an interest in naval and maritime affairs. Established in 1873 at the U.S. Naval Academy in Annapolis, Maryland, where its offices remain today, the Naval Institute has members worldwide.

Members of the Naval Institute support the education programs of the society and receive the influential monthly magazine *Proceedings* and discounts on fine nautical prints and on ship and aircraft photos. They also have access to the transcripts of the Institute's Oral History Program and get discounted admission to any of the Institute-sponsored seminars offered around the country. Discounts are also available to the colorful bimonthly magazine *Naval History*.

The Naval Institute's book-publishing program, begun in 1898 with basic guides to naval practices, has broadened its scope in recent years to include books of more general interest. Now the Naval Institute Press publishes about one hundred titles each year, ranging from how-to books on boating and navigation to battle histories, biographies, ship and aircraft guides, and novels. Institute members receive discounts of 20 to 50 percent on the Press's more than eight hundred books in print.

Full-time students are eligible for special half-price membership rates. Life memberships are also available.

For a free catalog describing Naval Institute Press books currently available, and for further information about joining the U.S. Naval Institute, please write to:

Membership Department
U.S. Naval Institute
291 Wood Road
Annapolis, MD 21402-5034
Telephone: (800) 233-8764
Fax: (410) 269-7940
Web address: www.navalinstitute.org